Laptops

for
dummies®
A Wiley Brand

Laptops

7th Edition

by Dan Gookin

A Wiley Brand

Laptops For Dummies®, 7th Edition

Published by: **John Wiley & Sons, Inc.,** 111 River Street, Hoboken, NJ 07030-5774, www.wiley.com

Copyright © 2021 by John Wiley & Sons, Inc., Hoboken, New Jersey

Published simultaneously in Canada

For general information on our other products and services, please contact our Customer Care Department within the U.S. at 877-762-2974, outside the U.S. at 317-572-3993, or fax 317-572-4002. For technical support, please visit www.wiley.com/techsupport.

Wiley publishes in a variety of print and electronic formats and by print-on-demand. Some material included with standard print versions of this book may not be included in e-books or in print-on-demand. If this book refers to media such as a CD or DVD that is not included in the version you purchased, you may download this material at http://booksupport.wiley.com. For more information about Wiley products, visit www.wiley.com.

Library of Congress Control Number: 2020952025

ISBN: 978-1-119-74027-8; 978-1-119-74028-5 (ebk); 978-1-119-74029-2 (ebk)

Manufactured in the United States of America

SKY10023679_010421

Contents at a Glance

Table of Contents

Introduction

t's lightweight, high-tech, and portable; the product of years of research, a longtime dream of engineers and scholars, something people all over the world crave. It's wireless. It's about communications. And it will help you become the ultimate mobile computer user. Of course, I'm talking about this book: *Laptops For Dummies*.

This is the seventh edition of *Laptops For Dummies*, updated and spiffed up for the latest in PC laptop hardware and software as well as for Microsoft's latest operating system, Windows 10.

This book covers your portable computer from laptop to lap-bottom, inside and out, on the road or resting at home. The information here runs the gamut, from introducing your laptop to making your first wireless connection at your favorite swanky cybercafé. You'll find this book useful whether you want to go laptop shopping or you consider yourself an old hand.

About This Book

I'm glad that you're still reading this introduction. Most people stop reading after a few paragraphs, or they don't even bother reading the introduction. Consider yourself special.

This book covers laptop computing, from buying and setting up to going on the road, from networking and the Internet to power management and security and everything in between. There's a lot of laptoppy advice to be had between this book's yellow covers.

I don't intend for you to read every chapter in sequence. That's because this book is organized as a reference: Find the tidbit of information, the knowledge nugget you need to know, and then be on your merry way. Everything is cross-referenced, so if you need to look elsewhere in the book for more information, you can easily find it.

In writing this book, I assume that you may know a bit about computers, as most folks do today. But you may be utterly fresh on the idea of *portable* computing. Despite what they tell you, a laptop computer isn't merely a desktop computer with a handle attached. There's more to it, and this book is here to show you the ropes — and to let you take full advantage of what the laptop has to offer.

And Just Who Are You?

Let me jump to the conclusion that you're a human being, not a cleverly disguised owl. Furthermore, either you own a laptop PC or you want to buy one. You may already have a desktop computer, or perhaps you had a laptop a long, long time ago and noticed that things have changed.

I use the word *laptop* to refer to all types of portable computers, from the traditional notebooks to the teensy Ultrabooks. A new category is the 2-in-1 laptop, which is more like a tablet. Those are covered here as well and fall under a general category that I term *tablet PCs.* Any laptop with a touchscreen display is a tablet PC, and I wax eloquently on that topic in Chapter 7.

This book assumes that your laptop is PC-compatible, that it runs the Windows operating system. The current version is Windows 10, which is a great operating system for laptop users. This book doesn't cover older versions of Windows, nor does it cover using Linux, which is fun but way too nerdy.

This book doesn't describe the basic operations of a computer, Windows, or your software. I've tried to keep the information here specific to the portable aspects of the laptop computer. Beyond that, if you need more information about running your computer, any standard PC or Windows reference works fine.

Icons Used in This Book

The Tip icon notifies you about something cool, handy, or nifty — or something that I highly recommend. For example: "Never make a bar bet with a guy wearing a bowtie."

Don't forget! When you see this icon, you can be sure that it points out info you should remember or something I said earlier that I'm repeating because it's important and you'll likely forget it anyway. For example: "There is no need to touch the electric fence a second time just to be sure that it's on."

WARNING

Danger! Ah-oogah! Ah-oogah! When you see the Warning icon, pay careful attention to the text. This icon flags something that's bad or that can cause trouble. For example: "The enormous sea monster slithering toward your village won't be using the legal system to settle its grievances."

TECHNICAL STUFF

This icon alerts you to something technical, an aside or a trivial tidbit that I simply cannot suppress the urge to share. For example: "My first laptop was a steam-powered, 8-bit 6502 that I breadboarded myself." Feel free to skip over this book's technical information as you please.

Where to Go from Here

You can start reading this book anywhere. Open the table of contents and pick a spot that amuses you or concerns you or piques your curiosity. Everything is explained in the text, and stuff is carefully cross-referenced so that you don't waste your time reading repeated information.

My email address is dgookin@wambooli.com. Yes, this is my real address. I reply to all email I receive, and you'll get a quick reply if you keep your question short and specific to this book. Although I enjoy saying hi, I cannot answer technical support questions or help you troubleshoot your laptop. Thanks for understanding.

You can also visit my web page for more information or as a diversion:

```
www.wambooli.com
```

This book's specific support page can be found at

```
www.wambooli.com/help/laptops
```

There you'll find updates, as well as frequent blog posts with laptoppy information, tips, and tricks.

The publisher also maintains a support page, complete with updates and such. You can visit the publisher's website at dummies.com. To search for specific information related to this book, including the bonus online Cheat Sheet, search for *Laptops For Dummies* from the site's main page.

Enjoy your laptop computer. I'll see you on the road!

1

This Laptop Thing

Discover how the modern laptop came to be.

Learn how to buy a new laptop that's just right for you.

IN THIS CHAPTER

» **Understanding portable computing**

» **Reviewing laptop history**

» **Discovering modern laptops**

» **Getting to know the subnotebooks**

» **Recognizing the tablet PC**

Chapter **1**

The Portable Computing Quest

One summer day, in his 42nd year, Eugene noted how pleasant the weather was outside. He was inspired to attach wheels to the room-size, vacuum tube computer. Then he and the other three computer scientists, despite their utter lack of muscle tone, pushed the 17-ton beast out of the lab to work outside. It was this crazy notion that sparked the portable computer revolution.

Today the revolution continues. Computers are not only shrinking — they're becoming more portable. Their names represent a pantheon of portable PC potential, including portables, laptops, notebooks, netbooks, convertibles, and tablets. Indeed, portable computing has a rich history, from the first dreams and desires to the multitudinous options now available.

The History of Portable Computing

You can't make something portable by simply bolting a handle to it. Sure, it pleases the marketing folk, who are interested in things that sound good more than things that are practical. For example, you can put a handle on an anvil and call it portable, but that doesn't make it so.

My point is that true portability implies that a gizmo has at least these three characteristics:

>> It's lightweight.

>> It needs no power cord or other wires.

>> It's practical.

In the history of portable computing, these three things didn't happen all at once, and definitely not in that order.

THE ANCIENT PORTABLE COMPUTER

Long before people marveled over credit-card-size calculators, merchants and goatherds used the world's first portable calculator. Presenting the *abacus,* the device used for centuries to rapidly perform calculations that would otherwise induce painful headaches.

Abacus comes from the Greek word meaning "to swindle you faster." Seriously, the abacus, or counting board, is simple to master. Schoolkids today learn to use the abacus as a diversion from more important studies. In the deft hands of an expert, an abacus can perform all the same operations as a calculator — including square roots and cubic roots.

In his short story *Into the Comet,* science fiction author Arthur C. Clarke wrote of stranded astronauts using many abacuses to plot their voyage home when the spaceship's computer wouldn't work because the Internet was down and their version of Windows couldn't be validated.

The Xerox Dynabook

The desire to take a computer on the road has been around a long, long time. Back around 1970, when Bill Gates was still in school and dreaming of becoming a chiropodist, Xerox PARC developed the Dynabook concept.

Today, you'd recognize the Dynabook as an eBook reader, similar to the Amazon Kindle: The Dynabook was proposed to be the size of a sheet of paper and only a half-inch thick. The top part was a screen; the bottom, a keyboard.

The Dynabook never left the lab, remaining only a dream. Yet the desire to take a computer on the road wouldn't go away. During the three decades after the Dynabook concept fizzled, many attempts were made to create truly portable computers.

The Osborne 1

The first successful portable computer was the Osborne 1, created by computer book author and publisher Adam Osborne in 1981. Adam believed that in order for personal computers to be successful, they must be portable.

His design for the Osborne 1 portable computer was ambitious for the time: The thing needed to fit under an airline seat — and this was *years* before anyone would even dream of using a computer on an airplane.

The Osborne 1 portable computer, shown in Figure 1-1, was a whopping success. It featured a full-size keyboard and two 5¼-inch floppy drives but only a teensy, credit-card-size monitor. It wasn't battery powered, but it did have a handy carrying handle so that you could lug around the 24-pound beast like an overpacked suitcase. Despite its shortcomings, 10,000 units a month were sold; for $1,795, you got the computer plus free software.

The loveable luggables

The Osborne computer was barely portable. Face it: The thing was a *suitcase!* Imagine hauling the 24-pound Osborne across Chicago's O'Hare Airport. Worse: Imagine the joy expressed by your fellow seatmates as you try to wedge the thing beneath the seat in front of you.

Computer users yearned for portability. They wanted to believe the advertising images of carefree people toting the Osborne around — people with arms of equal length. But no hipster marketing term could mask the ungainly nature of the Osborne: Portable? Transportable? Wispy? Nope. Credit some wag in the computer press for dreaming up the term *luggable* to describe the new and popular category of portable computers ushered in by the Osborne.

Never mind its weight. Never mind that most luggable computers never ventured from the desktops they were first set up on — luggables were the best the computer industry could offer an audience wanting a portable computer.

In the end, the Osborne computer's weight didn't doom it. No, what killed the Osborne was that in the early 1980s the world wanted IBM PC compatibility. The Osborne lacked it. Instead, the upstart Texas company Compaq introduced luggability to the IBM world with the Compaq 1, shown in Figure 1-2.

The Compaq Portable (also called the Compaq 1), introduced in 1983 at $3,590, proved that you could have your IBM compatibility and haul it on the road with you — as long as a power socket was handy and you had good upper-body strength.

Yet the power cord can stretch only so far. It became painfully obvious that for a computer to be truly portable — as Adam Osborne intended — it would have to lose its power cord.

The Model 100

The first computer that looked even remotely like a modern laptop, and was fully battery powered, was the Radio Shack Model 100, shown in Figure 1-3. It was an overwhelming success.

FIGURE 1-2:
The luggable
Compaq Portable.

WHAT'S A PC?

PC is an acronym for *politically correct* as well as for *personal computer*. In this book's context, the acronym *PC* stands for personal computer.

Originally, personal computers were known as *microcomputers*. This term comes from the microprocessor that powered the devices. It was also a derisive term, comparing the personal systems with the larger, more intimidating computers of the day.

When IBM entered the microcomputer market in 1982, it called its computer the *IBM PC*. Though it was a brand name, the term *PC* soon referred to any similar computer and eventually to any computer. A computer is basically a PC.

As far as this book is concerned, a PC is a personal computer that runs the Windows operating system. Laptop computers are also PCs, but the term *PC* more often implies a desktop model computer.

FIGURE 1-3:
The Radio Shack
Model 100.

The Model 100 wasn't designed to be IBM PC compatible, which is surprising considering that PC compatibility was all the rage at the time. Instead, this portable computer offered users a full-size, full-action keyboard plus an eensie, 8-row, 40-column LCD text display. It came with several built-in programs, including a text editor (word processor), a communications program, a scheduler, and an appointment book, plus the BASIC programming language, which allowed users to create their own programs or obtain BASIC programs written by others.

The Radio Shack Model 100 was all that was needed for portability at the time, which is why the device was so popular.

» The Model 100 provided the *form factor* for laptops of the future. It was about the size of a hardback novel. It ran for hours on standard AA batteries. And it weighed just 6 pounds.

» So popular was the Model 100 among journalists that it was common to hear the hollow sound of typing on its keyboard during presidential news conferences in the 1980s.

» Despite its popularity and versatility, people wanted a version of the Model 100 that would run the same software as the IBM PC. Technology wasn't ready to shrink the PC's hardware to Model 100 size in 1983, but the Model 100 set the bar for what people desired in a laptop's dimensions.

PORTABILITY AND COMMUNICATIONS

Long before the Internet came around, one thing that was deemed necessary on all portable computers was the ability to communicate. A portable computer had two communications duties: First, it had to be able to talk with a desktop computer, to exchange and update files; second, it needed a *modem*, to be able to communicate electronically over phone lines.

Nearly every portable computer, from the Radio Shack Model 100 onward, required a modem, or at least an option for installing one. This was before the Internet era, back when a modem was considered an optional luxury for a desktop computer. Out on the road, away from a desktop at the office, early proto-road-warriors needed that modem in order to keep in touch.

The lunch buckets

Before the dawn of the first true laptop, some ugly mutations slouched in, along with a few rejects from various mad scientists around the globe. I call them the *lunch bucket* computers because they assumed the shape, size, and weight of a hardhat's lunch box. The Compaq III, shown in Figure 1-4, was typical of this type of portable computer.

>> The lunch box beasts weighed anywhere from 12 to 20 pounds or more, and most weren't battery powered.

>> The lunch bucket portables were the first PCs to use full-screen LCD monitors. (The Osborne and Compaq portables used glass CRTs.)

>> Incidentally, around the same time as the lunch bucket computers became popular, color monitors were becoming standard items on desktop PCs. All portables at the time, even those with LCD monitors, were monochrome.

>> Honestly, the lunch bucket did offer something over the old transportable or luggable: less weight! A late-model lunch bucket PC weighed in at about 12 pounds, half the weight and about one-eighth the size of the suitcase-size luggables.

Dawn of the PC laptop

The computer industry's dream was to have a portable computer that had all the power and features of a desktop computer yet was about the same size and weight as the Model 100. One of the first computers to approach this mark was the Compaq SLT, back in 1988, as shown in Figure 1-5.

FIGURE 1-4:
The Compaq III.

FIGURE 1-5:
The Compaq SLT.

The Compaq SLT was the first portable computer to resemble a modern laptop: A hinged lid swings up and back from the base, which contains the keyboard. This design is known as the *clamshell.*

Feature-wise, the SLT had what most PC desktop users wanted in a portable system: a full-size keyboard, full-size screen, floppy drive, and 286 processor, which meant that the computer could run the then-popular DOS operating system. The computer lacked a hard drive.

Weight? Alas, the SLT was a bowling ball at 14 pounds!

What the Compaq SLT did was prove to the world that portability was possible. A laptop computer was designed to feature everything a desktop computer could and to run on batteries for an hour or so. Believe it or not, consumers were *delighted.*

The search for light

Just because the marketing department labeled the computer a *laptop* didn't mean that it was sleek and lightweight. For a while there, it seemed like anyone could get away with calling a portable PC a laptop, despite the computer's weight of up to 20 pounds — which is enough to crush any lap, not to mention kneecaps.

In the fall of 1989, NEC showed that it could think outside the laptop box when it introduced the UltraLite laptop, shown in Figure 1-6.

The UltraLite featured a full-size screen and keyboard but no disk drives or other moving parts! It used battery-backed-up memory to serve as a *silicon disk,* similar to today's solid-state drives (SSDs). The silicon disk stored 1 or 2MB of data — which was plenty back in those days.

As was required of all laptops, the UltraLite featured a modem, and it could talk with a desktop computer by using a special cable. Included with the UltraLite was software that would let it easily exchange files and programs with a desktop PC.

The weight? Yes, the UltraLite lived up to its name and weighed in at just under 5 pounds — a feather compared to the tumid laptops of the day. And the battery lasted a whopping 2 hours, thanks mostly to the UltraLite's lack of moving parts.

CALCULATING LAPTOP WEIGHT: THE MISSING PIECES

When computer companies specify the weights of their laptops, I'm certain that they do it under ideal conditions, possibly on the moon or at another location where gravity is weak. The advertised weight is, as they say, "for comparison purposes only."

Commonly left out of the laptop's weight specs is the *power brick*, the AC adapter that connects the laptop to a wall socket. When the laptop isn't running on batteries, you need the power brick to supply the thing with juice, so the power brick is a required accessory — something you have to tote with you if you plan to take the laptop on an extended trip.

Back when laptops were novel, the advertisements never disclosed how much the power brick weighed — sometimes half as much as the laptop itself! Either that or the power brick was even bulkier than the laptop, as shown in the figure, in the obnoxiously big Dell 320LT power brick (and its cumbersome 30-minute batteries). Lugging around those items isn't convenient. Things are better today.

FIGURE 1-6:
The NEC UltraLite.

Modern Laptops

As technology careened headlong into the 21st century, it became apparent that computer users were desperate for three things from their laptops — in addition to the basic PC compatibility, portability, and communications features that had long ago been deemed must-have items:

>> Light weight

>> Long battery life

>> Full hardware compatibility with desktop systems

Over time, all these qualities were achieved — at a price. Today, the holy grail of a lightweight, PC-compatible laptop that boasts a long battery life isn't elusive; it's just expensive!

The notebook

The modern PC laptop is dubbed a *notebook*. It can sport a full-size keyboard and numeric keypad but often has a compact keyboard. The notebook weighs in anywhere from 2 to 6 pounds, and the battery lasts somewhere between 4 to 6 hours.

The rest of the typical notebook offers features similar to a desktop PC: fast processor, lots of memory, plenty of storage, LCD screen, wireless networking, and so on. Putting all these features into a laptop computer gives you today's notebook.

The subnotebook

Human laps aren't getting any smaller. Human eyes can comfortably read text that's only so big. Most important, human fingers have trouble with keyboards that are too tiny. Despite these limitations, a popular notebook category is the *subnotebook,* which is the smallest, lightest, and most portable type of laptop.

Several kinds of subnotebooks are available, such as the Ultrabook, the netbook, and the Ultra Mobile PC (UMPC). Each of these offers compromises on the notebook design, primarily to accommodate for the smaller size and weight. Figure 1-7 illustrates a typical netbook computer from the 2000s.

FIGURE 1-7:
A netbook PC,
circa 2008.

The tablet PC

Computer manufacturers have long attempted to create the electronic equivalent of a pencil and pad of paper — a very *expensive* pencil and pad of paper. What they seek is a portable computer with a monitor but no keyboard. A digital stylus is used to write directly on the screen.

Over the years, this digital triptych has had various names attached to it: the PenGo computer, the Apple Newton, Pen Windows, and eventually the tablet PC.

The *tablet PC* can be one of two things. First, it can be a traditional laptop or notebook, but one that features a touchscreen interface. The screen can even bend and twist to cover the keyboard. This type of system might also be called a *convertible* laptop.

An even lighter and thinner version of the tablet PC exists, such as the Microsoft Surface, shown in Figure 1-8. These computers are essentially laptops without a keyboard, though a keyboard is often included as a type of cover; it's shown attached in the figure.

FIGURE 1-8:
A tablet PC.

Tablet PCs can offer pen input by using a digital pen or stylus, or your stubby human finger. This device effectively brings the laptop quest full circle to a pad of paper and pencil, although fully entrenched in the digital realm.

>> Don't confuse the tablet PC with mobile devices, such as the iPad or the Samsung Galaxy Tab. A tablet PC differs from these gizmos in that it offers features associated with traditional computers and, thanks to a keyboard, behaves as a laptop computer.

TECHNICAL STUFF

>> The ancients used something called a *tabulae ceratea* to write temporary messages. Every Greek or Roman schoolboy took with him to class a folding wooden tablet. Its insides were coated with a black wax. Using a stylus (basically a stick), the student would write into the wax, again and again. Oh, we've truly come such a long way.

Chapter **2**

A Laptop of Your Own

When you go out to buy something new and scary, like a computer or a floor-vacuuming robot, it helps to know two things: First, it helps to identify what you want to do with the new thing; second, it helps to know as much as possible about what you're buying.

For a laptop, you probably want freedom and portability, if not the social status that comes with being a smart, handsome laptop owner. For a floor-vacuuming robot, the only thing that you mustn't do is alter its programming so that it suddenly becomes hellbent on enslaving your family. Therefore, comparatively speaking, buying a laptop is far less risky.

Do You Need a Laptop?

The dream of portable computing has been realized. Laptops in all their glorious variety are everywhere.

For you as a consumer, and as someone who needs a computer in order to survive in the 21st century, the question is simple: Do you need a laptop?

As you might guess, if the answer were "No," this book would be a lot thinner.

Why you need a laptop

I can think of several reasons for buying a laptop computer:

To have a laptop as your main computer

A desktop computer cannot pretend to be a laptop, but a laptop can certainly fake being a desktop: You can use a full-size keyboard and monitor with your laptop (see Chapter 12). You can also connect any number of popular desktop peripherals, such as a printer, a scanner, or external storage. The advantage is that, unlike with a desktop system, you're free to disconnect the laptop and wander the world whenever you want.

To use a laptop as a space-saving computer system

Unlike with desktops, you don't have to build a tabletop shrine to your laptop computer — that is, you don't need a computer desk. If space is tight where you live or work, store the laptop on the shelf or in a drawer. Then set it up on the kitchen table or a coffee table whenever you're ready to work. Forget about the constant mess and clutter that orbit the typical desktop computer station.

To get a laptop as a second computer

Why buy a second desktop computer when you can get a laptop and enjoy not only the presence of a second computer but also its portability? Furthermore, you can network the two computers, allowing them to share the Internet connection and printers as well as each other's data and files.

To take the laptop on the road

Laptops let you take your work on the road. Thanks to cloud storage and other synchronization tricks, you can be off and running to anywhere you like.

>> Laptops let you escape the confines of your office and work anywhere you like for a few hours. Eventually, the battery must be recharged.

>> The laptop lets you take your work with you when you travel. It lets you experience the reality of using a computer on an airplane (which isn't as cool as it sounds).

MR. LAPTOP GOES TO COLLEGE

Setting up a computer in a college dorm room in the 1980s was the sure sign of being a nerd. Today, not setting up a laptop computer in a college dorm room is the sure sign of being a social outcast. I implore future students to pester their parental units early — say, starting in the second grade — to ensure that they leave for college armed with the best portable computing power possible.

No, I'm not being silly. Some colleges *require* students to arrive with laptops in tow. Those institutions may even publish laptop guides so that campus compatibility is guaranteed and issues such as viruses and spyware are dealt with before classes start. My advice: Follow those guidelines. Look for a laptop based on the school's recommendations. But there's still more you need to do.

Be sure to prepare a college-bound laptop for the onslaught of malware. See Chapter 19 for vital information about laptop security. Also see Chapter 20 for dealing with another college laptop issue: theft. You've probably spent a lot of time preparing for college; you should prepare the laptop for college as well.

Why you don't need a laptop

Thanks to the fees charged by the miniaturization lab, laptops are generally more expensive than their desktop counterparts. They're also more expensive to fix. Forget about upgrading the hardware. Laptops are easily stolen. The battery life never lives up to the printed specifications. It's tough to get work done on a jet or in a café unless you're really, really motivated to do so — *ack!* These are but minor quibbles.

You can dither about whether to get a laptop or a mobile device, à la the iPad. It's a legitimate debate: If all you want to do is read email, browse the web, engage in the social networking thing, take pictures, watch films, or listen to music, you don't need a laptop. Sure, the laptop can do all that, but if you don't plan to create anything or do anything else requiring a full-on PC, get a laptop or tablet PC instead.

Laptop Shopping

The best computer you can buy is the one that does what you need it to do. To find this computer, you must familiarize yourself with some issues and deliberately ignore others.

Things to ignore when buying a laptop

When it comes to spending your money on a useful computer, especially a laptop, feel free to ignore these items:

Slick marketing campaigns: You'll never be as cool as the person in the ad, no matter how much effort you put into it. As a tool, a laptop is judged by whether it offers features that you need, not by how nifty its advertising looks.

Brand name: Too many people consider brand name first and don't even know which components they need. Similarly, you don't need to buy a laptop from the same manufacturer as the one who made your desktop PC. As long as the laptop runs the software you need, you're fine.

Low price: An abundance of cheap laptops are available. In haste, you may buy a laptop, thinking that you're getting a deal — but get stuck with a brick instead.

High price: It's easy to be duped into believing that the most expensive laptop is the best. Buying too much is not a wise buying decision.

Things to heed when buying a laptop

Throughout laptop history, five key items have been vital to the laptop-choosing decision:

Weight: Nearly all laptops weigh between 2 and 7 pounds. The heavier laptops, the notebooks, have more features, such as a larger display or a numeric keypad next to the keyboard. The lighter models, the tablet PCs and subnotebooks, don't necessarily have fewer features; they might actually have more lightweight or advanced features, which makes them more expensive.

Size: Most laptops are thinner than an inch. Tablet PCs are the thinnest. Subnotebooks are the smallest.

Display: Recently, manufacturers have discovered that people love the larger screen on a laptop — even though the larger display adds to the laptop's size and weight (and consumes more battery power). For a laptop being used at one location and only rarely going on the road, a huge display is wonderful. If you want portability, though, and a longer battery life, consider a smaller display.

Touchscreen display: If the laptop advertises itself as a tablet PC, or a convertible notebook, it has a touchscreen display. You can use your finger to manipulate the touchscreen. If the laptop comes with a digital stylus or pen, all the better.

Battery life: Despite their manufacturers' claims, most laptops run anywhere from three to five hours unplugged. Subnotebooks and tablet PCs hold the record, with many of them lasting as long as ten hours. Regardless, it's possible and necessary to manage the laptop's power; see Chapters 10 and 23.

>> Stuff that's important to the overall weight of the laptop — the power brick and cord, keyboard cover, extra batteries, portable storage, and other gizmos — aren't included in the basic tonnage calculation. Keep these items in mind when weight is important to you.

>> Convertible laptops, especially those with a twisting-folding lid, are thicker than standard laptops because of the extra circuitry required for their touchscreen displays. See Chapter 7.

>> If you desire both a large display and portability, consider getting an external monitor for your laptop. This way, you can enjoy the big, roomy screen when the laptop is at your workstation and still have the portability you need when taking the laptop on the road.

Software for Your Laptop

A computer system is composed of two parts: hardware and software. When you buy a new laptop, you probably pay more attention to the hardware. This approach is understandable, but it isn't the reason you bought the device: Laptops, like all computers, exist to run *software*. If you want a laptop that does everything you need, I recommend looking for software first and then finding hardware to match that software.

The operating system

The main program that controls your laptop is the *operating system*. It's the computer's brain, giving the laptop its personality and giving you, the human, a way to control the computer.

For nearly all PC laptops, the operating system is Microsoft Windows. This book is specific to Windows 10, which has been around since 2015. Given that most laptops last perhaps six years at the most, my guess is that all PC laptops today run Windows 10.

>> There's no special laptop version of Windows. The operating system offers features specific to laptops with touchscreens, but otherwise it's the same Windows you would use and dislike on a desktop computer system.

>> If you have an older laptop that runs a previous version of Windows, please back up your data and consider buying a new laptop at once!

>> See Chapter 8 for more information on Windows.

Other software

Laptop computers run the same software as desktop computers. Most major computer applications, such as Microsoft Office, are commonly used on laptops and might even come preinstalled. Just about everything you can run on a desktop PC runs on a laptop.

>> Laptops are okay for playing computer games, but you need to ensure that your laptop has the graphics horsepower to run high-end computer games, such as *Call of Duty* or *Mass Effect*. Such hardware makes the laptop larger, which is good because those games benefit from a bigger display.

>> If you plan to run graphics editing programs, get a laptop with a high-end video card, larger display, and lots of memory.

>> If you plan to edit video on your laptop, you need the maximum amount of internal storage. I recommend an SSD, if you can afford one. It's also advisable to get an external hard drive or another type of storage, which many video editing programs require.

>> See Chapter 9 for information on installing new programs, as well as on removing some of those "free" programs that are included on a new laptop.

Laptop Hardware Buying Decisions

In the balance between computer hardware and software, it's the software that determines what type of hardware, and how much of it, you need. After you know the software's needs, choosing the matching hardware is a snap.

Important laptop hardware guts

For a laptop, weight, size, and battery take center stage. However, these components aren't the only hardware specs you should pay attention to. As with all computers, other hardware items play a role in computer performance and must also be part of your laptop purchase decision. They are described in this list:

Processor: Spend the extra money to invest in a fast processor. Doing so extends the useful life of your laptop by ensuring that you can run tomorrow's software before tomorrow comes, but not before yesterday. You'll be thankful later.

Memory: *Memory* is where the action happens in a computer, where the work gets done. Not having enough memory in your laptop limits its performance. Having enough (or way too much) memory makes Mr. Laptop very happy.

Mass storage: The mass storage device is the electronic closet where the laptop stores your stuff. The mass storage device is either the traditional *hard drive* or a *solid-state drive (SSD)*. It must have room for the computer's operating system, all the software you get and later install, all the data files and junk you collect, plus room (lotsa room) to grow.

TIP

>> The *processor* is the main chip inside a computer. It's not the computer's "brain." Software is the computer's brain. No, the processor is more like the computer's muscle.

>> Laptop processors are more expensive than their desktop counterparts. The reason is that laptop processors are designed to use less power and generate less heat. These improvements take time, so their development cycle is longer; hence the added cost.

>> How do you know how much memory or storage is enough? Easy: Look at the software you want to use. For example, if the software states that it wants 2GB of memory, get a laptop with at least that much memory. If the software requires at least 100GB of drive storage space, factor that amount into your laptop's mass storage capacity requirements.

>> If you cannot afford a faster processor, get more RAM.

>> The things that consume huge amounts of drive storage space are video, music, and photos, in that order. If you plan to collect any of these types of files on your laptop, get a humongous hard drive!

>> I recommend a laptop with at least 500GB of mass storage. If you need more storage, obtain a traditional hard drive because high-capacity SSDs are expensive.

>> Tablet PCs don't require as much storage as traditional laptops. The reason is that tablet PCs are used primarily for nonproductivity purposes — reading email, browsing the web, or enjoying digital entertainment.

>> Few, if any, laptops today come with an optical drive. If you need such a drive, buy an external, USB DVD drive. You can attach this drive to your laptop when needed; you don't need to lug the gizmo around with you.

REMEMBER

» By investing in the latest, fastest processor, lots of RAM, and copious amounts of mass storage now, you're extending the life of your laptop. That's a good thing. You want your laptop investment to last for years. Pay more now, and you earn it back down the road, when you're still using your laptop while others are forced to buy a new one.

TECHNICAL STUFF

» *GB* is the abbreviation for *gigabyte*. It means 1 billion characters of computer storage. A GB is approximately 1,000MB. *MB* is the abbreviation for *megabyte*, or 1 million characters of computer storage. One MB stores about one minute of music, a 3-by-4-inch digital photo of low quality, or as much text as you'll find in a typical novel with or without a decent plot.

Communications options

Your laptop must have gizmos that quench its communications thirst. Here are the options, in order of importance:

Wireless networking: It's a given that your laptop must come with some type of wireless Ethernet adapter. Connecting to a Wi-Fi network is a must. See Chapter 16 for details.

Wired networking: Traditional laptops come with a wired Ethernet port, allowing you to connect the device to a wired network when one is available. Most of the time, the laptop uses the Wi-Fi connection. Ethernet ports aren't available on netbooks and many tablet PCs.

» Long gone from the laptop landscape is the dialup modem. Quite frankly, long gone is the dialup phone line once used to host this antiquated type of Internet access.

» Another communications option is sharing a smartphone's mobile data connection with your laptop. This process, called *USB tethering*, is covered in Chapter 16.

The green laptop

As human beings, it is our duty to be good stewards of the environment. If you care about your mom (the other mom, Mother Earth), you can be wise about how you spend the planet's resources when you make your laptop-buying decision. Two issues are important: power usage and materials.

In power usage, laptops have always been ahead of the computer desktop curve when it comes to getting the most from our planet's energy resources. See Chapter 10 for information on power management.

Beyond power usage, you can check the greenness of your laptop's materials: Some laptops are designed from environmentally friendly materials or at least contain no lead, mercury, plutonium, mayonnaise, or other toxic materials. Even better, some laptops are designed to be recycled. The only way to know is to check with the manufacturer; they love boasting about such things.

Service, Support, and Warranty

The issue of service and support is much more important for a laptop than for a desktop computer. A laptop is a unit. It lacks the easily replaceable components of a desktop. As such, it's not an item that just anyone can fix.

To ensure that you start out your laptop experience on the best foot possible, I have three recommendations:

First, determine where your laptop will be repaired. Odds are good that it won't be in the back room at the local Mega Mart where you purchased the thing. The laptop will probably take a trip through the mail. If that's not what you want, ensure that you buy an onsite support option when you buy the laptop. (Yes, some manufacturers offer this service.)

Second, research technical support for your laptop. Most manufacturers offer phone support. Is it good? Terrible? In your native tongue? Maybe a superior support option is available for an extra price. If you need it, buy it.

Finally, definitely buy a long-term warranty with your laptop. Most manufacturers offer a standard 90-day or even 1-year warranty. I recommend at least a 3-year warranty. This long-term warranty is recommended because if the laptop breaks, the *entire unit* must be replaced. Doing so isn't cheap.

>> Some manufacturers offer you a replacement laptop by way of mail-in service while yours is being fixed. Consider this offer a bonus.

>> A lack of service and support is one reason that some dealers (and large department stores and discount houses) offer laptops at ridiculously cheap prices. Don't ever expect the employees in such a place to be able to help you, and the guy who cuts meat in the back can't fix your laptop, either.

WARNING

>> Don't buy a service contract! It's not the same thing as a warranty. A service contract is basically a way for the big box store to make *even more* money from suckers. The extended warranty that I recommend is offered by the manufacturer, not the store. This warranty covers your laptop just fine and dandy. The service contract does nothing.

The Final Step: Buying Your Laptop

When you're ready to buy your laptop, buy it!

Don't sit and wait for a better deal or a lower price. You can *always* find a better deal and a lower price. Hardware gets faster and better. The price always comes down. Therefore, when you're ready to buy, take the plunge and buy! Waiting gets you nowhere.

TIP

>> If possible, use a credit card to pay for your laptop. The law offers far more protection to credit card users than to people who pay by check or — don't even think about it — cash.

>> See Chapter 4 for information on migrating information from your old laptop to a new one.

2

Say Hello to Your Laptop

Chapter **3**

From Laptop Box to Lap

After being awarded a huge government grant, scientists have proven that any computer works best when you first remove it from its shipping box. Yes, I was surprised. Even more so, I was surprised that removing a laptop from its box and getting it onto your lap involves more steps than you might expect.

Laptop Box 101

I write this section with the full knowledge that it's probably too late: The box that your laptop came in is open. The foam packing material has been removed. Plastic has been peeled off. The laptop most likely sits in front of you. Great! Now you can get to the real point of this section: things to observe and pay attention to regarding that box and all the goodies inside.

> » When you're lucky enough to find instructions on how to unpack the box, heed them! I refer specifically to labels such as Open Other Side and Remove First.

>> Ensure that you open and free the packing slip if it's attached to the outside of the box. The slip contains the shipping invoice, which you should examine to confirm that what was shipped is exactly what you ordered. If the packing slip isn't on the outside of the box, look for it on the inside.

WARNING

>> Always open computer equipment boxes with your hands. Never use a box cutter, because you can slice into something important.

>> Beware of those big, ugly staples often used to close cardboard boxes. They can go a-flyin' when you rip things open, poking out eyeballs or just lying in wait on the floor for a bare foot.

>> Always look for boxes within boxes. Also be on the lookout for items stuck in the sides or ends of the packing material.

>> Do not eat the foam packing material. When people say that rice cakes taste like foam packing material, they're being facetious.

REMEMBER

>> Fill out warranty and registration information only after you're certain that the laptop works.

Removing the laptop from the box

Laptops, like all computers, come with lots of bits and pieces. Some of that stuff isn't junk, and you want to keep it for as long as you own the laptop. Other stuff is junk, and you can throw it away. The problem: It's difficult to determine what's worth keeping and what to toss. My advice is to keep everything for now.

Here's a handy way to approach this unpacking and pre–setup stage of your lap-top's introduction to your lap:

1. Unpack the laptop.

Remove the laptop from any plastic bag or shrink-wrap. Don't worry about opening the laptop's lid yet (though the temptation may be great). Just set the thing on a table by itself. When you do this, say "There."

2. Find all the various hardware pieces that came with the laptop.

Primarily, look for the power adapter and power cord. If your laptop came with only these scant items, wonderful.

Secondarily, locate the battery (if it's not installed), extra batteries (if any), cables, connectors, weird and tiny gizmos that you'll probably lose eventually, and other mystery junk.

TIP

A handy trend for many manufacturers is to include a computer road map with the laptop. It's often the first thing you find when you open the box. Unfold the map to see a visual guide to your laptop, including setup directions.

3. **Make a pile for all the paperwork.**

Separate the product keys, manual, warranty, special offers, and weird piece of paper, the importance of which cannot be determined. Most important are the product keys, which help install or activate any software that comes with the laptop. The manual, if one exists, is so brief as to be a joke.

4. **Place all packing material back into the box.**

This material includes plastic bags, twist-ties from the cables, and those silica pouches they tell you not to eat (probably because the stuff inside would give you superhuman powers).

Later, after your laptop is all set up and you're starting to become familiar with it, you can further organize the detritus from the box. As you work, you need to keep various items with the laptop at all times — for example, the power cord, extra batteries, and other objects, depending on how you use the laptop. You need a place, such as a laptop case, for those items.

Other stuff that comes with your laptop you might want to keep for as long as you own the laptop, such as any manuals or documentation. These things need not be kept with the laptop all the time, so storing them in a drawer or on a shelf is okay.

Only after using the laptop for a while should you consider throwing stuff away, such as the special-offer cards you don't need. Oftentimes, you can just toss those things in the laptop box. See the next section to find out what to do with the box.

TIP

>> If the laptop comes with a how-to manual, consider yourself lucky. Most laptops have no how-to material whatsoever.

>> Sometimes, the only manuals that come with the laptop are directories listing the locations where you can get it fixed. Sometimes, this material is in English.

>> Don't lose the product keys!

>> See Chapter 13 for information on finding the best laptop bag. Even though your laptop may come with a genuine imitation-leatherette case, you want to see what else is available.

>> I have a shelf in my office where I store important material that comes with every computer I own. Each one has its own container, and each container holds all the stuff that came with the computer that I want to keep: spare parts and manuals and other documentation. I suggest that you have a similar shelf or location for a container or special box for your laptop's extra stuff. Or throw it all in the everything drawer. I won't judge you.

"How long should I keep the box?"

I recommend keeping the box and the packing material for as long as you own the laptop. That way, if you need to ship the laptop to a repair center or return it to the dealer, you have the original box.

When the laptop dies, you can then bury it in its original box, throwing out both at the same time or using them for recycling purposes.

>> Many dealers and repair centers accept laptop returns only when packed in the original boxes.

>> You might actually have *two* boxes: the laptop box and the shipping box that the laptop box comes in. Feel free to toss out or recycle the shipping box.

>> If you don't have the original box, you can order another one — but why pay for it when you can just save the original?

>> No, you don't need to pack the laptop in a box when you take it on the road; slipping the laptop into a suitable bag is fine for that purpose. You need the boxes only if you plan to mail or ship the laptop.

Submitting the warranty

Wait a week to ensure that the laptop works and that you have everything you ordered. When you're satisfied, submit the warranty card: Fill in the card and mail it or visit the proper website to fill out the online warranty.

>> When you order a computer directly from the manufacturer, you usually don't need to fill out a warranty.

WARNING

>> In some cases, activating the warranty sets the start date for the warranty period. Otherwise, the warranty may start on the day the laptop was manufactured, which could have been three months ago! Read the card or other information to be sure.

Set Up Your Laptop

All laptops have a generic look to them. At first glance, you might even say that all laptops look alike. Even so, they have subtle differences. Anyone who replaces an older laptop with a newer model recognizes instantly that the power button isn't in the exact same place. And those newer laptops? The keyboard may just pop off like it's some kind of peripheral.

When your laptop has come with specific setup directions, follow them. If not, or in addition to those directions, follow the information in this section to get your laptop all set up and ready for use.

Finding a place for the laptop

Yes, you can put the laptop in your lap. But what happens to your lap when you stand up?

Ah-ha!

Unlike desktop PCs, laptops can go anywhere or be put anywhere. No wonder they're popular! With a fully charged battery, your laptop has a home wherever you go. Beyond that, you can place your laptop anywhere you like: on the kitchen table, the coffee table, a real desk, or a computer desk — or in bed with you.

Here are some general laptop-location tips:

TIP

>> Use the laptop on a flat, steady surface.

>> Yep: Your lap is not a flat, steady surface. It's okay for short spells, but, otherwise, I recommend that you find something more stable.

>> The flat surface is a must: The laptop has air vents to help keep it cool. Setting the laptop on a pillow or another nonflat surface makes the laptop run hotter than it would like.

>> Keep the laptop away from the sun, if possible. Heat isn't good for any computer, and you can't see the screen in direct sunlight (or else you'll waste battery power turning up the screen-brightness level).

>> Likewise, use your laptop in a well-ventilated area. Don't cover the laptop while it's on and open.

>> Keep Mr. Laptop away from, or out of spilling range of, any drinks or food you might be consuming.

>> If possible, connect the laptop to a power source while you use it.

>> Have a place to store your laptop when it's not in use: in a drawer or on a shelf. Keeping it in the same place means that you can always find it when you need it.

» Though you can use the laptop anywhere, be aware of ergonomics! For example, when you're using the laptop on a coffee table, if you start to feel a pain in your back from hunching over, stop! Find a better, more comfortable place to work.

Charging the battery

Your laptop may or may not have a fully charged battery when you first take it out of the box. Therefore, one of the things you need to do after finding a place for the laptop is to charge its battery.

If necessary, insert the battery into the laptop. Plug in or attach the battery per the directions that came with the laptop or, quite handily, etched into the bottom of the laptop case. Few laptops today feature removable batteries, so consider yourself fortunate if you can skip this step.

Plug in the laptop, as illustrated in Figure 3-1.

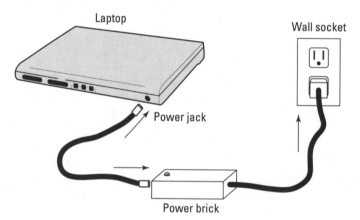

FIGURE 3-1:
Plugging in your laptop.

Insert one end of the power cord into the laptop's power cord connector. Attach the power cord to the power brick, if necessary. Plug the power brick into the wall. Note that the power brick may also contain the plug that connects directly to the wall.

That's it. The laptop's battery is charging. Yes, the battery charges even when the laptop's power is off.

» Laptops with removable batteries sport different methods for inserting, installing, or attaching the battery. Clues can be found on the laptop's case or on the battery itself. You might even find an instruction sheet, but don't count on it.

>> The advantage of a removable battery is that you can keep both charged to effectively double the laptop's useful, unplugged life.

>> It usually takes a while to charge a laptop's battery. The length of time depends on the type of battery and power management hardware and on whether you're using the laptop at the time. Even so:

>> The good news is that you can start using your laptop right away — just keep it plugged in so that the battery can charge.

>> Refer to Chapter 10 for more information on using the laptop's battery and power management system.

"Should I plug the laptop into a UPS?"

I advise my desktop computer readers in *PCs For Dummies* (Wiley) to consider investing in an uninterruptible power supply, or UPS — specifically, one with both surge and spike protection. This device serves to protect the computer from nasty electrical intruders that can come through the power lines, but also to provide emergency power if the electricity goes bye-bye.

A UPS for a laptop is unnecessary. The main reason is that your laptop already has a battery for backup power. If you're running your laptop from an electrical outlet and the electricity goes off (or some doofus unplugs it), the laptop quickly and happily switches its power source to the internal battery. Nothing is lost!

>> Although you don't need a UPS for your laptop, I still highly recommend plugging your portable 'puter into a power strip that offers surge protection and line filtering. Such a gizmo helps keep your laptop's power source clean and steady.

>> Generally speaking, if a lightning storm is nearby, don't plug your laptop into the wall unless you're using a spike protection filter. This admonition holds for the network cable as well. Wait until the storm passes before reconnecting the laptop.

Bye-Bye, Old Laptop

Getting a new laptop is so enjoyable that you'll probably forget about the old laptop. Above all, recognize that electronics lack feelings. Jealousy isn't part of the computer's programming. Yet.

As long as the old laptop still works, don't throw it away. First, migrate your old files and programs to the new laptop, as covered in Chapter 4. Second, remove the old laptop's battery (if possible). Third, put the laptop back in its original box, or store it someplace where it won't be thrown out accidentally.

Deciding when to retire an old laptop

Laptops should last at least three years, which is magically the same length of time as the maximum warranty provided by most manufacturers. I've had laptops last even longer, but after a point they do run slow or just start acting silly. Eventually new technology passes your laptop in terms of price and performance.

More key than hardware failure is battery failure. Even with modern battery technology, eventually a laptop's battery no longer keeps a charge. At that point you can buy a replacement battery, if available. Or you can run the laptop purely from AC power.

Disposing of the old laptop

After you officially retire the old laptop and replace it with a new one, keep the old one around for a bit longer. I store old laptops in my computer bone yard. They sit in their boxes (which I save), along with all other pieces and parts. I do reuse items such as external mice and thumb drives, but the laptop itself gets retired.

>> Every five years or so, I purge old computers and laptops. Don't let nostalgia cloud your resolve: Dispose of your ancient technology.

>> Before letting the laptop sail off into the digital sunset, I remove its mass storage device — the hard drive or SSD. Because it may still contain sensitive data, I dispose of the old hard drive at a data recycling center, which properly destroys the drive and all its data.

>> Along with the drive, I remove the battery. Dispose of old laptop batteries per the rules and regulations of your locality. Batteries are *not* to be tossed in with the rest of the rubbish.

>> The laptop might also be recyclable. Many waste transfer stations harvest the precious metals and other valuables from old electronics. Inquire with your local sanitation or recycling service for details.

>> Old technology holds no value. If your laptop was old enough to replace, it's too old to be of value to anyone — even a nonprofit or charity.

TECHNICAL STUFF

What to Do Next

My guess is that after setting up your laptop, you'll want to turn it on and see how it works. This desire is understandable, but it's a separate task from unpacking the laptop, so I've put that information in Chapter 4. Here are some other spots in the book that you should consider visiting to help start out your laptop journey on the proper foot:

>> You can find information in Chapters 4 and 5 about turning a laptop on or off. Turning it off can be an interesting adventure, especially if you've never used a battery-powered computer.

>> Chapter 6 helps you overview the various parts of your laptop.

>> For a tablet PC, check Chapter 7 to review the special tablet features.

>> Power management on a portable computer is a big deal, so consider putting Chapter 10 on your homework reading list.

>> Whether you're new to the concept of wireless networking or just eager to set things up, visit Chapter 16. There you find a rundown of the basic wireless networking ordeal for a laptop computer.

>> Before taking your laptop on the road, read Chapter 13, which covers a few nifty things you might want to consider before you venture out into the cold, cruel world with your new computer companion.

Chapter **4**

To Turn On a Laptop

O h, please! How tough can it be to turn on a laptop computer? Does the author really need to write an entire chapter on the topic? Or am I misreading the title and this chapter has a romantic subject? Or perhaps one of betrayal?

Turning on a laptop is more than flipping a switch. First, it's not a switch: It's a *power button*. Second, the power button is typically under the lid, which is something you're not used to if you're a desktop PC user. Finally, you need to contend with Windows. Details on this information just can't squeeze into a single paragraph. No! You need paragraphs and lovely illustrations. Yes, a chapter is required, a whole chapter.

Turn On Your Laptop

Turning on a traditional notebook-style laptop computer involves four steps: Open the lid, adjust the lid for optimal viewing, find the power button, and then push the power button. Oh, and you end up adjusting the lid after the power is on, but this isn't an initial step.

Turning on a tablet PC involves hunting down the power button, pushing the power button, and then using the device with either one hand, two hands, or all three hands.

These descriptions describe the easy part. Now come the details.

Step 1: Open the lid

Of all the notebook-style laptops I've owned, it seems that no two open the same way. The current trend is to have the device open without working any latch mechanism; you just open the lid. Still, your laptop may feature one or more latches. These may be in front or on the sides. The latch may be a slider or a button. Use Figure 4-1 as your guide to finding the latch.

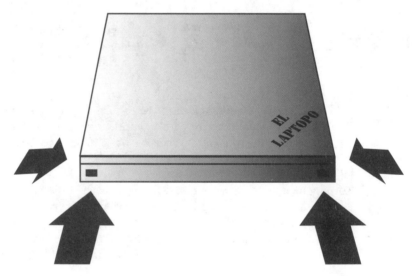

FIGURE 4-1:
Likely locations
for laptop lid
latches.

After you work the latch, lift the lid. If the laptop has no latch, lift the lid and rejoice that your portable PC lacks a latch.

>> Obviously, tablet PCs lack a latch because the laptop is the lid. Or the keyboard cover might be the lid.

>> The front side of the laptop is the side opposite the lid's hinge. This orientation is often difficult to remember because the logo on the lid appears upside-down when the lid is closed. This arrangement is so that the lid appears right side up when the lid is open.

>> You can configure the laptop to remain on when the lid is closed — for example, when you're using the laptop with an external monitor, keyboard, or mouse. See Chapter 12 for details.

Step 2: Adjust the lid for optimal viewing

Raise the lid to an angle best suited for viewing; use Figure 4-2 as your guide.

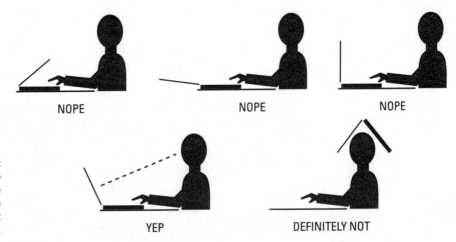

FIGURE 4-2:
Adjust the lid so that you view the screen at an angle that's just right for you.

Convertible laptops might allow you to open, twist, and reset the lid so that the monitor faces up when you lay the laptop flat.

Some tablet PCs feature a kickstand on the back. Pop out the kickstand to prop up the tablet. Other tablet PCs may feature a folding lid or cover, which you can arrange to help prop up the screen for better viewing.

TECHNICAL STUFF

Employees at the Apple Store adjust the lids on all the demo laptops to precisely 70 degrees. The idea isn't to present the laptop at the perfect viewing angle but rather to encourage potential buyers to touch the machine by adjusting its lid.

Step 3: Locate the power button

Laptop designers have grown adept at hiding or masking the power button. I've seen it on the side of older laptops, though to keep the computer from being turned on inside a briefcase, most manufacturers now put the power button inside the laptop, up near the lid hinge. Look for it there.

A tablet PC sports its power button on the device's edge.

 As a clue to finding the power button, look for the universal power button symbol, shown in the margin. This symbol appears on or near the power button, or not at all.

>> Sometimes, the power button symbol is different from the circle/slash icon, shown in the margin: The symbol can be a solid dot, a line-and-a-circle for On and Off, respectively, or, occasionally, the crescent moon symbol.

>> The power button may be a spring-slide switch that you must push in one direction and then release.

>> Some power buttons are tiny push buttons, or what I call *press-and-pray* buttons. There's no click or bump to the button's feel; you press it in with your finger and then pray that the laptop obeys you.

>> On a convertible laptop, the power button is most likely located on the monitor. This way, it can be accessed when the monitor is folded flat, when the laptop is in Tablet mode. In this configuration, look for a special power-button lock. The lock prevents the power button from being punched accidentally when the tablet laptop is in full Tablet mode.

Step 4: Punch the power button

To turn on your laptop, press the power button.

Sometimes, you can turn on the laptop by opening the lid. Sometimes, you can *wake up* a laptop by tapping a key on the keyboard. Whether these tricks work depends on how the laptop was shut down. But for all intents and purposes, punching the power button does the job most of the time.

REMEMBER

>> It's a *power button,* not an On–Off switch.

>> The power button may illuminate while the laptop is on.

>> If nothing happens when you punch the button, the battery is most likely dead: Plug the laptop into a wall socket by using its AC adapter cord (or module or power-brick thing).

>> Check all power cables! The power brick may wiggle loose from the wall socket cable.

>> When everything is plugged in and nothing happens, you have a problem. Contact your dealer or laptop manufacturer for assistance.

NERDY TERMS FOR STARTING A COMPUTER

Despite years of effort to come up with better words, the computer industry struggles with antique and obscure jargon to say "Start the computer." Among the lingo, you find these terms:

boot: To turn the thing on, or to "pull it up by its bootstraps." In fact, *bootstrap* is an even older version of this term. *Boot* is the oldest computer term, but the easiest to spell.

cold boot: To turn on the computer when it has been off for a while. *See also* warm boot.

cycle power: To turn off the computer by waiting a few seconds and then turning it on again. This process is often required when you try to fix something.

Das Boot: Not a computer term; rather, the title of a German film about a World War II U-boat.

power up, power on: More human terms for "Turn on the computer."

restart, reboot: To shut down a computer and then start it without turning off the power.

start, turn on, switch on: Additional human terms for "Turn on the computer."

warm boot: Another term for *restart, reboot,* or *reset.*

It's Windows!

When your laptop starts up, you see some initial messages and perhaps the manufacturer's logo or graphic, and then the computer's *operating system* — its main program — comes to life. For all PC laptops covered in this book, this program is Windows.

Laptops use the same version of Windows that's used on desktop PCs. Extra options are made available for laptops; specifically, for power management and battery monitoring. Plus, other utilities and fun junk may have been installed by the laptop manufacturer. Otherwise, it's the same Windows you know and despise.

>> This book covers Windows 10, which is the current and most fabulous version of Windows for today's laptops, notebooks, and tablet PCs.

>> Chapter 8 notes those places in Windows with which laptop computer owners should be familiar.

>> Messages may appear before Windows starts, especially when the laptop was improperly turned off or the laptop's battery expired the last time you used it. These messages are expected as the laptop recovers from mishaps and improper shutdowns.

Running Windows for the first time

When you first turn on a brand-new laptop, Windows completes some gyrations and prompts you to set up and configure various system settings. These include items such as the language you'll use on the laptop (I'm guessing English), the time zone, and your name. It's routine computer housekeeping stuff.

You may also be prompted to use or create a Microsoft account, which includes an account name and a password.

Another important step is to connect with the Internet. If a Wi-Fi network is available, sign in to that network to help expedite the Windows configuration process. See Chapter 16 for information on connecting to Wi-Fi networks.

After you answer the questions, Windows is fully installed. More configuration may be necessary, such as specifying networking options and customizing the Windows environment. You can mess with these options later.

TIP

>> When you're asked to create user accounts, create only one, for yourself. Don't bother creating them yet for every member of the whole fam-damily as well as for your pets. You can do that later, and then only when other people *really* need to use the laptop.

>> Though you don't need to use a Microsoft account to sign in to Windows, using or creating such an account has advantages. For example, Windows remembers your settings across multiple computers. I've not had any issue with using my Microsoft account, but, again, it's not a requirement.

>> The main Windows account is known as *Administrator*. This account is the one that's used to modify the computer, add new software, and tend to other

administrative chores. Even when you don't intend it, when you're the only person using the computer, *you* are the administrator.

>> Do not forget the administrator's password! The password cannot be recovered if it's lost.

>> See Chapter 20 for more information on passwords and Windows security issues.

Activating Windows

Soon after you complete the initial setup, you're asked to "activate" Windows. Activation requires an Internet connection so that your laptop can chat with the Microsoft mothership. The purpose behind activation is to ensure that your laptop is running a legitimate copy of Windows. If it isn't, or if you elect not to activate, Windows won't function on your laptop. My advice: Activate when prompted.

Signing in to Windows

After the initial setup, and every time you start your laptop after that, you're greeted with the graphical fun and folly of the Windows operating system.

The first step is to sign in to Windows, which is like identifying yourself to the warden. It involves supplying a user account name and a password to verify that you are who you claim to be.

The very first screen shown in Windows 10 is called the *lock screen.* Press Enter or swipe the screen to summon the sign-in screen. A sample sign-in screen is illustrated in Figure 4-3. Here's what to do:

1. **Type your password in the box or, if it's enabled, type your PIN.**

Click the mouse or tap the screen to activate the box. For a tablet PC, an onscreen keyboard appears.

If you've set up a PIN and you type it in, you're done signing in. Otherwise:

2. **Press Enter or, on a touchscreen, tap the arrow.**

When the stars are aligned in your favor, you're granted access to Windows.

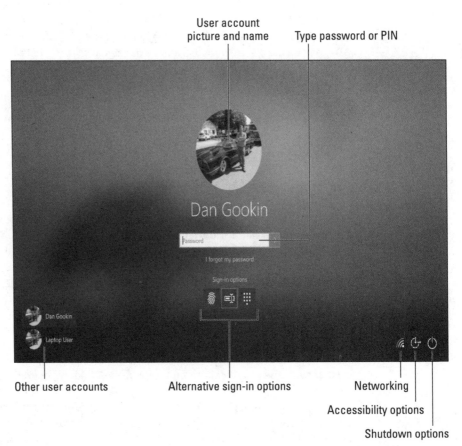

User account
picture and name

Type password or PIN

Dan Gookin

Password

I forgot my password

Sign-in options

Other user accounts

Alternative sign-in options

Networking

Accessibility options

Shutdown options

FIGURE 4-3:
The Windows 10
sign-in screen.

After a few frantic moments, you see the Windows desktop and you can start using the laptop. See Chapter 8 for a discussion on using Windows after you sign in.

>> If your laptop comes with a fingerprint reader, you can use it to identify yourself: Swipe or press your finger (or thumb) on the reader bar. That's all you need to do.

>> Yes, the fingerprint reader works whether your finger is attached or not. And yes, you watch too many spy movies.

>> The Accessibility Options button (refer to Figure 4-3) displays options for folks needing physical assistance when using the laptop.

>> The Shutdown Options button in the lower right corner of the screen displays a menu with various choices for turning off the laptop. See Chapter 5 for a description of these options.

» Windows 10 uses the term *sign in* to refer to the process of identifying your account on the laptop. Other terms include *log on* or *log in*. These differing terms are offered to help foster confusion among Windows users.

» By the way, it's *log,* as in *to write down.* It has nothing to do with timber.

What's Next?

Just because you have a new laptop doesn't mean you must start over. If you're moving from an old laptop to a new one, you probably want to keep your favorite files, documents, photos, videos, music, and all those programs. The process is called *migration.* Once, Windows made it easy. Not any more.

Migrating your files

I'll be blunt: It's not easy to move files over from your old laptop to the new one. In earlier versions of Windows, the process was seamless, thanks to a program called the Windows Migration Wizard. It worked so well that Microsoft decided not to include this program with Windows 10.

Your only alternative is to connect both new and old laptops to the same network and then transfer files manually. This can be avoided for all cloud storage, because files stored on the cloud (such as OneDrive) are automatically synchronized, but the rest of the lot must be copied manually.

Here are the general steps to take to migrate files from your old laptop to the new one:

1. Ensure that both laptops are on and connected to the same network.

The network can be wired or wireless. If you need confirmation, refer to Chapter 17 for information on using the Network window. The network must be private, and file and folder sharing must be active. Chapter 17 holds the details.

If both laptops see each other in the Network window, you're good to go.

2. On the old laptop, find your User Profile folder.

The *user profile* is your main account folder. Press Win+E to open a File Explorer window. Into the address bar, type **%userprofile%** and press Enter.

3. Share your User Profile folder.

Right-click the folder (not on a specific file or folder) and choose Properties. In the folder's Properties dialog box, click the Sharing tab. Click the Advanced Sharing button. Ensure that the item Share This Folder is checked. Click the OK button. Refer to Chapter 17 for info on sharing folders.

After the folder on the old laptop is shared, you can access your files and copy them to the new computer.

4. On the new laptop, open the Network window and browse to the shared User Profile folder on the old laptop.

Choose Network from a File Explorer window, as shown in Figure 4-4. Open the old laptop's icon, and then open the shared User Profile folder. You see all your old folders in the window, which is how you access the old laptop's files.

Path to the User Profile folder   The User Profile folder

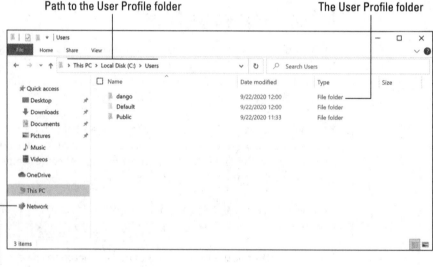

The Network folder

FIGURE 4-4:
Finding your User
Profile folder.

5. Visit your User Profile folder on the new laptop.

Follow the directions for Step 2, although you're hunting down your User Profile folder on the new laptop, not the old.

In the end, you have two open folder windows: one representing files on the old laptop and the second showing files on the new laptop.

6. **Copy from one window to the other those files you want to keep.**

For example, open the Pictures folder from your old laptop, and then select and copy all the files. Open the Pictures folder on your new laptop and paste the files.

Repeat this step for each folder on the old laptop. Yes, it's tedious, but that's how it's done. And it doesn't take that much time, especially considering the alternative methods, crude and ugly.

Alas, these steps don't copy over your programs. Even the old Migration Wizard didn't perform this task. See the next section for more information on reinstalling your favorite software.

REMEMBER

>> The crude-and-ugly alternative is to copy files from the old laptop to a thumb drive or another type of external storage. Then you add the storage to the new laptop and copy over the files, which is an extra, bothersome, painful step.

>> Any files you have on cloud storage are copied over as soon as you install the cloud storage software on your new laptop. This storage includes Microsoft's own OneDrive but also Dropbox, Google Drive, Amazon Cloud, and other storage. Install those cloud storage programs and you'll instantly see the files. See Chapter 18 for details.

Reinstalling your programs

Lamentably, you can't just copy software from the old laptop to the new. Software is installed, not copied. As long as you have the setup program, you reinstall the software. Here are the methods for accessing the setup program:

>> Locate the original software download, which was copied from the old laptop and most likely found in the Downloads folder. Run this program again to reinstall.

>> For subscription software services, visit the web page to download the software and configure the new laptop's subscription.

Yes, these are tedious things to do, but the method is proper: Run the installation program or obtain new software from the website. You may need to verify your registration and unregister the other computer if you're allowed only a given number of software installations. For example, you may have a license to run Microsoft Office on only one computer.

>> The product keys and other software installation information are details you should keep with all the papers and whatnot that arrived with your laptop. Refer to Chapter 3.

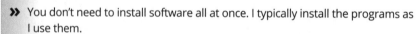

>> If your software arrived on an optical disc, use this disc to reinstall the program. You need the product key, and if your laptop lacks an optical drive, you need to use a USB optical drive. (See Chapter 12.)

>> After downloading programs, you may invariably need to download updates and patches. The onscreen directions explain what to do.

>> You don't need to install software all at once. I typically install the programs as I use them.

TIP

Adding other accounts

It's rare but entirely possible to add another user account to your laptop. This might be an account for a pesky relative who doesn't want to buy their own laptop or an account for a child, who is another type of pesky relative.

Not many people add second accounts to their laptops. It's not required to have more than your own account on the computer. Should the need arise, follow these steps to add a second account in Windows 10:

1. Press Win+I to summon the Settings screen.

2. Click the Accounts button.

3. On the left side of the screen, choose Family & Other Users.

4. Click Add a Family Member.

5. If you're creating a child's account, choose the link Create One for a Child.

More restrictions can be placed on a child's account, as covered in Chapter 19.

6. Type the person's email address.

Or, better, hand the laptop to the other person and let them expend the typing energy.

Yes, you need an email address to verify the account.

7. Click the Next button.

8. Click the Confirm button.

An email is sent to the address specified in Step 6.

The additional account is set up and the user can sign in. The account must be confirmed, however. Further steps are provided in the email sent to the account holder.

See Chapter 5 for information on switching from one account to another.

Chapter **5**

To Turn Off a Laptop

The concept of an Off button is lost on the computer industry. Using extreme logic that few sentient beings harbor, the same button that turns on a laptop also turns off the laptop. Even worse, that button — the power button — may not turn off the laptop at all!

End Your Laptop Day

Given the rich variety of ways to properly dismiss a laptop, many users overlook the most obvious way: Heave the thing through a window. Until the laptop lid is spring-loaded and defenestration software is perfected, you can explore the aero-dynamic potential of a flying laptop all by yourself. What remains are the multi-tudinous existing options for ending your laptop day.

Keeping the laptop on all the time

The first option for ending your laptop day is not to end it at all. Leave the laptop on! Eventually, the laptop enters Sleep mode, which keeps the screen dark and saves power. Sleep mode is covered in Chapter 10.

Though I can see the reason for leaving a desktop computer on all the time, I don't recommend doing so for a laptop. The primary reason is that laptops run hot. It's a good idea to shut them down, one way or another, when you're done working.

Finding the shutdown options

As you might suspect, Windows does a magnificent job of obscuring the available methods of dismissing your laptop. Three different locations are available for the several sets of choices.

The first location is the Power menu, which lists the more traditional shutdown choices. The Power menu is found on the Start button menu, as illustrated in Figure 5-1.

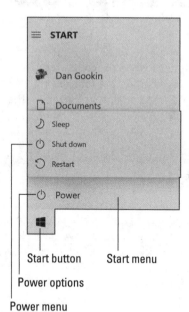

Start button   Start menu

FIGURE 5-1: Power options on the Start menu. Power options

Power menu

To display the Power menu, follow these steps:

1. **Click or tap the Start button.**

You can also press the Windows logo key on the laptop's keyboard.

2. **Choose Power.**

The Power menu appears, as illustrated in Figure 5-1.

3. **Choose a power option.**

Or press the Esc key to dismiss the menu.

The three power options are

>> Sleep

>> Shut Down

>> Restart

The second location deals with user account options, which don't affect whether the laptop is on or off. These options are displayed in Figure 5-2. Here's how to access the options:

1. **Click or tap the Start button.**

2. **Choose your account name or image.**

Use Figure 5-2 as your guide.

The account options are

>> Lock

>> Sign Out

>> Switch to another user

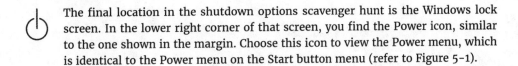

The final location in the shutdown options scavenger hunt is the Windows lock screen. In the lower right corner of that screen, you find the Power icon, similar to the one shown in the margin. Choose this icon to view the Power menu, which is identical to the Power menu on the Start button menu (refer to Figure 5-1).

User account

Account options

≡ **START**

⚥ Change account settings

🔒 Lock

⤷ Sign out

⚇ Arthur

🎖 Dan Gookin

🗋 Documents

🖼 Pictures

⚙ Settings

⏻ Power

FIGURE 5-2:
Account options
on the Start
menu.

Start button   Start menu

Shutting down your laptop

It's the end of the day, or perhaps you see a low-battery notification. Whatever the reason, you need to properly turn off your laptop. Heed these steps:

1. **Save your work and close all programs.**

   The generic Save command is Ctrl+S.

2. **Summon the Power menu.**

   Click or Tap the Start button and choose the Power item.

3. **Choose Shut Down.**

   The laptop turns itself off.

Yes, that's correct: The laptop turns itself off. You need not touch the power button. When the screen goes dark and the power lamp is dimmed, you can shut the lid and put away your laptop.

>> If you don't remember to save your work and close all open programs, you see a reminder as the laptop shuts down. Cancel the shutdown process, save your work, and then attempt to shut down again.

>> Shutting down might trigger Windows to install updates. If so, the shutdown process takes longer than anticipated and might even require an Internet connection. See Chapter 19 for information on how to configure Windows to help avoid this situation.

>> Closing the lid doesn't necessarily turn off your laptop! See the later section "Determining what happens when you shut the lid."

REMEMBER

Restarting Windows

Occasionally, you're directed to restart the laptop, which is often referred to as *restarting Windows.* To do so, heed these steps:

1. **Save your work and close all your programs.**

This is the step everyone forgets, so let me repeat it:

2. **Save your work and close all your programs.**

3. **Click or tap the Start button.**

4. **Choose Power.**

5. **Choose Restart.**

After you choose the Restart command, the laptop seems to be turning itself off, but just before it does, it starts right back up again. It's kind of like trying to put a toddler to sleep.

TIP

>> Restarting Windows is often necessary when installing software, adding hardware helpers called *device drivers*, or performing Windows updates. You're generally given a choice: "Would you like to restart Windows now?" If so, choose Yes or whatever option restarts the laptop.

>> Shutting down Windows and then starting your laptop (described in Chapter 4) also qualifies as a restart, though this process doesn't work as fast as the restart procedure described in this section.

>> Occasionally the laptop may restart itself to perform a critical update. This surprise restart occurs only if you keep your laptop on all the time. See Chapter 22.

Putting Mr. Laptop to sleep

(If you're reading this book out loud, now is the time to whisper.)

Sleep mode is a generic term that refers to the laptop's low-power operating mode. In this mode, the laptop is still on, but the screen goes dark, the processor throttles back to low speed, and activity reduces to a low simmer. The idea is to keep the laptop ready to use but not to waste power.

To sleep your laptop, follow these steps:

1. **Click or tap the Start button.**
2. **Choose Power.**
3. **Select the Sleep command.**

Unlike with a shutdown or restart, you don't need to save anything before the laptop enters Sleep mode, though it's a good idea anyway.

To revive a snoozing laptop, press a key on the keyboard, tap the mouse pad, or touch the screen.

After waking up the laptop, you may have to unlock Windows: Sign in again. This level of precaution is okay — in fact, it's what you want; Windows should be locked after the laptop wakes up from Sleep mode.

TECHNICAL STUFF

>> You can also sleep the laptop by closing the lid, although this function isn't guaranteed: See the later section "Determining what happens when you shut the lid."

>> If the laptop is conditioned to sleep when you close its lid, opening the lid wakes it up.

>> The laptop may automatically go to sleep after a period of inactivity — say, 30 minutes or so. Setting this timeout is part of the laptop's power management scheme, which is covered in Chapter 10.

>> Some laptops might feature a Sleep button, although this feature isn't as popular as it once was. Though the Sleep button can be configured to perform a number of tricks, generally speaking you press the button to place the laptop into Sleep mode.

>> You can stop whispering now.

Hibernating the laptop

When the laptop's hibernation feature is enabled, you see a fourth option on the Power Options menu: Hibernate (shown in Figure 5-3).

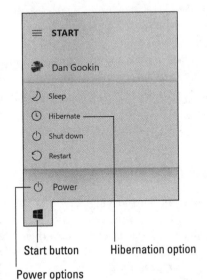

≡ **START**

🦔 Dan Gookin

☽ Sleep

🕐 Hibernate

⏻ Shut down

↺ Restart

⏻ Power

FIGURE 5-3:
The Power
Options menu,
featuring the
Hibernate
command.

Start button   Hibernation option

Power options

The Hibernate option is a blend of Sleep mode and shutdown. When this option is chosen, the laptop saves its current state; all running programs, the contents memory, even the laptop's smell is saved. Then the laptop shuts down. No power is consumed.

When you start the laptop again, you sign in to Windows as you usually do, but then your previous session is restored — just like coming out of Sleep mode, though the laptop's power was off the entire time.

>> Hibernation is the default setting for closing the laptop's lid while the laptop is on battery power. This feature is enabled whether you see the Hibernate command on the Power Options menu or not.

>> See the later section "Activating hibernation" for details on placing the hibernation feature on the Power Options menu.

Locking Windows

A quick way to protect your laptop when you're away for a spell is to lock it: Press the Win+L keyboard shortcut. The Windows lock screen appears. Only by choosing an account and typing a password can someone gain access to the laptop.

To unlock the laptop, sign in to Windows.

>> You don't need to save any files or close any programs when you lock the computer. Locking doesn't turn off anything or suspend any activities.

>> The Lock command is also found on the Account Options menu, illustrated earlier, in Figure 5-2.

Signing out of Windows

Somewhere between shutting down and locking Windows is a way to end your Windows day and keep the laptop ready and active. The solution is to sign out of Windows, also known as *logging off* or *logging out.* Follow these steps:

1. **Save your work and close your programs.**

   If you forget to save your work, Windows reminds you in a suitably rude fashion.

2. **Click or tap the Start button.**

   Up pops the Start button menu.

3. **Choose your account picture at the top of the Start button menu.**

   You see the Account Options menu, similar to the one shown earlier, in Figure 5-2.

4. **Choose the Sign Out command.**

   You're signed out of Windows.

The laptop remains on and you see the lock screen. At this point, another user can sign in, or you can use the Power icon on the lock screen, shown in the margin, to sleep, shut down, or restart the laptop.

Only rarely is it necessary to sign out of Windows. It's a good way, however, to shut down errant programs without having to restart the laptop: Sign out, and then sign back in again.

TIP

Switching to another user

If your reason for signing out of Windows is to let someone else use the laptop — say, your precious Peanut wants to play a game — a fast option is to switch user accounts. Heed these directions:

1. **Click or tap the Start button.**
2. **Choose your account picture.**
3. **Select the other user from the Account Options menu.**

You're signed out of Windows, and the laptop immediately displays the other user's sign-in screen.

Shutting down when the laptop doesn't want to

Unlike with a desktop computer, you can't just yank that power cord from the wall to deliberately force a laptop into electronic submission. The reason it doesn't work is that with the AC power gone, the laptop immediately starts using its battery. "So there," the laptop exclaims, as it continues to stubbornly labor against your will.

If the laptop continues to ignore you, press and hold the power button. Keep holding it: hold, hold, hold. Continue holding down the button, usually for five to ten seconds. Eventually, the laptop turns itself off.

See Chapter 21 for more laptop troubleshooting information.

Shutdown Options and Configuration

The power button always turns on your laptop. That's a given — well, as long as the laptop is healthy and has a charge. The real mystery surrounding the power button is what happens when you punch that button while the laptop is on.

Setting the power button's function

While the laptop is on, you may not think about the power button's function. You might just accept that pressing the button does something — you don't know what. If you're discontent not knowing the power button's "while on" function, you can change it. The reason is that the power button is programmable.

To set the power button's function, obey these steps:

1. **Pop-up the Start button menu.**

   Press the Windows key on the keyboard, or click or tap the Start button.

2. **Type** control panel **to locate the Control Panel app.**

3. **Choose the Control Panel app.**

   The Control Panel window opens, a relic of Windows versions gone by.

4. **Choose the Hardware and Sound category.**

5. **From beneath the Power Options heading, click the link labeled Change What the Power Buttons Do.**

   You see the Power Options System Settings window, illustrated in Figure 5-4. It has two columns — one for when the laptop is battery powered and another for when it's plugged into the wall. One row is for the power button, and the other is for closing the laptop's lid.

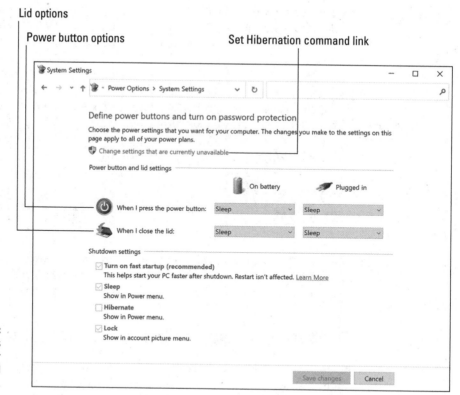

FIGURE 5-4:
Setting options for various power buttons and the lid.

6. **Choose what happens when you press the power button on battery power.**

   Click the top right button to view these options:

   Do nothing: The laptop does nothing when you press the power button. This option effectively disables the power button while the laptop is on.

   Sleep: The laptop immediately enters Sleep mode.

   Hibernate: The laptop hibernates.

   Shut down: The laptop turns itself off.

7. **Choose what happens when you press the power button while the laptop is plugged in.**

   Click the top left button to view the same options as shown in the preceding step.

8. **After choosing the various options, click the Save Changes button.**

9. **Close the window.**

Generally speaking, having both options (on battery and plugged in) set to Shut Down is most likely what you'd expect from the power button.

REMEMBER

» A row of settings for the Sleep button row appears when your laptop features this button.

» When the laptop is off, pressing the power button turns it back on again. You cannot change that function, nor would you really want to.

» You're not totally screwed if you change the power button's function from shutdown to something other than shutdown. In this case, to shut down the laptop, choose the Shutdown command from the Power menu.

Determining what happens when you shut the lid

As with setting the power button's function, you can direct the laptop to carry out specific actions when you close its lid. As with the power button, the actions you choose are different, depending on whether the laptop is operating on battery power or plugged into the wall.

Follow the steps in the preceding section to summon the Power Options System Settings window. (Refer to Figure 5-4). Use the lower left and lower right buttons to set the laptop's behavior when the lid is closed.

» As an example of setting the close-lid function, if you connect a large-format monitor and full-size keyboard to your laptop, you can choose to have the laptop "Do Nothing" while the lid is closed. With this choice made, you can continue to use the laptop with the lid closed.

» I choose to have my laptop sleep when I close its lid when it's plugged in. When the laptop is on battery power, closing the lid hibernates the laptop.

Activating hibernation

The hibernation feature isn't normally displayed on the Power menu. To activate this command, follow these steps:

1. **Click or tap the Start button.**

2. **Type** control panel **to search installed programs.**

3. **Choose the Control Panel app item.**

4. **Choose the Hardware and Sound category.**

5. **From beneath the Power Options heading, click the link labeled Change What the Power Buttons Do.**

   The Power Options System Settings window appears, as shown in Figure 5-4.

6. **Click the Link that says Change Settings That Are Currently Unavailable.**

   This step is necessary because adding or removing an item from the Power menu requires a higher level of system security.

7. **Place a check mark by the Hibernation item.**

   The item says *Hibernate,* with the text Show In Power Menu underneath.

8. **Click the Save Changes button.**

   You may also close the Control Panel window.

The Hibernation command now appears on the Power menu, as illustrated earlier in this chapter, in Figure 5-3.

Chapter **6**

Traditional Laptop Tour

I f a laptop computer were merely a miniaturized desktop computer, using one would be simple — providing you were miniaturized as well. Most likely, this isn't the case.

As laptop evolution has demonstrated, users rejected a tiny PC as their portable computer of choice. So the modern laptop exists with all the capabilities of a desk-top computer, but presented in their own, unique way. It's not that any item found on a laptop is weird; it's just different from what you might otherwise be used to.

>> Review Chapter 1 for details on laptop history.

>> Also see Chapter 7 for information on tablet-style laptops.

Around Your Laptop

As you manhandle a typical laptop computer, you'll discover that it's festooned with a festival of features. Bumps. Knobs. Holes. Each of these has a significance, and not every laptop sports all the possible features.

Locating removable storage slots

Replacing the old optical drive, laptops now sport media card slots. This change makes sense because most media cards store much more information than the old CD or DVD format. The memory card of choice is the SD Card, where SD stands for Secure Digital. This postage–stamp–size card has a smaller sibling, the MicroSD card.

Either the SD Card or the MicroSD card is inserted into a slot on the laptop's edge. Locate this slot on your laptop's case, if you haven't already. Sometimes the slot is hidden: On the Microsoft Surface laptops, it's behind the kickstand and flush with the laptop's rear.

Insert the card into the slot label up. An arrow on the card indicates the proper insertion direction. Push the card in all the way until it catches. If the card doesn't insert, reorient it and try again. You can't insert the card upside down or backward.

After the card is inserted, Windows takes over. See Chapter 9 for details.

WARNING

You must follow a specific procedure to eject a media card. You don't just pop it out of the slot. Chapter 9 discusses the process.

LAPTOP HARDWARE RELICS

For years, the primary way to expand laptop hardware was the PC Card. Also known by the acronym PCMCIA (Personal Computer Memory Card International Association), this card was a thick, credit-card-size gizmo you inserted into a roomy garage on the laptop's side.

The PC Card added features to the laptop's basic hardware configuration, such as a modem, removable drive, or network connection. This standard was replaced by USB for adding laptop peripherals.

A more recent relic is the optical drive, though some large "aircraft carrier" laptops may still feature an optical drive slot or tray. This format proved to be too large and store too little to an ongoing standard for laptop computers. SD cards and cloud storage have replaced it as an alternative to internal storage for a laptop.

If for any reason your laptop needs to read an optical disk, get a USB optical drive. It has the bonus of being powered from a wall socket, which saves the laptop's battery. Also, you can use the drive with a desktop PC, seeing how these computers are no longer shipping with optical drives, either.

Attaching the laptop to something sturdy

Some laptops feature a special "belt loop" through which you can snake a security cable. This feature may not have a specific name, though the Universal Security Slot, or USS, is popular. Another option is the Kensington Security Slot, or K-Slot. The slot looks like a tiny oval labeled with the Padlock icon and sporting a *K* in the middle.

Of course, this security feature means nothing unless the security cable is attached to something solid and immovable, like a heavy desk or a pipe organ. The idea is to prevent the laptop from being stolen, not to add a cool chain to your portable PC.

See Chapter 20 for more information on laptop security.

Keeping the air circulating

Like you, your laptop must breathe. Discover where its breathing slots are located. They might not be obvious; they might not even be visible. If they are, note their locations and try to keep the vents clean and clear of obstruction.

TIP

>> Your laptop prefers that you set it upon a flat, hard surface.

>> Avoid using your laptop for too long on a soft surface, like setting it on a couch or bed.

>> Never block the vents, lest the laptop become too hot and malfunction in various amusing-yet-annoying ways.

Discovering the webcam

Something you might find on the laptop's lid, on the monitor side, top center, is the laptop's webcam. As with other laptop features, not every laptop sports a video camera. Some tablet PCs have a second camera on the back. And sometimes the camera is at the bottom of the screen, which is odd but I didn't design those laptops.

The *webcam* is your laptop's eyeball, used to capture still images or video. Specific software that comes with the laptop activates and uses the webcam, allowing you to video-chat, snap pictures, or compose video messages for email. See Chapter 15 for more information on using your laptop's webcam.

The Pluggable-Innable Holes

Yes, laptops are supposed to be light and portable. Then again, laptops are also computers, and computers are notorious for having lots of things plugged into them. They plug into various holes and use various cables with various ends, variously. These are the same holds used on desktop computers for the same purpose: to add more hardware and expand the computer's capabilities.

Table 6-1 lists the official name, configuration, symbol, color, and description of the various holes you might find located around your laptop. This table should give you an idea of what a hole is used for and what you might eventually want to plug into it.

TABLE 6-1   **Laptop Ports and Their Symbols, Designs, and Colors**

Port Name	Configuration	Symbol	Color	What You Can Do with It
Display Port			None	Connect an external monitor.
eSATA		eSATA	Black	Connect an external hard drive.
HDMI		HDMI	Black	Connect to an HDMI TV or monitor.
Headphone			Forest green	Plug in headphones, which automatically disables the laptop's speakers.
Mic			Pink	Connect a microphone.
Mini DisplayPort			None	Connect an external monitor.
Power			Yellow	Plug the laptop into an AC power socket.

Port Name	Configuration	Symbol	Color	What You Can Do with It
RJ-45/ Ethernet			None	Add your laptop to an Ethernet network, or connect to the Internet.
USB			White, Black, Blue	Add a variety of components to the laptop, including printers and thumb drives.

As usual, keep in mind that not every laptop sports all these items. Smaller laptops and netbooks have only a few of the essentials, if that.

>> These holes are officially known as *ports*.

>> Keyboards and external mice are attached to your laptop by using the USB port. When you need more USB ports, you attach a portable USB hub to your laptop. See Chapter 12 for more information about USB.

>> The power jack might look different from its description in Table 6-1. Ensure that you don't plug the power cable into a microphone port!

>> The USB port colors depend on the USB version: 1.0 is white, 2.0 is black, and 3.0 is blue. Other colors are available, as covered in Chapter 12.

>> Check out Chapter 7 for some specific items to look for on a tablet PC.

Look at the Pretty Lights!

What would a computer be if it weren't for all the blinking lights? Even before personal computers were popular, the monster computers of science fiction came equipped with banks and banks of blinking lights. Though I'm certain that a modern laptop could easily replace all the Batcomputers in TV *Batman*'s Batcave, it just wouldn't be visually impressive — or credible — to a 1960s television audience.

Your laptop most likely has many more lights than the typical desktop computer. I'm trying to think of a reason, but it honestly baffles me. Suffice it to say that Table 6-2 lists common lights, lamps, and bright, blinking things that you might find on your laptop and describes what they do or why they're necessary.

TABLE 6-2

Pretty Laptop Lights

Symbol	What It Could Possibly Mean
🌙	The laptop is in Sleep mode.
🔋	The laptop is running on battery power. This lamp can change color when the laptop is charging.
🔌	The laptop is plugged in.
⬆A A	The Caps Lock state is on. You might also see a light on the Caps Lock key.
⬆ 1	The Num Lock state is on. You might also see a light on the Num Lock key.
📶 ((•))	Wireless networking is active.
ᛒ	Bluetooth wireless is active.

Other pretty lights doubtless exist, such as the bright light that may appear next to the webcam when you're recording video or taking a picture. Plus, some lights are specific to your laptop's manufacturer. Thanks to the International Symbol Law, most symbols are pretty common.

>> Some lights can blink or change color. For example, the battery indicator might change from green to amber to red as the battery drains. The wireless network lamp might flicker as data is transferred.

>> The plugged-in lamp and the battery lamp (refer to Table 6-2) may be lit when the laptop is plugged in, whether the laptop is turned on or not. That's normal for some laptops.

>> Some netbooks have no lamps on them — not enough room, I suppose.

This Isn't Your Daddy's Keyboard

The standard computer keyboard has 105 keys, not counting any special web keys, media keys, or other fancy knobs. That's a lot of buttons. You just can't squeeze that many keys on a laptop and keep it portable, let alone keep the keyboard on one side of the thing. Oh, sure, some of those laptops the size of aircraft carriers — the models with the 18-inch displays — can sport a full-size PC keyboard. But most laptops opt for portability over the need to use your laptop as a surfboard.

Exploring the keyboard layout

Figure 6-1 illustrates a typical laptop keyboard layout. The standard typewriter keys are a normal size, but the many other keys have been miniaturized and clustered around the standard keys in a confusing and arbitrary manner. Observing your own laptop's keyboard easily confirms how wacky the arrangement can be on the keyboard's periphery.

FIGURE 6-1: Typical laptop keyboard layout.

As with a desktop keyboard, you should be able to identify these basic items on your laptop keyboard:

Alphanumeric, or "typewriter," keys: These are the basic typing keys, each of which is labeled with a character (a letter, number, or punctuation symbol). When you're typing on the computer, pressing a key produces its character on the screen.

Shift keys: The keyboard sports various shift keys, used either alone or in combination with other keys. These include Shift, Alt, Ctrl.

Fn key: It's the feature key, although I suspect *Fn* stands for *function* or *fun*.

Windows key: The Windows key appears between the Ctrl and Alt keys. It's used like a shift key, although it can also be used by itself. In this book, I refer to it as the Win key.

Function keys: These keys, labeled F1 through F12, are on the top row of the keyboard, right above the number keys. On some laptops these are secondary keys, accessed only by pressing the Fn key at the same time as a function key. Sharing these keys are laptop feature keys.

Cursor-control keys: These keys can be anywhere around the keyboard. In Figure 6-1, the cursor keys plus Page Up and Page Down are in the lower right corner of the keyboard. Home and End are toward the top. Of all the keys on a laptop keyboard, the cursor keys wind up in the most bizarre and unpredictable spots.

Numeric keypad: This area is covered in the next section.

In addition to the keys described in this section, your laptop may feature specific keys for special Windows functions, such as switching tasks, or keys for adjusting the laptop's speaker volume, and so on.

>> The Fn key is usually color-coded with other keys on the keyboard. These keys map to specific laptop functions. See the later section "Having fun with the Fn key."

>> Though the alphanumeric keys are approximately the same size as found on a desktop PC's keyboard, their *travel,* or feel, has less depth.

>> European laptops often sport the AltGr key — the Alt (or Alternative) Graphic key. It helps produce the many diacritical marks and special characters that are part of various European languages.

>> European laptops also have the euro symbol, €, on the keyboard. Likewise, laptops in the United Kingdom feature the £ symbol on the 3 key, where the # symbol is found on keyboards in the United States.

>> A one-time popular PC key may or may not be available on your laptop. The Menu key, also known as the Context key, is labeled as shown in the margin. It appears to the right of the spacebar. The Menu key serves the same function as right-clicking an item, but this key was never widely used, so many laptops omit it.

Finding the secret numeric keypad

The first thing the laptop designers decided to sacrifice to the Size Gods was the keyboard's numeric keypad. Rather than just saw off that end of the keyboard, laptops since the Radio Shack Model 100 have used a combination of numeric keypad and alphabetic keyboard.

The shared numeric keypad is illustrated in Figure 6-2. Examine the 7, 8, and 9 keys. These three keys are also the top three keys on a numeric keypad. Because of this similarity, a shadow numeric keypad uses the right side of the alphabetic keyboard. The trick, of course, is knowing how to turn the thing on and off.

If your laptop features a Num Lock key, press it to switch the keys illustrated on the left in Figure 6-2 into a numeric keypad.

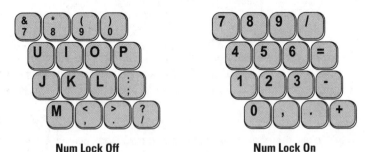

FIGURE 6-2:
The hidden
numeric keypad.

Num Lock Off

Num Lock On

If your laptop lacks a Num Lock key, look for a color-coded key that you can use in combination with the Fn key.

When you still can't find a Num Lock key, your laptop lacks the ability to use a shared numeric keypad. If you're desperate for such a thing, get a USB numeric keypad for your laptop.

Having fun with the Fn key

To make up for their lack of keys, laptop keyboards feature the Fn key. It's used in combination with other keys, just like a Shift key, giving those keys multiple purposes. Typically, these other keys occupy the top row; they are similar to the function keys on a desktop computer keyboard.

In Figure 6-3, you see how the Fn key is used to alternate between the traditional keyboard function keys and special laptop feature keys, as labeled in the figure.

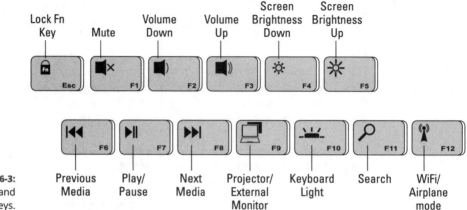

FIGURE 6-3:
Fn keys and
function keys.

Be aware that in some cases the Fn key activates the function keys, and in others the Fn key is used to access the key's features. Often a lock key (refer to Figure 6-3) is available to lock the Fn key on to access the keys one way or the other.

>> Take a moment to peruse your laptop and look over its available Fn keys. They may not be in the same order shown in Figure 6-3, and more or fewer symbols may be used.

>> Some laptops use alphanumeric key combinations with the Fn key as well as function-key combinations.

>> The Home, End, Page Up, and Page Down keys often appear as Fn keyboard combinations.

>> The Fn key and its companion keys are often color-coded and flagged with various icons. Sadly, there's no standard for naming or assigning the various Fn keys and their functions.

TECHNICAL
STUFF

>> Having an Fn key is an old, old laptop trick, dating back to the prehistoric days of portable computing. In those days, the Fn key was used to help produce keystrokes not available on a laptop's limited keyboard.

This Isn't Your Momma's Mouse

Laptops have had mice as long as desktop computers have. The problem was that the marriage never really worked out well. Though you can add a USB or wireless mouse to your laptop, the main pointing device is the *touchpad*. It has variations and inconsistencies, as you might expect, which require further explanation.

Using a touchpad

Your laptop features a touchpad pointing device, though everyone calls it "the mouse." Like a desktop computer mouse, the touchpad manipulates the pointing device on the display, which lets you fully enjoy the graphical goodness of the Windows operating system.

The touchpad dwells just below the spacebar, in the front center of the laptop. Typical laptop touchpads are shown in Figure 6-4. Two varieties are common. One is a flat pad with touch-sensitive areas. The other offers buttons akin to the traditional computer mouse buttons.

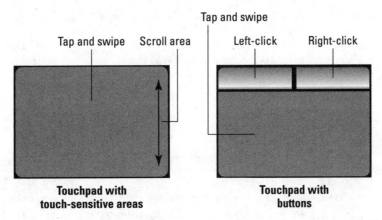

FIGURE 6-4:
Touchpad
varieties.

**Touchpad with
touch-sensitive areas**

**Touchpad with
buttons**

To adjust the touchpad, heed these directions:

1. Press the Win+I keyboard shortcut.

The Settings app appears.

2. Choose the Devices item.

3. From the list on the left side of the window, choose Touchpad.

Behold the various controls and settings for the keyboard's touchpad input gizmo.

The nifty thing about the Settings app's Touchpad screen is that it may offer suggestions for, or help with, various features. For example, if your laptop's touchpad features multiple finger-swiping shortcuts, you may see an onscreen tutorial or description of its features.

OOH, THAT LENOVO TrackPoint MOUSE!

Some Lenovo laptops feature a joystick-like mouse that looks like a pencil eraser jammed between the keyboard's G, H, and B keys. It's officially named the TrackPoint, though I prefer to call it the *happy stick*. Regardless, the gizmo is quite handy to use as a pointing device in addition to the touchpad.

The idea behind the happy stick is that you can manipulate it by using the index finger of either hand. You can then use your thumb (on either hand) to click the left or right "mouse" buttons on the touchpad. The TrackPoint can be used with a middle button to scroll the screen: Press the Scroll (center) button on the touchpad and slide the TrackPoint up or down.

Here are some terrific touchpad touch tips:

>> Use your forefinger to move the mouse pointer.

>> Tap your finger to click the mouse. A light touch is all that's required, although some touchpads let you mash down to click.

>> To right-click, use two fingers to tap the touchpad. This trick may not work on every touchpad.

>> Swipe your finger up and down on the right edge of the touchpad to scroll the screen. This action works similarly to using the scroll wheel on a traditional computer mouse. If it doesn't work, use two fingers to swipe the touchpad to scroll an object on the screen.

>> The most difficult mouse operation is the *drag*. That's where you have to hold down a button while moving the pointer. With practice, it can be done — but you must practice!

Obtaining a real mouse

The best type of input device you can use on your laptop is . . . *a real mouse*. No, not the furry rodent kind. Silly. A computer mouse.

You can use a full-size, desktop computer mouse on your laptop instead of, or along with, the touchpad. Yes, it's one more thing to carry, but because desktop computer mice are familiar and people are used to them, it often makes sense for the laptop to have a "big computer" mouse.

Rather than use the same, full-size (and wired) computer mouse with your laptop, consider buying a portable mouse — specifically, a wireless mouse. This type of mouse uses a wireless connection to transmit its movement from the mouse into the laptop. Further, the wireless mouse is light, portable, and tiny, which makes it easy to use on an airplane or on your thigh, when an airplane isn't available.

TIP

If your laptop features Bluetooth, obtain a Bluetooth wireless mouse. Otherwise, the mouse relies upon a USB dongle for its wireless connection. By using Bluetooth, however, you free up a USB port for another external device.

Chapter **7**

The Tablet PC Tour

The tablet PC may be a miraculous improvement over the traditional laptop, but it's nothing new. Two thousand years ago, the Romans called it a *tabulae ceratae*, a wax writing tablet. Back then, it was *the* high-tech recording device: The wax was black. A sharp, metal stick, or *stylus*, was used to write on it. The pointy end of the stylus was for writing, and the wider, flat end was for erasing. The *tabulae* was used for all kinds of writing, including important documents. And I'm certain that more than one Roman schoolkid used the excuse once too often, "I left my homework in the sun."

Fast-forward 2,000 years and you can have, in your lap, a tablet PC that does all that the *tabulae ceratae* could do — and more! You can use a digital stylus to write on a computer screen rather than use an iron stylus to write on beeswax. Such a marvel seems like a must-have extension to the whole laptop concept.

WARNING

» Don't confuse the tablet PC with the mobile device also called a *tablet*. A tablet PC runs Windows, which is nothing like the iPad or Android tablets.

» A common variation on the *tabulae ceratae* was the trifold version (three tablets tied together). Medieval scholars referred to it as a *triptych*.

» By the way, Roman schoolboys didn't do math on a *tabulae ceratae*. They learned to do math on the abacus. (Roman girls did not go to school.)

Tablet PC Types

The name *tablet PC* is generic. As far as Windows is concerned, the name refers to any laptop with a touchscreen, though a true tablet has a detachable keyboard, hidden keyboard, or no keyboard at all. The Windows operating system offers special touchscreen features on a tablet PC, features that other laptops lack.

Figure 7-1 shows several types of tablet PCs. Of the lot, the convertible and tablet varieties are the most common.

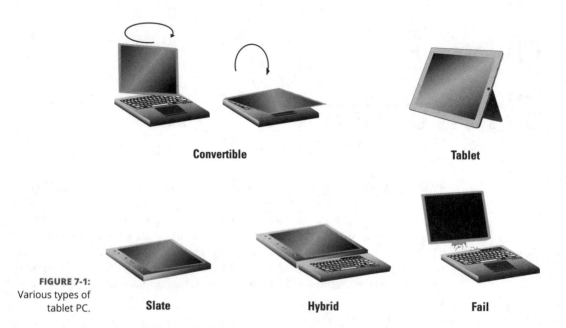

Convertible

Tablet

FIGURE 7-1:
Various types of
tablet PC.

Slate

Hybrid

Fail

A *convertible* is a traditional laptop (also called a *notebook*) with a swiveling lid. When the screen is up and facing the keyboard, the computer looks like a laptop. If you rotate the screen and fold it over the keyboard, the system becomes a tablet.

The tablet model is similar to a mobile device, such as an iPad or Android tablet. A tablet such as the Microsoft Surface is simply a thin-format touchscreen laptop without an attached keyboard.

Less common are the slate and hybrid models. The *slate* is a traditional laptop without a keyboard. The *hybrid* is the same thing, but with a detachable keyboard.

REMEMBER

>> Just because your laptop has a touchscreen doesn't make it a tablet. It may employ tablet-like features, but it's not the same as a keyboard-less model, such as those illustrated in Figure 7-1.

>> Tablets are also referred to as *2-in-1 laptops* because the keyboard/cover is often sold separately.

>> Most tablet users buy a keyboard/cover combination as well as a digital pen or stylus as accessories.

>> The slate and hybrid models feature physical buttons around the screen, which a tablet model lacks.

TECHNICAL STUFF

>> The germination of the tablet PC had to be the Xerox Dynabook concept, back in the 1970s. The Dynabook never appeared, but other attempts have been made to bring tablet computing to the masses. See Chapter 1.

The Tablet PC Tour

As a computer, a tablet PC features more expansion options than an iPad or Android tablet. Due to its thin size, however, the tablet PC sports fewer expansion options than a notebook–style laptop. And thanks to improvements in the Windows touchscreen interface, today's tablet PCs sport fewer buttons and knobs than the convertible, slate, and hybrid models from just a few years ago.

Take a moment to examine your tablet PC and look for the following items on the front and around the sides:

Touchscreen: The main part of the tablet, on the front. This is where information is displayed and where you interact with the device. Frequently covered in fingerprint smudges.

Cameras: Above the touchscreen you find a camera. This is the tablet PC's front-facing camera, used for video conferencing or for taking selfies. Some tablet PCs also feature a rear camera, designed for taking pictures of things other than yourself. These cameras may or may not feature an LED flash.

Windows button: Some tablets feature the Windows button, labeled with the Windows 10 logo, as shown in the margin. Push this button to wake up the tablet or, when the tablet is on, to display the Start button menu.

Power button: This button turns on the tablet PC, most definitely. As covered in Chapter 5, it may or may not turn off the device.

Power connector: This hole is where you connect the tablet's power supply. It often doubles as a USB connector, although you may not be able to connect USB peripherals to the power connector port.

USB connectors: You can plug various external gizmos into the tablet PC, which defeats the whole "mobile" nature of the device, but for camping out in one spot, having access to peripherals is a must.

Mini Digital Video port: Use this hole to connect an external monitor. If the monitor cable is incompatible with the Mini Digital Video port, you can obtain an adapter or a converter.

Pen dock: Tablets with a pen or stylus often feature a hole where the pen lives. See the next section.

Headphone jack: Use this hole to connect a headphone so that you can listen to music or videos or noisy things on the Internet without annoying those around you.

Microphone jack: Sometimes this item is a port into which you can plug a microphone, but most often it's a tiny hole that serves as a microphone.

Keyboard/cover connector: Along one of the tablet's edges you'll find the spot where the keyboard or cover attaches. For most tablets, the detachable keyboard pops on or off, often by using a magnetic connector. When the keyboard is off, use the onscreen keyboard, as covered elsewhere in this chapter.

Volume control: Locate the volume buttons on one side of the tablet. You may find separate buttons or a single, rocker-style button for raising and lowering the tablet's volume.

Your tablet PC may have some or all of these items, and it may have even more, depending on what the manufacturer has tossed in as a bonus.

TIP

>> The Microsoft Surface line of tablets feature a kickstand on the back. Pop out the kickstand to prop up the Surface for easy viewing. You might also locate other features behind the kickstand, such as a MicroSD card slot.

>> The most common video cable adapters attach to a USB C port. If you need an adapter, find one that connects to this versatile port.

>> See Chapter 6 for information on finding hardware tidbits on a convertible laptop, which is more of a traditional laptop anyhow.

>> Some tablet PCs feature only one USB connector. If you need more USB peripherals, you need to get a USB hub for your tablet PC. See Chapter 12 for details on USB.

The Pen Is Mightier than the Mouse

Tablet PCs feature a touchscreen. You can use your finger as an input device, but your finger is short and stubby and, please, you need a manicure. A better option is to use a *digitizer pen*, which I call a *stylus*.

Introducing the digital pen

The *stylus* is a pointing device, like the mouse. For the most part, it works just like a mouse: Tap the screen to click, double-tap, right-tap, and so on.

Okay: There's no such thing as a right-tap. See the next section for information on using the stylus. Before using it, however, take a look at the pen. Some important parts are illustrated in Figure 7-2.

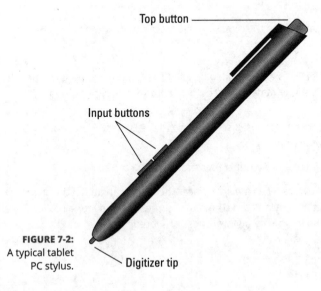

Top button

Input buttons

FIGURE 7-2:
A typical tablet PC stylus.

Digitizer tip

The stylus works by touching the tablet's screen, which is a *digitizer.* In Windows, the stylus's touch is interpreted similarly to mouse movement. You can point the pen at the screen, touch the screen, and manipulate items in interesting ways, as covered elsewhere in this chapter.

The function of the pen's buttons varies. Generally speaking, one of the input buttons is the right-click button. On a two-button stylus, the second button is the Erase button.

Some tablet PCs come with a stylus. If not, the stylus must be purchased as an add-on. As long as the stylus is Windows-compatible, you can use it on your tablet PC. But remember:

Just because your laptop features a touchscreen doesn't imply that a digital pen works as an input device.

REMEMBER

To confirm that your tablet PC can use a digital pen, obey these steps:

1. **Tap the Start button.**

2. **Choose the Settings icon.**

   This icon is shown in the margin.

3. **Tap Devices.**

4. **From the categories on the left side of the window, choose Pen & Windows Ink.**

   If you see a Pen heading on the right side of the screen, your tablet PC can use a digital pen.

The Pen item in the Settings app can also be used to adjust aspects of the pen. The number of options available depend on the pen's hardware capabilities.

>> Some digital pens use batteries. If so, rush out to the Battery Store right now to buy a spare battery or two.

>> If the digital pen features one button, it's the right-click button.

>> Some tablet PCs feature a *pen tether,* a place where you can attach the stylus to the tablet by using a nylon cord. The tether comes in handy for all of us pen-droppers, who loathe the awkwardness of searching underneath an airline seat for *anything.*

TIP

>> The Microsoft Surface Pen is a Bluetooth wireless peripheral. It connects automatically to the Surface tablet. Other styluses may require additional setup, such as Bluetooth pairing or another type of interface. Some simpler styluses may work by simply interacting with the laptop's touchscreen. See Chapter 12 for information on Bluetooth.

Using the pen as a mouse

Most of the time, you use a digital pen with your tablet PC just as you'd use a mouse on a desktop computer. It makes an excellent pointing device, but it does have its quirks.

Table 7-1 lists pen and mouse equivalents.

TABLE 7-1 **Pen and Mouse Actions**

Mouse Activity	Pen Equivalent	Description
Point	Hover	Hover the stylus above the touchscreen. (Don't touch!)
Click	Tap	Tap the stylus on the screen.
Double-click	Double-tap	Tap the stylus twice on the same spot.
Right-click	Long-tap	Tap and hold the stylus on the same spot.
Drag	Drag	Touch the stylus to the screen and move the stylus a little.
Right-drag	Right-drag	Press and hold the stylus button while keeping the stylus on the screen.

As you hover or point the mouse on the screen — without touching the screen — you see a pen pointer appear, similar to the one shown in the margin. This tiny target is called the *pen cursor*.

TIP

>> It's easier to navigate menus when you hover the pen, as opposed to dragging the pen.

>> You can simulate a right-click by pressing the pen's button and then tapping the screen. If the pen features two buttons, the right-click button is the top one.

REMEMBER

>> You can always use your finger to tap or drag items on the screen. I find it easier to use my finger to swipe through a document or move a window.

Touchscreen Text Typing

To answer the question of why anyone would want to fork over hard-earned money for a tablet PC keyboard cover, simply take a look at the keyboard. What keyboard? Exactly.

To make up for the lack of a keyboard, tablet PCs offer a touchscreen keyboard called the *touch keyboard.* Using this keyboard is definitely a new experience. And it's apparently so dreadful that people buy the expensive keyboard covers.

Summoning the touch keyboard

The touch keyboard pops up anytime you tap the screen on a text field or any-where that typing is required. When the touch keyboard doesn't pop up, tap the Touch Keyboard icon, shown in the margin, which appears on the taskbar at the bottom of the screen.

If you don't see the touch keyboard icon, switch the laptop into Tablet mode; see the later section "Windows Does the Tablet PC."

To dismiss the touch keyboard, tap the X button in the upper left corner, just as you would close any window on the screen.

Exploring the touch keyboard varieties

During the PC-to-laptop transition, certain sacrifices were made to the keyboard gods. These sacrifices allowed the laptops to sport smaller keyboards. The transition from laptop keyboard to touchscreen keyboard met with further sacrifices. Yes, the keyboard gods are merciless; some keys had to go.

To help you deal with the missing keys, the touch keyboard offers several presentations. Figure 7-3 illustrates the standard layout. Tap the &123 key to view the symbol keyboard, which features two pages, as illustrated in the figure. Tap the left or right arrows to switch between symbol palettes.

If you find the standard keyboard lacking, you can select another keyboard presentation: Tap the Keyboard Preferences key (refer to Figure 7-3) to view a keyboard selection menu, shown in Figure 7-4.

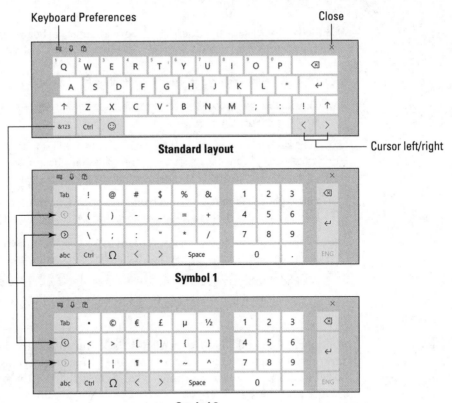

FIGURE 7-3:
The touch
keyboard keys.

Standard layout

Keyboard Preferences

Close

Cursor left/right

Symbol 1

Symbol 2

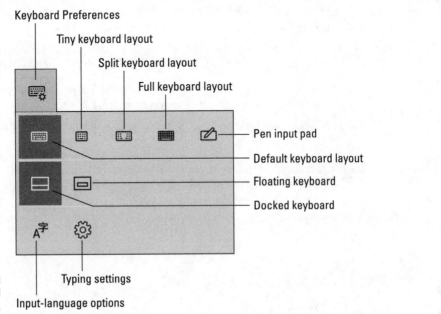

Keyboard Preferences

Tiny keyboard layout

Split keyboard layout

Full keyboard layout

Pen input pad

Default keyboard layout

Floating keyboard

Docked keyboard

FIGURE 7-4:
The keyboard
selection menu.

Typing settings

Input-language options

Use the keyboard selection menu to choose another keyboard layout. The options shown in Figure 7-4 include

Default keyboard layout: This layout is shown in Figure 7-3.

Tiny keyboard layout: This option shows the default keyboard layout, but in a smaller (one-quarter size) presentation.

Split keyboard layout: This layout is smaller than the standard keyboard layout. It splits the keyboard in half, showing it on both the right and left sides of the keyboard. People who type with their thumbs prefer this layout.

Full keyboard layout: This option presents an onscreen keyboard with the similar keys as a full-size desktop computer keyboard.

Pen input pad: This keyboard isn't a keyboard at all, but is a scribble pad for using the digital pen. See the later section "Scribbling text on the screen."

Docked/floating keyboard: These options set the keyboard at the bottom of the screen (docked) or allow it to be moved to any convenient onscreen position (floating).

The touch keyboard, in all its varieties, lacks function keys and perhaps other favorites. Though the touch keyboard is useful for quick typing, sending email, social networking, and performing other light activities, I strongly recommend getting a real keyboard for your tablet PC, if it doesn't already have one.

>> To type a capital letter, press the Shift key and then tap the letter. Some tablet PCs may let you press and hold two keys at one time when using the touch keyboard.

>> Tap the Shift key twice to enter Shift-Lock mode, similar to Caps Lock on a physical keyboard. Tap the Shift key again to exit that mode.

>> To access special characters, long-press a key. For example, long-press the A key to view a pop-up palette of accented *A* characters.

>> Long-press one of the keys on the keyboard's top row to access numbers 1 through 9 and 0.

>> Not shown in Figure 7-3 are the emoji keyboard keys. Tap the Happy Face icon to view the various emojis — pages and pages of them.

Typing control-key combinations

To generate control-key combinations on the touch keyboard, first press the Ctrl key. Next, tap the next key in the combination, such as S for the Ctrl+S keyboard shortcut.

When you tap the Ctrl key, certain keys on the touch keyboard are highlighted. These include the standard editing keys: A, Z, X, C, and V for the commands Select All, Undo, Cut, Copy, and Paste, respectively.

Some onscreen keyboards may let you press and hold the Ctrl key and then tap another key, as you're used to doing on a full-size keyboard. This capability depends on how the touchscreen interprets different touches.

Scribbling text on the screen

In a nod to the *tabulae ceratae,* you can use your finger or a digital pen to scrawl text as input for your tablet PC. Please: Do not use an iron stylus, because it may seriously damage the laptop's touchscreen.

To use the stylus or your finger to draw text, activate the pen input pad for the touch keyboard: Tap the Keyboard Preferences button (refer to Figure 7-3), and then tap the Pen Input Pad item. The pen input pad is illustrated in Figure 7-5.

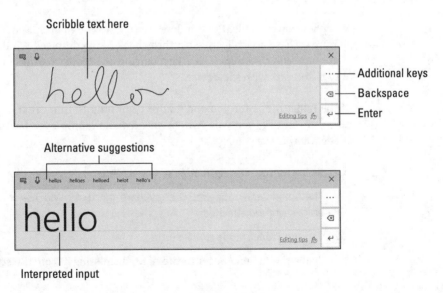

FIGURE 7-5:
The pen input pad.

To input text, use your best penmanship and write in the box, as illustrated atop Figure 7-5. You can print or, if you were educated in the last century, use cursive. Your input is interpreted, as shown on the bottom in the figure; suggestions appear atop the input pad. Choose a suggestion to fix the lousy interpretation of your scrawl.

As you write, the text is inserted into whichever program you're using.

TIP

>> You can move the touch keyboard to a different position on the screen, one that may be more comfortable for you while writing.

>> Turn the tablet PC to a vertical orientation for a more natural writing setup.

>> You can write single words or an entire line. To clear a line, tap the Space or Enter key buttons.

>> To erase a word or character, drag horizontally across it.

>> Obviously, the pen input pad won't help you with keyboard shortcuts and other special keys used to control Windows or your programs. I consider this input technique more of a curiosity than something I use on a regular basis.

Windows Does the Tablet PC

When you have a tablet PC, Windows is eager to cough up special fun and frivolous features. These are collectively a throwback to the despised Windows 8, but given that your tablet PC may lack a keyboard, these features offer a more convenient way to interact with the device.

If the tablet life is for you and you're beginning to think that keyboards are oh-so-20th century, you can switch your lovable laptop over to full-screen Tablet mode. Obey these steps:

1. **Swipe in from the right edge of the screen.**

The Action Center appears. The keyboard shortcut is Win+A — if your tablet has a keyboard attached.

2. **Tap the Tablet Mode quick setting.**

3. **Swipe the Action Center to the right, dismissing it from the screen.**

Behold! Windows has regressed to its eighth and most despised version, with full-screen apps and windowless windows. The taskbar has changed as well, serving more as an anchor than a program-switching tool, as illustrated in Figure 7-6.

When you tap the Start button, you see the old Windows 8 Start screen, though an alternative is App view, shown in Figure 7-6. To start an app, tap its tile or button.

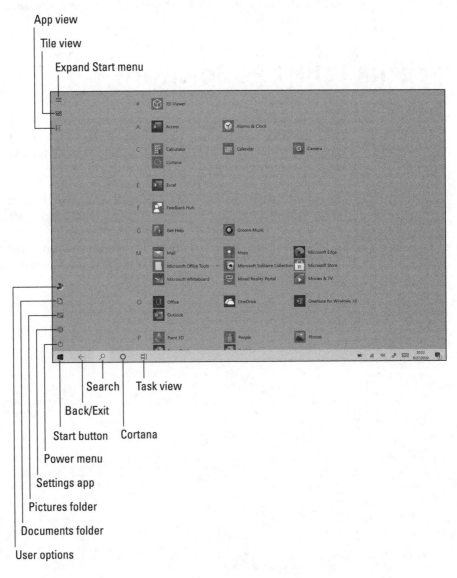

To exit Tablet mode, repeat the steps in this section.

>> Tap the Task View button (refer to Figure 7-6) to switch to a running app. You can also swipe in from the left side of the screen to page through running apps.

>> Windows may prompt you to switch to Tablet mode whenever you detach the tablet's keyboard or switch a convertible laptop into tablet position.

Special Tablet PC Software

When your tablet PC demands include special treatment, you'll be happy to know that Windows is ready to meet your needs. Special programs are available to tablet PC users, which take advantage of your laptop's touchscreen and pen input abilities. These programs include OneNote and Sticky Notes.

I'm not sure what OneNote does, though it allows you to scribble notes, mix in images, and collaborate with others. This program is part of Microsoft Office.

Sticky Notes works like Post-it® brand notes from 3M, although putting the notes on your tablet PC doesn't gunk up the monitor. This program is rather easy to figure out if you've ever used a Sticky Note.

Chapter **8**

Your Laptop and Windows

Someone must be in charge. On a ship, you find the captain; on the playground, it's the bully; and in the Milky Way galaxy, it's the Mulvanian Empire, which is right now hurtling a fleet of stellar battle cruisers toward Planet Earth. Before they arrive, you should know that the kingpin in charge of all the software in your laptop is Windows, which is your laptop's *operating system,* or the main program in charge of everything.

Using Windows on a laptop works similarly to using Windows on any computer. Coupled with the disappointment and frustration that everyone experiences with Windows, you find a few laptop-specific issues. It's important to understand those issues, because the Mulvanian Empire is on its way.

The Big Windows Picture

Windows is easy to use in the same way that a nuclear reactor control room is easy to use: You see knobs and buttons and dials, and you can operate these items easily. Knowing what they do and the potential danger involved is the problem.

Don't press the A3-5 button.

Viewing the desktop

The *desktop* is the traditional place where Windows programs lurk; it's the spot where you get your work done. After signing in to Windows, the next thing you see is the desktop.

Windows 10 also offers a Tablet mode interface, which looks like the old, disliked Windows 8 Start screen. See Chapter 7 for a discussion of this feature. For now, most adult laptops use the desktop, as illustrated in Figure 8-1.

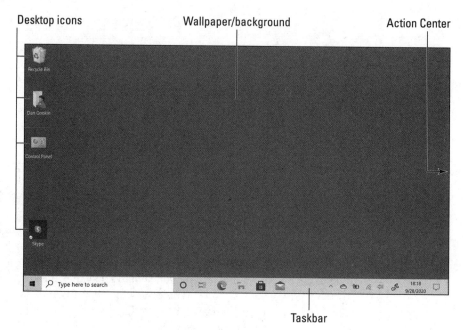

Desktop icons   Wallpaper/background   Action Center

FIGURE 8-1: The Windows desktop.

Taskbar

Here are a few important things to note on the desktop:

Icons: These tiny pictures represent files, folders, or programs. Microsoft wants you to call them *apps* in Windows 10. They're programs.

Wallpaper, or background: The wallpaper is the image you see on the desktop, or it may be a solid color, such as the one used in Figure 8-1. You change the background when the mood hits you; see Chapter 9.

Action Center: This panel is hidden off to the right. Swipe in, right-to-left from the right edge of the screen to view various notifications or access options. See the later section "Visiting with the Action Center."

The taskbar: This doohickey skirts the bottom of the desktop, displaying a host of icons and controls. Buttons appear on the taskbar that represent programs or windows open on the desktop; plus, it plays home to lots of junk. See the later section "Working on the taskbar" for specific knowledge nuggets.

Take a moment right now to find each item on your laptop screen. Don't touch the display! Just find them and point. (And maybe even say, "Oh, there it is!")

TIP

>> The desktop is the workspace background. Programs and apps appear on top of the desktop as you work.

>> To quickly view the desktop, press the Win+D key combination.

>> The Win+D keyboard shortcut is disabled when the laptop is in Tablet mode, as covered in Chapter 7.

Exploring the Start button menu

The most important gizmo on the Windows desktop is the Start button, found on the left end of the taskbar at the bottom of the screen. Click the Start button to behold the Start button menu, lovingly illustrated in Figure 8-2.

The Start button menu is a fun slab-o-stuff that includes a list of programs, fun places to visit in Windows, and other things to start. Primarily, the Start button lists programs to start (get it?), arranged alphabetically, as illustrated in Figure 8-2. Scroll or swipe the list to view the lot.

If you tap the three-line, or *hamburger*, button atop the Start menu, the icons on its left side expand, as shown in Figure 8-2. Each icon is a shortcut to an important place in Windows, such as the Documents folder or the Settings app. The Power item shows options for ending your computer day.

Not shown in Figure 8-2 on the right are program and promotional tiles, which is how the Start menu is originally configured. I have removed these tiles, a painstaking process involving right-clicking a tile and choosing the Unpin from Start command. To add program tiles, right-click a program in the Start button list and choose Pin to Start.

>> Dismiss the Start button menu by clicking the mouse on the desktop or tapping the Esc key on the keyboard.

>> Tablet mode changes the appearance of the Start button and the Start button menu. All apps and programs run full-screen. See Chapter 7 for information.

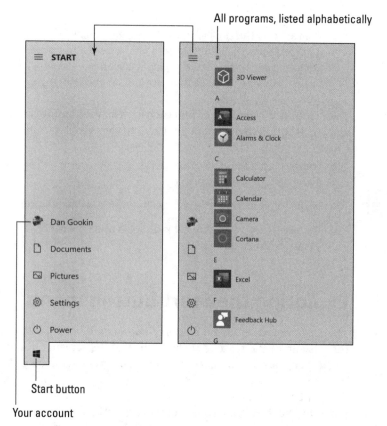

All programs, listed alphabetically

FIGURE 8-2:
Things to look for
on the Start
button menu.

Start button

Your account

Working on the taskbar

An important tool for working on your laptop is the Windows taskbar. It's home
to a smattering of important locations, but its largest role is in helping you work
with multiple programs at a time.

Figure 8-3 illustrates the major provinces on the taskbar.

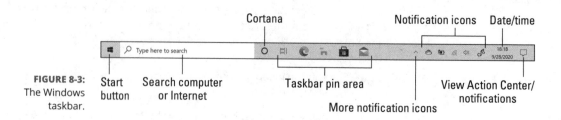

FIGURE 8-3:
The Windows
taskbar.

Cortana

Notification icons   Date/time

Start
button

Search computer
or Internet

Taskbar pin area

More notification icons

View Action Center/
notifications

Here's how each taskbar goober works:

Start button: This button is the main control on the desktop. Click the Start button to pop up the Start button menu. This menu contains options for controlling the computer and for starting programs.

Search box: Use this item to search for files on the computer or items on the Internet.

Cortana: This button is your gateway to the Cortana voice-activated search thing.

Taskbar pin area: In this region, you find icons representing popular programs or features, such as the web browser, File Explorer, and Microsoft Store.

Notification icons: These teensy icons pester you with pop-up balloons from time to time. They can also help you do things or monitor events and show you the date and time.

Date/Time: Use this item to check the date and time, or click it to view a pop-up calendar.

Action Center: Tap this icon to view the Action Center. Its appearance changes to indicate pending notifications visible in the Action Center.

In addition to the pinned programs, buttons appear on the taskbar for each program or window you open. Click the button to switch to that program, or right-click it for a pop-up menu of common activities, recently opened files, and other goodies.

REMEMBER

>> The taskbar isn't welded to the bottom of the screen. It can hippity-hop to any screen edge, but traditionally it's stuck to the bottom of the screen. That's probably gravity in action, though I'm not certain.

>> To move the taskbar, or relocate it to the bottom of the screen, you must first unlock it: Right-click the taskbar and choose the Lock the Taskbar command. After it's unlocked, you can drag the taskbar to any edge of the screen. Choose the Lock the Taskbar command again to cinch it down.

>> The icons in the notification area serve two purposes. First, they can notify you with pop-up bubbles. Or you can simply point the mouse at an icon to view status information, such as whether the network is connected or how much battery juice remains. Second, the icons provide instant access to some common features, such as networking, antivirus, volume control, and others to keep handy.

>> To use the icons in the notification area, click the mouse. Either you see a pop-up menu of options or something else happens. The icon's behavior is grossly inconsistent, so sometimes you right-click, sometimes you left-click, and sometimes you double-click.

Visiting with the Action Center

 The notification icons are a traditional Windows feature. Messages, updates, and controls are offered in the Action Center to supplement the notification icons. When new information is available, an icon appears on the far right edge of the taskbar, as illustrated in the margin.

To view the Action Center, swipe in from the right edge of the screen. The keyboard shortcut is Win+A. And you can click or tap the Action Center icon.

Figure 8-4 illustrates the Action Center. It features two parts. The upper part lists ongoing notifications, such as new email, calendar reminders, instant messages, and other constant annoyances.

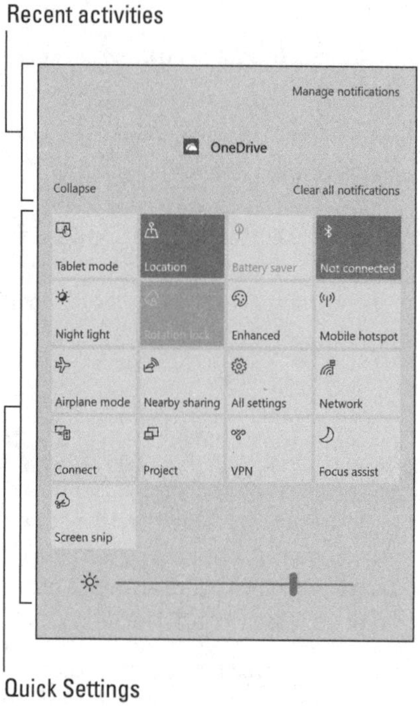

Recent activities

FIGURE 8-4:
The Action
Center.

Quick Settings

The lower part of the Action Center contains Quick Settings. These tiles let you instantly activate or deactivate various laptop features. Some tiles give you quick access to certain apps, such as the All Settings button, which launches the Settings app.

Swipe the Action Center to the right to dismiss it, tap the Esc key, or press Win+A a second time.

Using the supersecret shortcut menu

TIP

If you're an old hand at Windows, you can appreciate what I call the supersecret shortcut menu. It appears in the lower left corner of the screen when you press the Win+X keyboard shortcut or right-click the Start button.

The supersecret shortcut menu lists locations that let you control various aspects of Windows, such as the Settings app, Mobility Center, and the all-cryptic Power-Shell. The commands and locations can be difficult to get to, which is why the supersecret shortcut menu is so handy.

Shouting at Cortana

Windows features a voice control and search system named Cortana. It's interactive, so you can bellow directions to your laptop and, hopefully, Cortana obeys, by either responding verbally or displaying additional information or websites. This tool has nothing to do with Apple's Siri or Android's Google Now, which are incredibly similar, and that's merely a coincidence.

Cortana dwells on the taskbar, as illustrated earlier, in Figure 8-3. Click its icon to activate Cortana and work the configuration process. After Cortana is set up, tap its icon to use it. Type a question, or tap the Microphone icon (shown in the margin) to pronounce your dictates. For example, ask Cortana what the weather will be like tomorrow.

TIP

Cortana works best with a headset. By using such a handy peripheral, you can ensure that the technology hears your utterances. Further, when you have headphones on, Cortana's replies aren't broadcast so that everyone in the café knows that you're a Dolphins fan.

Windows and Your Stuff

One key part of any computer system is *storage*. Storage is important because it's where all your stuff is kept on the laptop. Yes, the stuff is "inside there, somewhere." All the programs, the Windows operating system, and all the files you create must be put somewhere inside the laptop.

Exploring your laptop's storage

In Windows, you can view the gamut of storage devices available to your laptop in a single, handy place. It's the This PC window, shown in Figure 8-5.

Pinned storage locations   Recent and popular folders

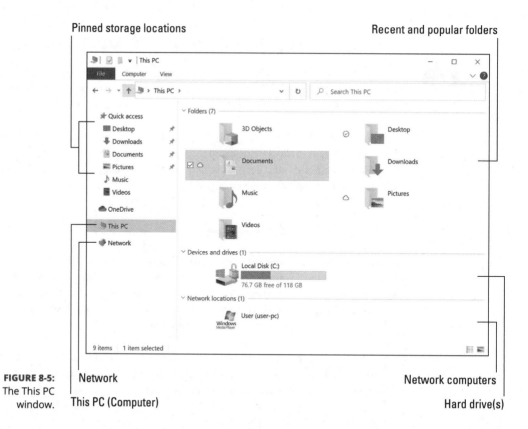

FIGURE 8-5:
The This PC
window.

Network

This PC (Computer)

Network computers

Hard drive(s)

To open the This PC window, follow these steps:

1. **Press the Win+E keyboard shortcut.**

This shortcut opens a File Explorer window.

2. **From the left side of the window, click the item titled This PC.**

The This PC window — a name which makes any sentence read awkwardly — shows folders and storage devices associated with your computer. You see popular folders, the internal hard drive or SSD, and any external devices, thumb drives, media cards, and other storage. Network storage or other computers may also appear in the window.

>> You can also open a Windows Explorer window by choosing the File Explorer icon on the taskbar; this icon is shown in the margin.

>> You can also choose File Explorer from the Start button menu to open a Windows Explorer window.

» The This PC window is your gateway to the laptop's storage devices. When you're told to "examine Drive C," for example, you open the This PC window, where you behold the Drive C icon.

» The Windows Explorer program opens to the Quick Access folder. This folder lists popular and frequently accessed folders and files.

» To add a folder to the Quick Access list, right-click the Folder icon and choose the command Pin to Quick Access.

» Another popular storage location is the Network window. It lists computers and other resources available to your laptop on the local network. See Chapter 17 for details.

Accessing your User Profile folder

In Windows, the User Profile folder is home to all your files and stuff. It's your personal storage area on the laptop's mass storage system.

The User Profile folder is given the same name as your user account name. So, if your login ID is Sponge Bob, the folder is named Sponge Bob. On my laptop, the folder name is Dan Gookin, which is also my human name but not my cartoon name.

To open your User Profile folder, follow these steps:

1. **Open a Windows Explorer window.**

   The quick way is to press the Win+E keyboard shortcut.

2. **Click the first chevron on the left end of the address box.**

   The chevron is illustrated in Figure 8-6. Clicking this icon displays a menu of top-level locations in the laptop's storage system.

3. **Choose your account name from the menu.**

   For example, in Figure 8-6, I chose Dan Gookin, which is still not my cartoon name.

The folders in your User Profile folder help you organize your stuff. Some of the folders are used automatically by various programs, such as the Paint program, which saves and opens its graphics files in the Pictures folder. And you're free to create new folders, such as the Programming folder I use on my laptop.

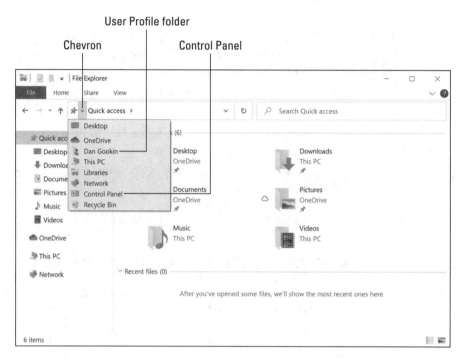

FIGURE 8-6:
The User Profile
folder.

Among the folders available in your User Profile folder, you find

Documents: The main place where you store documents and other random files.

Music: A place to store all audio files, especially songs stolen from the Internet or "borrowed" from your friend Skeetch.

Pictures: The folder where graphics files live. Most graphical applications automatically store images in this folder.

Videos: A special folder for storing digital video.

Even more custom folders are available: 3D Objects, Contacts, Desktop, Downloads, Favorites, Links, Saved Games, and Searches. Each of these folders is used somehow by one or another program in Windows or by Windows itself. You're also free to create and use your own folders or to create *subfolders* within the folders that are created for you.

Finding programs

As with your own stuff, the laptop stores all your programs, software, and applications. These items are accessed from the Start button menu, covered earlier in this chapter.

To run a program, summon the Start menu by heeding these steps:

1. **Press the Windows key on the keyboard, or click or tap the Start button on the taskbar.**

2. **Scroll to locate a program in the list.**

3. **Click or tap the program's icon to start it.**

TIP

To quickly locate a program, summon the Start button menu and type the first few letters of the program's name. For example, press the Win key and type **chro** to display matching program names. If Google Chrome is the top choice, press the Enter key to run the program.

>> I keep my most common programs pinned to the taskbar, including Word, the web browser, and my email program. To do so, locate the program on the Start menu and right-click its icon. Choose More, Pin to Taskbar.

TECHNICAL
STUFF

>> Internally, the laptop stores programs on the primary storage device, either the hard drive or SSD. They're located in the Program Files folder or Program Files (x86) folder. Windows itself is found in the Windows folder. Though you can use the Windows Explorer program to browse to these folders, I strongly recommend that you not mess with any files located there.

Settings and Options

A primary duty of any operating system is to control the computer's hardware. The operating system's responsibility to you, the user, is to provide you with access to the tools necessary to control the laptop's hardware. For the sake of confusion, Windows 10 uses two locations to handle that task: the Settings app and the traditional Control Panel.

Opening the Settings app

The modern approach to controlling the laptop's settings, as well as perusing various options in Windows 10, is to open the Settings app, shown in Figure 8-7. It's your first destination in the quest to tame your beastly laptop.

The fast way to visit the Settings app is to press the Win+I keyboard shortcut. The less-fast way is to choose the Settings icon from the Start button menu, shown in the margin. The most frustrating way is to ask Cortana to open the Settings app.

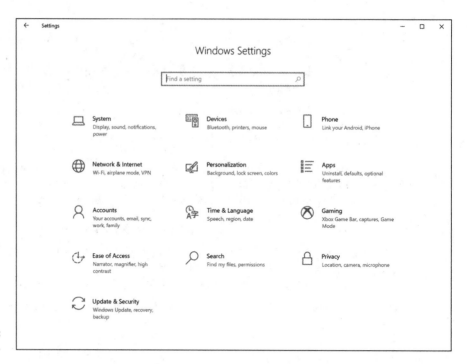

FIGURE 8-7:
The Settings app.

To use the Settings app, click or tap one of the main tiles. You see a second screen with categories on the left and controls on the right. Choose a category, and then mess with the controls. Various chapters throughout this book offer specific directions for using the Settings app to adjust various laptoppy things.

Visiting the Control Panel

When the Settings app fails you, or you consider yourself a grizzled Windows veteran, turn to the traditional Control Panel for making adjustments or setting options in Windows. In fact, some of the items chosen in the Settings app open portions of the Control Panel.

Figure 8-8 illustrates the Control Panel window. Category view is shown. To use the antique icon view, choose the Large Icons or Small Icons item from the View By menu, illustrated in the figure.

To access the Control Panel, summon a File Explorer window: Press the Win+E keyboard shortcut. Click the chevron on the far left end of the address box and choose Control Panel from the menu. (Refer to Figure 8-6.)

Windows Explorer address box chevron   Change Control Panel view

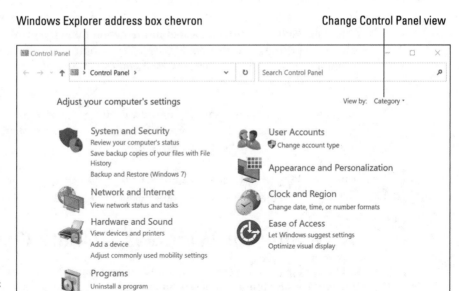

FIGURE 8-8:
The Control
Panel.

For tablet PCs, locate important items in the Control Panel by choosing the Hardware and Sound category. On the next screen, you see a few items listed that can help adjust your laptop's hardware. These items include

Power Options: Select items in this category to help conserve battery life and manage power settings. Details are covered in Chapter 10.

Pen and Touch: Choose this item to adjust how the touchscreen monitor works and how the digital pen interacts with the monitor. For example, you can configure how the double-click and right-click mouse actions translate to the digital pen.

Tablet PC Settings: Choose an item in this category to control settings specific to your tablet computer.

Other Control Panel locations are referenced throughout this book. For example, information about your user account is found in Chapters 4 and 9.

Using the Quick Settings

Many of your favorite laptop settings are accessed from the Quick Settings area of the Action Center, illustrated earlier, in Figure 8-4. To see the Action Center, press the Win+A keyboard shortcut or tap/click the Notification icon, illustrated in the margin.

The Quick Settings buttons located in the Action Center control various features mentioned throughout this book. Click or tap a button to access the feature. For example, click or tap the Airplane Mode button to activate this mode when you take your laptop on a trip.

In some cases, tapping a button controls a setting. For example, tap the Brightness button to interactively adjust the laptop's screen brightness level. Tap the Tablet Mode button to activate this feature.

TIP

On tablet PCs or laptops with touchscreens, you can quickly access the Action Center by swiping your finger inward from the right edge of the screen.

Accessing the Windows Mobility Center

A clutch of popular and useful laptop settings is found in a central location called the Windows Mobility Center, shown in Figure 8-9. You may see more items than those shown in the figure; your laptop manufacturer may have added to the list custom features and other useful or fun items.

To quickly summon the Windows Mobility Center window, press the Win+X keyboard shortcut and choose Mobility Center from the supersecret menu.

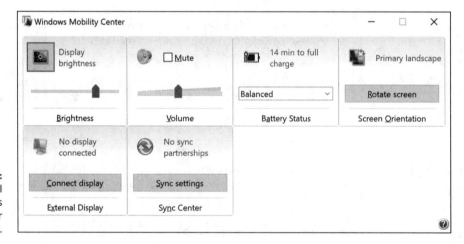

FIGURE 8-9:
The Control Panel's Windows Mobility Center window.

3

Out and About with Mr. Laptop

Chapter **9**

You and Your Laptop

No two laptops are alike. Sure, they may come from the same manufacturer or have the same case design or both be named Winston. After you set up Windows, add your account, and install software, things change. The system changes further as you customize Windows, which truly means no two laptops are alike. Even if your Winston laptop is exactly the same as someone else's laptop named Winston, you can customize things to your heart's content.

User Accounts

Perhaps the greatest thing that makes your laptop yours is your user account. The laptop sports your account name, which is probably your own name, as well as your unique password. The settings and changes you make in Windows are associated with your user account, which is why having such an account is an important thing.

Oh, well, yes: Security is also a big issue. User accounts help add security.

>> Your user account was configured when you first started or installed Windows on your laptop.

>> In Windows 10, user accounts can be associated with an online identity, such as an email account.

>> See Part 5 of this book for information on laptop security.

Accessing your user account info

No one can use Windows 10 without signing in to an existing user account. You can't even configure Windows without an account. So, my guess is that you already have a user account, possibly the only account on the laptop. To review this account's information, follow these steps:

1. **Click the Start button.**

   Up pops the Start menu.

2. **Click your user account picture from the Start menu.**

   The picture can be generic or specific to you.

3. **Choose Change Account Settings.**

   The Settings app opens to the Accounts area. Your account information is shown on the screen, similar to what appears in Figure 9-1.

Each of the items on the left side of the Accounts screen lets you change an aspect of your own account or add other accounts to the laptop.

>> Most basic account information is managed on the Internet by accessing your Microsoft online account. In the Settings app, choose the Manage My Microsoft Account link (refer to Figure 9-1) to visit the web page and make changes.

WARNING

>> Changing your Microsoft account affects all your Microsoft products, which include other computers with that account, subscriptions to the Office 365 service, Skype, as well as email and other Microsofty things.

Eschewing an online account

If you prefer not to surrender your laptop to the Microsoft hegemony, you can opt for a local account instead of an online one. To do so, follow these steps:

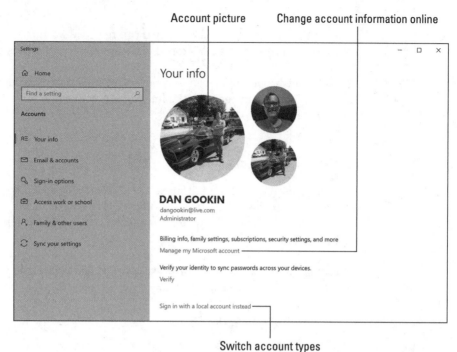

Account picture   Change account information online

Your info

Settings

⌂ Home

Find a setting

Accounts

R≡ Your info

✉ Email & accounts

🔍 Sign-in options

🗗 Access work or school

👤 Family & other users

🔁 Sync your settings

DAN GOOKIN
dangookin@live.com
Administrator

Billing info, family settings, subscriptions, security settings, and more
Manage my Microsoft account

Verify your identity to sync passwords across your devices.
Verify

Sign in with a local account instead

Switch account types

FIGURE 9-1:
Account information in the Settings app.

1. **Ensure that you've saved all your stuff and closed all open programs.**

   You must sign out of Windows to complete this process.

2. **Choose your account image from the Start button menu.**

3. **Choose the Change Account Settings item.**

4. **On the Accounts screen, choose the link Sign In with a Local Account Instead.**

   Refer to Figure 9-1 for this link's location.

5. **Work the steps onscreen to first verify your existing account, and then create a new password for the laptop.**

   You're signed out of Windows.

6. **Use your new account to sign in.**

The advantage of a local account is that you squarely tell a big American corporation to buzz off. Lots of people enjoy doing so.

The disadvantage is that some of your online information isn't synchronized; specifically, your Windows desktop and files shared on Microsoft's OneDrive cloud storage. Also, when you use a Microsoft account, Windows settings are saved across multiple computers. Especially if you're a road warrior with a desktop PC at home or the office, using a Microsoft account on both systems is the best choice.

To reestablish your Microsoft account as your laptop's account, summon the account screen again and click the link Sign In with a Microsoft Account Instead. Follow the onscreen directions.

Setting an account PIN

For a password to be useful, it must be complex. This added degree of difficulty makes such a password a pain in the rump to type on a tablet PC, or any other time you turn on a Windows computer. To alleviate the pain, you can assign a PIN to your account.

You're prompted to set up a PIN when you first add your account to Windows 10. If you haven't yet done so, follow these steps to set a PIN for your account:

1. **Press the Win+I keyboard shortcut.**

   The Settings app appears.

2. **Choose Accounts.**

3. **On the left side of the screen, choose Sign-in Options.**

4. **Choose Windows Hello PIN.**

5. **Click the Add button.**

6. **Continue following the onscreen directions.**

To sign in to Windows on your laptop, type the PIN. You don't even need to press the Enter key — just type the numbers. Try it now. Sign off and then sign back in: Choose your account item from the Start button menu and select Sign Out. Sign in again by using the PIN.

REMEMBER

>> To change the PIN, repeat the steps in this section but choose Change at Step 5.

>> I recommend against removing the PIN. If you desire to do so, at Step 5 click the Remove button.

>> Don't forget your PIN!

Changing your user account picture

Obviously, the most vital element of your user account is the picture. It's what you see when you first sign in to Windows. It appears atop the Start button menu. Is it a picture of you? Or is it a flower, a chess piece, a fish?

Your laptop most likely features a camera right above the screen. If so, you can use this camera to snap an account picture. Follow these steps:

1. **Click the Start button.**

2. **From the Start menu, choose your user account picture.**

   It's found atop the Start menu.

3. **Choose the Change Account Settings item.**

   The Settings app starts, zooming you to the Accounts area. On the right side of the window, you see your current account picture (refer to Figure 9-1).

4. **Swipe down the screen to see the Create Your Picture heading.**

5. **Choose the Camera option to use the laptop's camera to take a photo, or choose the Browse for One option to browse for suitable media stored on your laptop.**

   Continue following the onscreen directions.

If you choose to use the Camera, the Windows Camera app starts. You see a live view from your laptop's camera, as shown in Figure 9-2, allowing you to preen and pose for your pending picture. Tap the larger Shutter button to snap a charming picture for your user account.

After snapping the image, crop it: Adjust the four handles in or out to set the new image size and area. To reject the image, click the X button to cancel and then redo the shot.

The photo you select takes over as your account image. If you use your Microsoft account to sign in to Windows, the photo populates to other Windows computers and Microsoft-related accounts.

TIP

If the laptop lacks a camera, you can choose an existing photo to use as your account visage: Click the Browse button in Step 5. Use the Open dialog box to locate an image stored on the laptop. Select the image. Open it. That image is assigned to your account.

Shutter button

FIGURE 9-2:
Taking a selfie for
your account
image.

Adding online accounts

You most likely have multiple online accounts for all your various incarnations, including email accounts, social networking, and other Internetty things you use and in which you participate.

To add these accounts, follow these steps:

1. **Press the Win+I keyboard shortcut to bring forth the Settings app.**

2. **Choose Accounts.**

3. **From the list on the left side of the window, choose Email & Accounts.**

4. **Use the Add an Account button to set up your laptop with an email or other online account.**

For example, choose Google from the Add an Account screen to add your Google (Gmail) account, choose Yahoo to add a Yahoo! account, and so on.

Further account setup may be required for various apps — specifically, non-Microsoft apps. For example, if you use a third-party email program, it may require you to add your various email accounts regardless of what settings you make elsewhere in Windows.

The Perfect Display

Unlike with a desktop computer, you can't run out and buy a new screen of any old size for your laptop. What you see is what you get — to a point. Windows still allows you to adjust and mangle the laptop's display.

Setting the display resolution

Don't even bother with the laptop's screen resolution. It's most likely set to the optimal number of pixels — horizontal and vertical. That value is also the highest-resolution setting available for the laptop's display hardware.

To check the resolution, follow these steps:

1. **Right-click the desktop.**

2. **Choose Display Settings.**

3. **Use the Display Resolution menu to set a new resolution.**

Of all the different values on the menu (and these aren't multiplication problems), choose the one that's flagged as recommended.

Another trick is to change the magnification. If the resolution makes the icons appear too tiny on the desktop, on the same screen where you set the resolution, choose a scaling percentage from the menu, such as 200% to make everything appear twice as large.

TIP

Also check out the Magnifier tool: Open the Settings app and choose Ease of Access. From the items on the left side of the window, choose Magnifier.

Changing the desktop wallpaper

The desktop *wallpaper* is the background image or solid color you see when you visit the Windows desktop. Changing this image is one of the most obvious ways you can customize your laptop.

To change the desktop wallpaper, follow these steps:

1. **Right-click the desktop.**

2. **Choose Personalize from the shortcut menu.**

3. **From the Background menu, choose Picture, Solid Color, or Slideshow.**

Your choice affects the desktop wallpaper in a number of ways.

For the Picture option, you can choose an image supplied with Windows or one of your own images.

For Solid Color, you can choose a preset color from the bland palette that's presented.

For Slideshow, you choose one of your photo albums stored on the laptop. The background changes images according to the time schedule you set.

Adding a screen saver

The screen saver is more than an amusing diversion: It's also part of laptop security. In addition to obscuring whatever information is displayed, the screen saver can be configured to lock the laptop after a period of inactivity.

Set up or confirm your laptop's screen saver settings by following these steps:

1. **Pop up the Start button menu.**

Tap the Windows key on the keyboard or tap the Start button on the taskbar.

2. **Type** screen saver **to locate the Screen Saver Control Panel item.**

3. **Choose the Change Screen Saver item from the list of search results.**

The Screen Saver Settings dialog box appears.

4. **Choose a screen saver from the Screen Saver menu button.**

The screen saver preview appears in the dialog box, showing you how it affects the display.

For some screen savers, click the Settings button to adjust how the screen saver operates. Click the Preview button to view the screen saver full-screen.

5. **Set the screen saver timeout value.**

For example, 10 minutes is a good time.

6. **Place a check mark in the box labeled On Resume, Display Logon Screen.**

This setting ensures that the lock screen appears whenever the screen saver is disrupted.

7. **Click the OK button.**

The screen saver kicks in after a period of inactivity. Tap any key or move the mouse to wake up the laptop and sign in to Windows again.

TIP

WARNING

>> To disable the screen saver, choose None from the menu in Step 4.

>> The screen saver timeout and power-saving timeout may conflict. Ensure that you set the screen saver timeout (refer to Step 5) to a number lower than the power-saving timeout. See Chapter 10 or, when following these steps, click the Change Power Settings link before you reach Step 7.

>> Avoid downloading screen savers from the Internet. Although many of them are legitimate, some are spyware or worse: They spew ads all over your screen, and the software is nearly impossible to remove.

Setting the display orientation

Tablet PCs can be held horizontally, like a traditional laptop, and they can be held vertically, like a sheet of paper. As the laptop is rotated, so goes the screen — as long as the screen rotation feature is enabled.

To set the screen orientation on a tablet PC, follow these steps:

1. **Right-click the desktop.**

2. **Choose the Display Settings command from the pop-up menu.**

3. **Click the Display Orientation button.**

4. **Choose Landscape or Portrait.**

5. **If the Rotation Lock item is enabled, use it to lock the display in the chosen orientation.**

6. **If you're pleased with the new presentation, click the Keep Changes button.**

The display changes to reflect the orientation you've chosen.

If the rotation lock is active (Step 5), the display stays in the given orientation no matter how you turn or twist the laptop. To have the display automatically change orientation, remove the orientation lock.

>> A rotation lock tile exists as a quick setting in the Action Center: Swipe in from the right edge of the screen and tap the Rotation Lock quick setting to turn the feature on or off. See Chapter 8 for more information on quick settings.

>> The Flipped options on the Orientation menu (refer to Step 4) don't reverse the information displayed on the screen. Instead, they turn the image upside down. This way, you can choose one of the four options presented on the

Orientation button menu to set the display's "up" side to any of the tablet PC's screen edges.

>> Horizontal orientation is known as *Landscape mode.*

>> Vertical orientation is called *Portrait mode.*

>> Some tablet PCs (specifically, convertible laptops) may feature a physical button or Fn keyboard shortcut that sets or locks the screen orientation.

Adjusting screen brightness

If you're fortunate, your laptop features keyboard buttons to adjust the laptop's screen brightness. These are used with or without the Fn key to instantly adjust the screen's brightness.

Windows harbors a software brightness item in the Action Center: Press the Win+A keyboard shortcut to view the Action Center. A brightness slider appears at the bottom of the Action Center pane.

TIP

If you find yourself constantly adjusting the monitor's brightness to reflect your surroundings — dim for indoors and bright for outdoors — use the Adaptive Brightness setting. Follow these steps:

1. **Right-click the desktop and choose Display Settings.**

    The Settings app appears.

2. **Check the item Change Brightness Automatically When Lighting Changes to have the laptop automatically adjust the screen brightness.**

REMEMBER

The brighter the screen, the faster the battery drains.

Removable Storage

As your laptop's Lord High User, it's your job to manage the laptop's storage system. The main media is the mass storage inside the laptop, either the traditional hard drive or the SSD (the solid-state drive). This storage cannot be removed. Other media, however, can pop in or out. These media include digital media cards, thumb drives, and external hard drives and SSDs. All these gizmos must be properly added or removed from the laptop, lest you incur the imperious wrath of Windows.

Adding storage

To expand your laptop's storage capacity, attach an external storage device. These devices are of two kinds:

» A media card, inserted directly into a media card slot on the laptop

» A USB device, such as an external drive or a thumb drive

No matter how it's connected, the storage is added to your laptop's storage system. The device shows up in the This PC window in Windows 10. You can immediately access the storage by using your programs or the Windows operating system or whatever other type of file magic you employ.

TECHNICAL STUFF

» You can leave the removable media attached to your laptop as long as you like. But be careful when you remove it! See the later section "Ejecting media and storage devices."

» Some external storage comes in two parts: drive and media. The drive reads the media, and the media can be inserted and removed without detaching the drive. Examples of this type of external storage include a DVD/CD drive, which reads optical discs, or a media card reader, into which you insert various media cards.

Using the AutoPlay notification

When new storage media is added to the laptop, Windows alerts you with an AutoPlay notification, like the one shown in Figure 9-3.

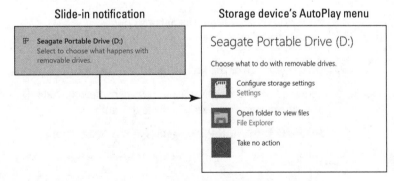

Slide-in notification   Storage device's AutoPlay menu

FIGURE 9-3:
An AutoPlay notification and options.

The notification slides in from the right edge of the screen. Tap it to view the AutoPlay menu, shown on the right in Figure 9-3. Even if you don't tap the notification, you can still use the storage; the notification simply presents the menu (on the right in Figure 9-3), which makes it easier to deal with the removable storage.

For example, to access files stored on removable media, tap the notification and choose the item Open Folder to View Files. You see a folder window appear, which lists the files and folders stored on the media.

To import photos from a freshly inserted media card, choose the item Import Pictures and Videos from the AutoPlay menu.

When you don't see the exact command you want on the AutoPlay menu, choose Open Folder to View Files and browse for available media, documents, or whatever is stored on the media.

>> The variety of options presented on the AutoPlay menu depends on which programs or apps are installed on your laptop as well as on the content of the removable media.

>> If the AutoPlay message doesn't appear, open the This PC window: Press Win+E and choose This PC from the list of locations on the left side of the window. Right-click on the storage device's icon and choose the Open AutoPlay command.

Controlling AutoPlay settings

Sometimes AutoPlay appears. Sometimes it doesn't. Sometimes the laptop gets a mind of its own and overrides your AutoPlay desires. To keep things in line, visit the AutoPlay screen in the Settings app. Obey these directions:

1. **Press Win+I to summon the Settings app.**

2. **Choose Devices.**

3. **On the left side of the screen, choose AutoPlay.**

   Items shown on the right side of the screen affect the AutoPlay settings, which are triggered when you add media to the laptop.

4. **Ensure that the AutoPlay toggle is in the On position.**

   Turning off this setting disables AutoPlay messages.

5. **Select the AutoPlay defaults.**

   Two menus are available, one for removable drives and another for memory cards. Choose a setting from the list.

6. **Close the Settings app window.**

If you want to view the AutoPlay menu whenever new media is inserted, choose the option Ask Me Every Time in Step 5.

Ejecting media and storage devices

By all that is holy, please don't yank out a media card from your laptop or disconnect a USB storage device without following the proper steps. Failure to abide by my admonition can result in damaged hardware and missing files.

To properly, sanely, remove media — such as media cards and thumb drives — follow these steps:

1. Display the This PC window.

Press Win+R to summon the File Explorer window, and choose This PC from the navigation pane on the left side of the window.

2. Right-click the media's icon.

Removable drives show up in the list of devices and drives.

3. Choose the Eject command.

4. When you see the safe-to-remove notification, remove the media from the laptop or from the media drive.

A chime plays when the safe-to-remove notification appears.

To detach a hard drive or any external storage device, such as a DVD/CD drive, you must use the Safely Remove notification. Follow these steps:

1. Click the Show More chevron on the taskbar's notification area.

The Show More icon is shown in Figure 9-4.

2. Click the Safely Remove notification icon.

The Safely Remove notification icon is shown in the margin as well as in Figure 9-4. Click this icon to display a pop-up menu, as shown in the figure.

3. Choose the drive you want to remove.

For example, in Figure 9-4, it's the Seagate Portable Drive (D:).

4. When you see the Safe to Remove notification, disconnect the drive from the laptop.

If you see a warning that the media cannot be removed, click the OK button. Locate whichever programs have open data files on the drive, save the files, and then close the programs. This process should allow the drive to be removed.

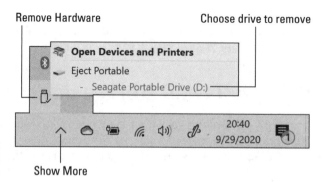

Remove Hardware   Choose drive to remove

FIGURE 9-4:
Safely removing a
storage device.

Show More

TIP

The easiest way to remove an external drive is to turn off the laptop. After it's off (not hibernating or sleeping), you can safely remove any external storage device.

The Software Side

Your laptop is hardware. To make it useful, beyond the social compliments for owning such a thing, it needs software. Software makes the hardware go. Windows is software, and bonus software was most likely included with your laptop, but that's not enough. To be productive, you need more software.

Adding new software

Unlike buying the laptop hardware, you buy or otherwise obtain new software for your laptop until the device dies or you sacrificially lay it before a herd of stampeding rhinos. Installing new software is considered a basic computer operator duty.

Most software obtained today is installed from the Internet. You can visit the developer's website or open the Microsoft Store app to see what goodies Microsoft urges you to buy. Obviously, an Internet connection is vital to obtaining software for your laptop.

>> Software you obtain from the Internet may force Windows to display a User Account Control (UAC) when it's first run. As long as you're sure the software is legitimate, allow it to run.

>> Software obtained from the Internet may require a code or a key. You enter this key to confirm that you have a purchased copy of the software and can use all of its features.

>> Legacy software packages may come on optical drives, though this format is rare. I've seen software available on thumb drives — which is nice because in addition to the software, you get a thumb drive.

>> Though software is often a one-time purchase, many programs such as Microsoft Office are offered as subscription services.

>> On the other side of the coin, lots of free software is available, though you should install such software only when you're certain it comes from a reliable source. And always run antivirus and anti-malware utilities on your laptop. See Chapter 19.

Removing software

Back in the days when you needed permission from the electric company to start your computer, you could easily uninstall or remove computer software: You deleted the program. Despite the fact that those days have been over for about 30 years, some people out there still believe — and spread the word — that you remove software by playing *Duck Hunter.* Not true!

To rid yourself of unwanted software, obey these steps:

1. **Open the Settings app.**

   Press the Win+I keyboard shortcut.

2. **Choose Apps.**

   On the right side of the window, a list of apps appears. These are the programs installed on your laptop.

3. **Scroll to locate the app you want to remove.**

4. **Click or tap the program's entry.**

5. **Click or tap the Uninstall button.**

   You see a second, redundant Uninstall button.

6. **Click or tap the second, redundant Uninstall button.**

   The program is removed.

WHAT DID THEY PREINSTALL THIS TIME?

TIP

Most laptops come with a bloat of software preinstalled. Don't feel compelled to use any of it. In fact, if the software annoys you, uninstall it. There's no point in keeping anything on your laptop's storage system when you don't plan to use it. *Remember:* It's *your* laptop!

Removing a program doesn't remove the files you created by using that program. So, if you remove a graphics program, the images you created or edited are not also deleted. Similarly, if you remove a screenwriting program, all your scripts that never sold remain on the laptop's storage system.

WARNING

You can't undo the uninstall action, though you can always reinstall the program — as long as you have the original installation files and any codes or keys required to verify that you own a legitimate copy.

Chapter **10**

Portable Power

Laptop manufacturers seem to have solved the issues of size and weight quite effectively over the past few decades. One issue that remains on hold, however, is that of battery power. For all laptop users, the question remains: How long can you use the thing without having to scramble desperately for a wall socket somewhere? Honestly, today's laptop batteries should last for days, not hours.

If the laptop's processor is the muscle, and software the brain, the battery is its heart. As long as that sucker keeps beating, you can use your laptop anywhere.

The Battery Will Get a Charge Out of This!

It's simple. The laptop's battery is what separates the laptop from the wall. Portable computers are portable only when they lack power cords. So, in a way, having a battery-powered computer gives you freedom.

Using the battery (or not)

Your laptop automatically uses the battery as its source of power — unless the power cord is plugged into an AC power source. When the cord is removed, the battery takes over. Plug in the cord again, and AC takes over and the battery charges.

>> The laptop's hardware monitors battery usage. You control only how quickly the battery drains. See the later section "When the Power Gets Low."

>> Most laptops use a Lithium-ion type battery.

>> Unlike older NiCad batteries, Lithium-ion batteries don't suffer from the dreaded memory effect: Feel free to use and charge the laptop's battery at any time. You don't need to wait for the battery to drain completely before recharging.

>> You can confirm which type of battery your laptop has by looking at its label. The label is found on the battery itself, although, if the battery isn't removable, the label might be located on the laptop's case. Battery information might also be found on those papers that came with the laptop. I recommended in Chapter 1 that you keep those papers, but you probably threw them away anyhow.

>> Your laptop might have *two* additional batteries inside. A secondary, alkaline battery inside is used to power the laptop's internal clock. An optional third battery keeps things powered for a battery swap. See the later section "Using a second battery."

TECHNICAL
STUFF

>> Batteries were developed in the 1700s, originally from a Leyden jar, which was a device used to store static electricity. Benjamin Franklin used Leyden jars arranged in a series like an artillery battery, which is where the term *battery* comes from.

>> By the way, those cylinder batteries used in your flashlight (and in many netbook laptops) were developed in the 1890s.

Locating the laptop's battery

If your laptop features a removable battery, take a moment to locate it. Odds are good that it loads into the bottom of the laptop, though a few laptop models have their batteries inserted through a hole or door in the side.

Battery details are found on the battery's label or on the laptop case. The information details the battery type model number, plus various stickers and tattoos from safety organizations, national and international.

DON'T BOTHER READING THIS TRIVIAL INFORMATION ON VARIOUS BATTERY TYPES

All batteries store electricity. How they store electricity depends on the chemicals inside the battery. Those chemicals determine the battery type and how the battery smells. Here are some popular battery types:

Alkaline: This type of battery is the most common. It's used in flashlights, remote controls, smoke alarms, and kids' toys. It's standard but not rechargeable, which makes it a poor choice for a laptop.

Lead acid: If ever two words could make an environmentalist blanch, they're *lead* and *acid*. Yet those two chemicals supply the robust power of a car battery. The batteries are durable, long lasting, and rechargeable, but they're too heavy and caustic for use in a laptop.

NiCad: Nickel-cadmium batteries were some of the first consumer batteries that could be recharged. Sadly, they suffered from a malady known as the *memory effect*, which makes them impractical for laptops.

NiMH: The nickel-metal-hydride battery proved to be longer lasting than the NiCad, but it too suffers from the dreaded memory effect.

Lithium-ion: This type of battery is the one you most likely have in your laptop. Lithium-ion, or *Li-ion*, batteries are lightweight and perform better than other types of batteries, and they don't suffer from the memory effect. Their power is managed by the computer, and they can be rapidly recharged.

>> Smaller-format laptops, Ultrabooks, and tablets such as the Microsoft Surface don't feature removable batteries.

>> A few netbooks operate using standard alkaline batteries.

>> Batteries get warm as they're being used. That's simply their nature. However:

>> Watch out if the battery gets too hot! For example, the battery can become too hot to touch or hold for more than a few seconds. The heat can be a sign of a malfunctioning battery, and such a thing is *dangerous*. Phone your dealer or laptop manufacturer immediately if you suspect that the battery is running hot.

Monitoring the battery

Your suspicions are confirmed: The laptop's battery drains as you use it. You should plan for at least two or three hours of active computer use under battery power. The rate of drain varies, however, depending on what you're doing with the laptop and how full the charge.

The best way to check the laptop battery status is to gander at the tiny Battery icon in the taskbar's notification area. The icon graphically shows how much power remains, but it's tiny. To see more details, click the icon to view a larger report, similar to what's shown in Figure 10-1.

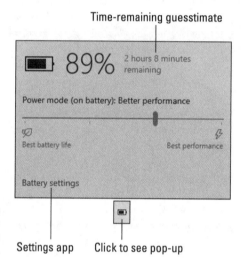

Time-remaining guesstimate

89% 2 hours 8 minutes remaining

Power mode (on battery): Better performance

Best battery life   Best performance

Battery settings

FIGURE 10-1:
Battery notification on the taskbar.
Settings app   Click to see pop-up

In addition to the percentage charge and a guesstimate of how much time remains, a button appears in the battery pop-up: Battery Settings. Tap it to visit the Settings app and view additional details about the battery — including using the Battery Saver feature. See the later section "Using the Battery Saver."

Click anywhere on the screen to dismiss the battery notification pop-up.

>> The Battery notification icon appears differently when the laptop is plugged into AC power, as shown in the margin.

>> When connected to AC power, use the Battery notification icon to confirm that the socket is working and power is flowing. If the icon doesn't appear as shown nearby, the laptop is using battery power and isn't being charged.

» Your laptop may feature a battery light on its case. The light may change color as the laptop drains. See Chapter 6 for more information on the pretty lights that festoon your laptop.

» The battery percentage isn't measured evenly as power drains. If the battery lasted for an hour and the meter is at 50 percent, it doesn't guarantee you another hour of battery life. The charge percentage, as well as the time remaining, are best guesses.

Charging the battery

This task is easy to do: Plug the laptop into a wall socket, and the battery begins to charge. Yes, you can continue to use the laptop while it's charging. Use it to the extreme! The charging rate is unaffected by whatever you're doing on the laptop.

» You can recharge your laptop's battery whether the battery is fully drained or not.

» I leave my laptop plugged into the wall whenever I can.

» There's no need to fully drain your laptop's lithium-ion battery every time you use it.

» The battery continues to charge even when the laptop is turned off (as long as it's plugged in).

Using a second battery

Thanks to improved battery life, as well as the fact that many laptops no longer feature removable batteries, the second battery option isn't as popular as it once was. But for a time, it was the best way to extend a laptop's operating life.

The second battery works like a spare: When the first battery runs low, a warning appears in Windows. You pop out the first battery and replace it with the second, fully charged battery. The laptop stays on the entire time.

» Even though the battery swap is supposed to be seamless, I strongly recommend saving all your work before performing a battery swap.

» If you've never swapped batteries, do a test-run at home or the office before you do so in the middle of the high desert during a critical operation.

» Ensure that the second or spare battery is fully charged. Either charge it in the laptop or use an external charger (if available). Put the fully charged spare battery in your laptop case or in any nonconducting (nonmetallic) container. Then head out on the road.

Replacing the battery

For most laptop users, when the battery dies, the laptop dies. When the battery is nonremovable, your carefree portable computer life is pretty much over.

Some laptops continue to work on AC power only; plug in the laptop and you're good to go. Other laptops may completely lock up and fail when the unreplaceable battery goes.

If your laptop features a removable battery, you can replace it. Use only approved replacement batteries and ensure that the replacement comes with a warranty.

WARNING

Using unapproved batteries in your laptop may lead to hazardous situations, such as, oh, the laptop catching fire and exploding. If you doubt me, search for *exploding laptop* on YouTube.

When the Power Gets Low

Nothing turns a casual afternoon of café computing into an urgent panic like a low battery warning on a laptop. Experienced laptop owners don't wait that long. They constantly monitor the battery's condition and take necessary action before the claxons sound. The idea is to be proactive, not reactive, before the power runs low.

Setting low-battery warnings

Windows peppers you with warnings as the battery power runs low. The Battery notification icon on the taskbar changes, and eventually pop-up messages appear. The idea is to alarm you: Either charge the battery, save your work, and shut down — or pray.

The good news is that you have control over the warnings. You can set when they appear and which actions are taken. The two warning levels are titled Low Battery and Critical Battery. Follow these steps to set each level and determine which actions are taken:

1. **Press the Win+E keyboard shortcut to see a File Explorer window.**

2. **At the left end of the address bar, click the chevron and choose Control Panel from the menu.**

   The creaky ol' Windows Control Panel appears.

3. **Choose Hardware and Sound.**

4. **Choose Power Options.**

You see the laptop's power plans, which are covered later, in the section "Reviewing the power management plan." The battery warning levels are set for a specific plan.

5. **Next to the active power plan, click the Change Plan Settings link.**

6. **In the Edit Plan Settings window, click the Change Advanced Power Settings link.**

Finally, the Power Options dialog box shows up. It's *the* happening place for all things having to do with power management in Windows.

7. **Scroll the list and locate the item labeled Battery.**

As you would expect, it's the last item in the list.

8. **Click the plus sign (+) by Battery to display various battery notification and action options.**

Each item has two subitems: one for settings when the laptop is on battery power and a second for when the laptop is plugged in.

9. **Set the battery level warnings.**

The warnings are illustrated in Figure 10-2. In chronological order, here are the items you can set:

(a) *Low battery notification:* Sets a warning for a low battery level, before the situation becomes critical. Values are set to On to set the low warning and set to Off to ignore it.

(b) *Low battery level:* Determines the battery percentage for the low-battery-level warning. This value should be generous, well above the critical level.

(c) *Low battery action:* Directs the laptop in what to do when the battery charge reaches the low battery level. I recommend the Do Nothing setting. Other options are Sleep, Hibernate, and Shut Down.

(d) *Critical battery level:* Sets the battery power level (percentage) for the crucial battery-level action.

(e) *Critical battery action:* Directs the laptop to sleep, hibernate, or shut down when the critical battery level is reached. I recommend choosing the Hibernate option.

10. **Click OK to confirm the settings.**

You can close any open dialog boxes and windows.

Click to expand

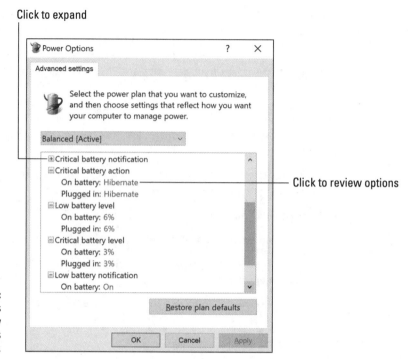

—— Click to review options

FIGURE 10-2:
Power Options
for setting low
battery warnings
and actions.

Setting the warnings is only one part of good power management. Hopefully, you never see the low battery notification and, most definitely, you never have the laptop automatically hibernate on you (for the critical–level action).

>> The low battery warnings are independent of the Battery Saver setting. See the next section.

>> When the low battery notice sounds or appears and you're blessed with a second battery for your laptop, pop it in and keep working! See the section "Using a second battery," elsewhere in this chapter.

>> That critical-battery notice is serious. Laptop time is over! You see no warning; the laptop simply hibernates or turns itself off — whichever option is set.

TIP

>> The best thing to do when power gets low: Plug in! This is the reason I take my power cable with my laptop wherever I go.

Using the Battery Saver

This section is brought to you by the word *parsimonious*. It's a polite word for *stingy*, which is an excellent adjective to describe how the Windows 10 Battery Saver feature works.

The Battery Saver kicks in automatically when your laptop's power percentage drops below a certain threshold — typically, 20 percent. You can, however, bolster the battery's life by activating the Battery Saver at any time. Follow these steps:

1. **Display the Action Center.**

    Swipe the screen from the right edge or, for non-touchscreen laptops, click the Notifications notification icon, as shown in the margin. The keyboard shortcut is Win+A.

2. **Click or tap the Battery Saver button.**

    If the button is disabled, the laptop is AC-powered, which means nothing needs saving.

When Battery Saver mode is active, the screen instantly dims. Laptop activity is curtailed, including Internet access. The idea is to power the laptop by using just a trickle of power. So don't be surprised if some of your favorite laptop features or programs don't work while Battery Saver is active.

Repeat the preceding set of steps to disable the Battery Saver.

To control the Battery Saver's features, visit the Settings app. Follow these steps:

1. **Open the Settings app.**

    Press the Win+I keyboard shortcut.

2. **Choose System.**

3. **On the left side of the window, choose Battery.**

    Use the toggle on the right side of the screen to activate the Battery Saver, but instead:

4. **Click the Battery Saver Settings link.**

5. **Set the percentage by the item Turn Battery Saver On Automatically At.**

    On my laptop, this item is set to 20 percent. This setting is in addition to the warnings set in the Control Panel, covered in the preceding section.

While you're viewing the Battery screen, scroll down to view apps that are consuming the most battery power. Tap an item to see whether you can control the app's background power usage. For example, you can suspend a program from running in the background if you suspect it's a battery hog and you don't currently need the program's features running all the time.

Reviewing the power management plan

A power management plan is where you configure Windows to perform specific actions based on whether the laptop is running from AC power or its battery. Specifically, you want to disable the screen or put the laptop to sleep after a period of inactivity. Face it: The laptop can get bored too — but this *ennui* is no excuse for the battery to drain.

You use the Settings app to determine specific timeouts for the display as well as when to thrust the laptop into Sleep mode. To review or adjust these settings, follow these steps:

1. **Press the Win+I keyboard shortcut to conjure the Settings app.**

2. **Choose System.**

3. **On the left side of the window, choose Power & Sleep.**

4. **On the right side of the window, choose a timeout value for the screen when the laptop is battery-powered.**

   For example, choose 5 minutes.

5. **Choose a screen timeout value for the laptop when it's AC-powered.**

6. **Set sleep timeout values for the laptop when it's battery-powered or AC-powered.**

   On my laptop, the sleep timeout values are set to 5 minutes for battery power, and 10 minutes for AC power (plugged in).

Obviously, the laptop's power manager can afford longer timeout durations when the device is plugged in as opposed to sucking juice from the battery.

REMEMBER

>> Adjust these settings if you find the laptop screen going blank or the thing shifting into Sleep mode too quickly for you. For example, if you use your laptop all the time, similar to a desktop computer, choose Never as an option for both settings (Display and Sleep) while the laptop is plugged in.

>> Windows is smart enough to know when you're using the laptop to watch a video. Especially when the video is enlarged to a full-screen presentation, the laptop may ignore the Display and Sleep power settings. Even so, be mindful that the battery is draining while you're entertaining yourself. A quick check of the battery status during intermission may be warranted.

Chapter **11**

The Printing Chapter

An important part of a computer system is the hard copy output device, commonly known as a *printer*. Lugging around a printer with your laptop doesn't really fit with the whole wireless–mobile–carefree motif promised in the laptop's brochure. This restriction doesn't preclude the capability to print something. It just means you must be clever.

The Great Printer Hunt

When it comes to using printers, your options on a laptop are pretty much identical to the options for a desktop: You peruse the list of available printers and then print something. The added goal, however, is to avoid the wire.

Finding printers in Windows

Pity the laptop user from decades past, when Windows was completely stupid with regard to finding printers. "Printer? What's a printer," Windows would ponder. Then you'd be forced to endure the ordeal of finding a printer, selecting a driver, and praying that it all worked.

Today, Windows 10 involves less frequent praying. It instantly locates all available network printers and presents them for your laptop's perusal, use, and abuse.

Any printer connected to the same network as the laptop is available for printing. Trust me. If you don't, open the Settings app to view the available lot of printing devices. Follow these steps:

1. Open the Settings app.

Press Win+I.

2. Choose Devices.

3. On the left side of the window, choose Printers & Scanners.

Available printers appear on the right side of the screen.

The printer list can get rather long, including some items you might not believe are printers, but they show up in the list anyway; refer to Figure 11-1.

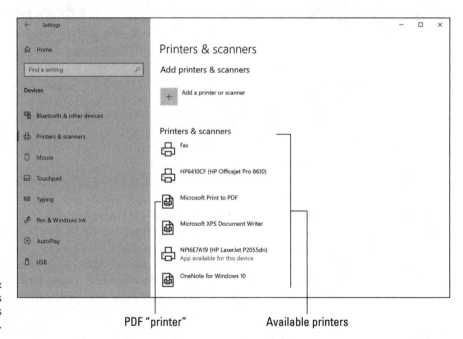

FIGURE 11-1:
The Add Printers
& Scanners
window.

The list of printers includes printers directly connected to the laptop (a rarity), printers found on the network, plus nonprinters that generate files as output, such as the Microsoft Print to PDF printer, illustrated in the figure.

» If your desired printer doesn't appear in the list, refer to the later section "Adding a network or wireless printer."

» A *network* printer is any printer connected directly to the network. It can also be a printer connected to a computer on the network, where the computer is sharing the printer as a network resource.

» Network printers can be wired or wireless. In fact, they both appear identically in the Printers & Scanners window.

» Not all items listed in the Printers & Scanners window are physical printers. Instead, consider them as output devices. For example, in Figure 11-1, you see the Microsoft Print to PDF "printer," which is really a utility to create PDF documents. The documents are printed to a file, not to a physical printer.

» Printers can be left on all the time. Most printers feature Sleep mode — just like your laptop — meaning that if the printer stays on and becomes bored, it snoozes to save energy.

» Be aware that a printer is available only when it's turned on and broadcasting its presence on the network. Printers in Sleep mode continue to be available.

» Network printers are also visible in the Network window. See Chapter 17.

Connecting a printer directly to your laptop

Here's something you can do: Plug a printer into your laptop. Today's printers use a USB cable, which connects to one of the laptop's USB ports. The connection is made. The printer is configured. You're ready to go — but not go far, because the printer has a cable and is most likely plugged into the wall for power.

If you need more specific installation instructions, follow these steps:

1. **Connect the USB cable to the printer and to your laptop.**

   What! The printer didn't come with a USB cable? That's true — and common. Get a standard USB A-to-B cable if you don't have one lying about.

2. **Turn on the printer.**

   At this point, Windows recognizes the printer and begins to install software to run the printer.

After the printer's software (driver) is installed, you can use it, as described elsewhere in this chapter.

When you need to go: Unplug the USB cable. You don't need to turn off the printer or the laptop to unplug. And when you return, reconnect the laptop to use the printer again.

TECHNICAL STUFF

» Refer to Chapter 12 for more information on what *USB* means and how it works.

» The software required to run the printer is called the *printer driver*.

Adding a network or wireless printer

Most network or wireless printers don't need additional setup. Windows is smart enough to find those printers (as long as the printers are turned on) and install the printer's software for you, making the gizmo instantly available.

When a network or wireless printer isn't automatically installed, you must attempt to do the setup yourself. Follow these steps:

1. **Start the Settings app.**

Press the Win+I keyboard shortcut.

2. **Choose Devices.**

3. **On the left side of the window, choose Printers & Scanners.**

4. **Click the Add a Printer or Scanner button.**

Windows puts on its pith helmet and explores the network's wild jungles, looking for printers. Any new printers located are added to the list. If not, continue with Step 5.

5. **Click the link labeled The Print That I Want Isn't Listed.**

The Add Printer Wizard appears. You thought he was dead at the end of Episode 2, but no.

6. **Choose an option in the wizard to continue the printer hunt.**

For example, if the printer is on a network and you just happen to know its name, you can type the name into the box by Select a Shared Printer By Name. Likewise, if you know the printer's network (IP) address, you can choose this option and type in the cryptic number.

7. **Continue working through the wizard to connect the lost printer.**

If the printer you're looking for still isn't found, consult its documentation. You may need to install special printer software first and then add the printer.

> » Also see the later section "Something Needs Printing" for information on using the newly installed printer.

> » To connect a Bluetooth printer, you must pair the printer with your laptop. This topic is covered in Chapter 12.

"What is the default printer?"

Your laptop can print documents to only one printer at a time. You can choose the printer when you print, or, when you don't specify a printer, Windows uses the *default printer.*

The default printer isn't a specific printer, and no manufacturer gives its printer that name. (At least not that I've ever seen.) Instead, it's one of the existing printers available on the network. If a printer is attached directly to your laptop, that printer is the default printer.

The default printer might appear as an icon along with other printers in the various "show me your printers" windows. To set the default printer, follow these steps:

1. **Open the Settings app.**

   Press the Win+I keyboard shortcut.

2. **Choose Devices.**

3. **Look through the list on the right side of the window for a printer flagged as Default.**

The default printer may not appear if you've opted to have Windows manage printers for you. Below the list of printers, look for a check box titled Let Windows Manage My Default Printer. With this option set, Windows sets the default printer based your previous printer choice. Disable this option if you prefer to set the default printer yourself.

To set a default printer, heed these directions:

1. **Display the Printers & Scanners part of the System app.**

   Work through Steps 1 and 2 in the preceding set of steps.

2. **Tap the printer's entry.**

3. **Choose Manage.**

4. **Choose Set As Default.**

    The selected printer is now the default, chosen automatically when you need to quickly print something.

Only one printer at a time can be set to the default. This device is the printer that's chosen when you use a quick-print command. See the later section "Something Needs Printing."

Something Needs Printing

The point of having a printer is to print something. When the need arises, even when a printer isn't present, printing is entirely possible.

What's the point in having a printer available to your laptop unless you're going to print something? Then again, you might not be near a printer when you need to print something. This section covers both situations.

Printing a document

The printing chore in Windows is handled by Windows itself. The Print command is found in many programs and apps, which opens the gateway to the common Print dialog box, shown in Figure 11-2. Some Windows programs, such as the Microsoft Office suite, use a Print screen, which features the same commands as the Print dialog box, but in a more attractive arrangement.

The Print command's location can vary, depending on the program you're using. Here are some places in which to look:

>> On newer programs, click the File tab on the Ribbon. Choose the Print item to view the Print screen.

>> Traditionally, the Print command dwells on the File menu.

>> Also look for the Print toolbar button.

>> When all else fails, the common keyboard shortcut to summon the Print dialog box or Print screen is Ctrl+P.

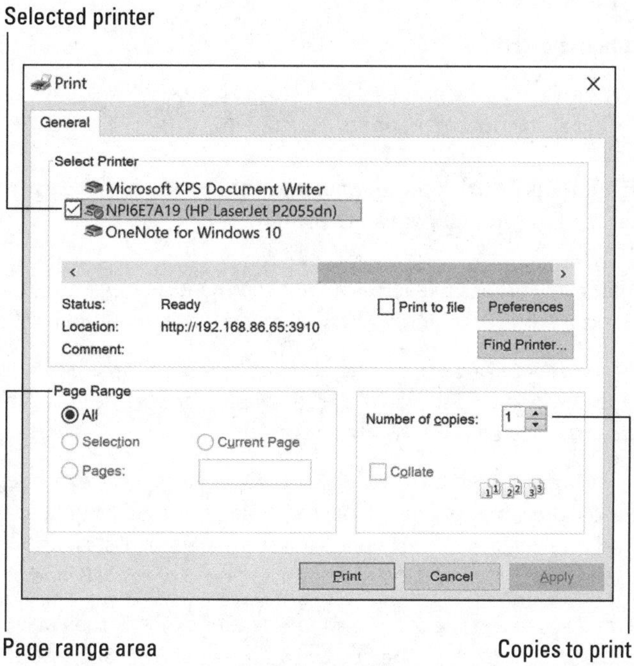

Selected printer

FIGURE 11-2:
A typical Print
dialog box.

Page range area   Copies to print

To best use the Print dialog box, obey these directions:

1. Save whatever it is you're planning to print.

Always save your stuff.

2. Summon the Print dialog box or Print screen.

Press Ctrl+P, which is the same keyboard shortcut used to help you sit through long movies after you drink too much soda pop.

The Print dialog box or Print screen appears.

3. Choose the printer.

The main or default printer is automatically selected. If you need to print on another printer, such as that fancy color printer that Ed hides in his office, choose it.

4. Select the page range.

Choose All to print the entire document, or if you need to print something specific, use the controls in the Page Range area to set what to print.

5. Set the number of copies.

6. **Click the Print button to print.**

   Assuming that the printer is ready to print, stocked with paper, and brimming with ink, the document prints.

If you opt to use a Print toolbar button, the document prints instantly: The default printer is used, and all pages are printed.

>> Not every program features a Print command. For example, the File Explorer lacks a Print command, which makes it difficult to output a list of files.

>> If you choose another printer, the same program or app may continue to use the new printer until you restart the laptop or quit the app. Afterward, the main or default printer is chosen again.

>> The Pages item in the Print dialog box lets you specify exact pages to print, which are set by typing the page numbers. Use the comma to separate individual pages or the hyphen to set a page range, such as **3-7** to print pages 3 through 7. Or use **3,7-9** to print page 3 and pages 7, 8, and 9.

>> You choose the paper size and set margins by using the Page Setup dialog box. Summon this dialog box by choosing the Page Setup command from the File menu or select it from the File tab on the Ribbon.

>> Sometimes, the Page Setup dialog box is found on a Print submenu.

Stopping a printer run amok

One of the most common printing issues, aside from a paper jam, occurs when the printer spews out page after page and you want it to stop. The correct solution for this situation varies, so I present several, from easiest to most drastic.

First, and easiest, look on the printer itself for the Cancel button. It's probably red and shaped like a stop sign or maybe a circle with an X in the middle. Mashing this button cancels the printing, though a modicum of text — up to a page or two — might still print. That's okay.

Second, you can cancel printing in Windows, although this technique never works, because printers are too fast and by the time you follow these steps, printing will be completed:

1. **Double-click the Printer notification icon.**

   It appears on the right end of the taskbar, shown in the margin. But be quick! This notification icon disappears as soon as printing is done.

2. **In the printer's window, click to select the print job.**

3. **Press the Delete key on the keyboard.**

   Or you can choose Document ➪ Cancel from the menu.

4. **Click the Yes button to confirm that you want to cancel the print job.**

Third, and most drastically, you can turn off the printer. This desperate act works. It may screw things up because turning off the printer may leave a page stuck, or *jammed,* in the printer. You can deal with this problem later. Additionally, after turning off the printer, heed the directions I give for the second option (in the preceding paragraph) to delete the print job from the printer's window.

TECHNICAL
STUFF

Things that are printed are called *jobs.* The list of jobs in a printer's window is the *queue.* The process of printing while you're doing other things in Windows is *spooling.* Good luck in Sunday's crossword puzzle.

Printing when you don't have a printer

The urge to print is seldom immediate. When printing can wait, let it wait: Save a document. Then open the document again, and print when your laptop is connected to the printer. Otherwise, I offer these nonprinter printing suggestions:

>> Decent hotels and airports have business centers. Use this service to temporarily connect to a printer to put your stuff on paper.

>> Some office supply stores offer printing services. Print shops and places such as FedEx Office (formerly Kinko's) also have printers available for rent by the hour or by the sheet.

>> You can also print to a PDF document, as covered in the next section.

Printing a PDF document

TIP

Before you print, consider whether what you're printing really needs to be on paper. Oftentimes, creating a PDF is easier. The Portable Document Format (PDF), also known as Adobe Acrobat, is extremely common, and has pretty much replaced the fax for all but the legal and medical industries.

To create a PDF document, abide by these steps:

1. **Finish your document.**

   Save! Save! Save! Always save.

2. **Press Ctrl+P to print.**

   The Print dialog box appears or, for some programs, the Print screen shows up.

3. **Choose the Microsoft Print to PDF printer.**

4. **Click the Print button.**

   The Save Print Output As dialog box appears. This is a necessary step because you're "printing" to a file, saving what would otherwise be hard copy as a new document.

5. **Work the controls in the dialog box to find a location for the file and give it a name.**

6. **Click the Save button to create the PDF file.**

   The PDF document is saved.

REMEMBER

Just because the PDF document is saved doesn't mean that your original document has been saved. I strongly recommend that you save the original document again before you quit the program.

» The PDF file is one of the most universal and common file formats available. Feel free to send this type of document as an email attachment, share it with others, or use it any way you like.

» In fact, in many instances, printing a PDF is better than sending a Microsoft Office document or even an image file.

» PDF files require the Adobe Acrobat reader software. The program is obtained free from this website: get.adobe.com/reader.

A Portable Printer for Your Laptop

When Adam Osborne originally proposed the portable computer, portable printing wasn't part of the big picture. He was right! How many times have you been in a café or at the airport and seen someone printing from a laptop? Never! The reason is that printing is a task you can do later.

If you really insist, you can obtain a portable printer. Though not of the same quality as a non-mobile printer, these models are small and light, battery-powered, and ideal for anyone who needs hard copy on the run.

The question you must ask is whether printing is of such an urgency that you just can't wait. The trade-off is one more thing to carry, which hampers the paradigm of portable computing.

>> The laptop and the printer don't need a physical connection between them. Wi-Fi and Bluetooth portable printers let you print without having extra wires to carry around.

>> Naturally, if your portable printer uses a cable, typically a USB cable, you need to pack that cable along with the printer in your laptop bag.

TIP

>> If you plan to use the portable printer in your car, get a model that features a *car adapter* — a thing you can plug into the car's 12-volt adapter (previously known as a cigarette lighter).

>> When the printer features rechargeable batteries, remember to fully charge the printer before you venture out on the road.

REMEMBER

>> Printers need paper! If you take a printer with you on the road, you also need to take some paper. There you go: *more* stuff to carry!

Chapter **12**

Expanding Your Laptop's Universe

When your laptop's contents don't meet up with your portable computing desires, you move into the forbidden territory of adding the dreadful peripheral. It's not that peripherals are bad. No, the problem with peripherals and various items clinging to a laptop is that such a configuration flies in the face of being "lite" and mobile. Still, an entire universe of external goodies is available to your laptop, like an electronic cafeteria of digital delights. If you can find room in your laptop bag, go for it!

USB Expansion Options

Similar to a desktop computer, the primary way you expand your laptop's universe is by adding USB peripherals. Whether your laptop has a single USB port or is festooned with USB ports like craters on the moon, your laptop's options for expansion are nearly limitless.

Understanding the USB thing

Three pieces comprise the USB system:

>> The USB port

>> The USB cable

>> The USB peripheral

Your laptop has one or more USB ports on its sides or rear. They may look like rectangular holes to you, perfect for inserting a Sucrets, but they're USB ports. The newer USB C standard features an oval end, which connects in any orientation. Many laptops feature the USB C port in addition to the traditional, rectangular ports.

The ports are color-coded based on the USB standard they support as well as on other features offered. These colors are listed in Table 12-1. They are found inside the USB port opening. For optimum peripheral efficiency, match the color of the cable with the color on the port.

TABLE 12-1   ## USB Color Codes

Color	Meaning
White	The port supports only the original USB 1.0 standard.
Black	The port supports the original USB 1.0 and USB 2.0 standards.
Blue	The port supports USB standard 3.0 and all previous standards.
Red	This USB 3.0 port also supplies power to charge a device. This port charges the device whether the laptop is turned off or not, though the laptop must be connected to power.
Yellow	This one is the same as a red USB port.

The USB cable, like most cables in our space-time continuum, has two ends. The end that plugs into your laptop is the A end, which matches the USB port. The other end sports different sizes, such as the B end, shown in Figure 12-1, and also the mini-USB and micro-USB connectors used to attach various devices.

The cable features different ends so that you can't plug a USB cable in backward, upside down, or sideways.

FIGURE 12-1:
The A and B ends
of a USB cable.

The A end   **The B end**

Finally, at the far end of the USB cable, lies the USB device itself. It can be any USB peripheral, including the entire pantheon of peripherals available to a desktop PC.

REMEMBER

The beauty of USB is that you can connect or disconnect peripherals without having to turn the laptop off or on or having to complete a complex setup or configuration. This is the number one reason why USB is so popular and why you use it to expand upon your laptop's hardware abilities.

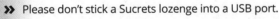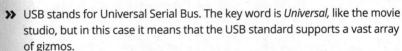

>> A *port* is a "hole" in the computer's case into which you plug something. The port is also the "smarts" that make useful whichever device you connect to the laptop.

>> Not every USB device comes with its own USB cable. For example, USB printers are notorious for not including USB cables in the box. You must buy a separate USB cable.

>> USB cables come in a variety of lengths, but they can be no longer than about 16 feet. And who needs to use a laptop with a USB gizmo sitting 16 feet away?

>> The USB cable isn't always necessary. Many USB devices are plugged directly into a USB port, such as a thumb drive or wireless adapter.

>> Please don't stick a Sucrets lozenge into a USB port.

WARNING

>> USB stands for Universal Serial Bus. The key word is *Universal,* like the movie studio, but in this case it means that the USB standard supports a vast array of gizmos.

>> All USB devices, even the cables and the spot where the USB port lives on your laptop, sport the USB symbol, shown in the margin.

Attaching and removing a USB gizmo

A USB device is a snap to connect — literally. You don't need to turn off your laptop, run a special program, or incant a spell in Latin. Just plug in the USB gadget and you're ready to go. The USB device adds its features to your laptop.

When you're done with the USB device, unplug it. The only time this operation isn't so easy is when detaching storage devices where your laptop is actively using the storage. See Chapter 9 for details on removing USB storage.

>> Many USB devices generate a notification after they're connected. The notification explains that software drivers are being installed, which allow Windows to access the device and, hopefully, make it useful.

>> Storage devices generate an AutoPlay notification. See Chapter 9 for information.

>> If the USB device has its own power switch, you must switch the thing on before the computer recognizes the peripheral.

>> Some wireless USB gizmos still require a USB connection. You plug a teensy USB transceiver into the laptop, which allows communications to a mouse or another wireless peripheral.

>> It's okay to leave those tiny USB transceivers plugged into your laptop at all times. The only drawback is that they occupy a USB port, which is often a precious commodity on a laptop.

REMEMBER

>> Be sure to read the manual that comes with the USB peripheral to determine whether you need to install special software before plugging in the device or turning it on.

TECHNICAL STUFF

>> The ability to plug and unplug USB devices without having to turn the computer off or on is known as *hot swapping*. It sounds risqué, but it's not.

Dealing with USB-powered devices

Quite a few USB doohickeys draw the electricity they need from the laptop's USB port. These USB-powered peripherals include external hard drives, cooling pads, and USB lamps.

The good news is that you don't need an extra cable, power supply, wall socket, or battery for a USB-powered device. The bad news is that these gizmos suck up the laptop's precious power juice. Generally speaking, when I'm using my laptop with a USB-powered device, the laptop is plugged into AC power.

>> Though you're free to use a USB-powered device when your laptop is running from battery power, keep a close eye on that battery meter. See Chapter 10 for tips.

>> Many USB-powered devices demand that they be connected directly to the laptop or to a powered USB hub. The device won't function when connected

to a nonpowered USB hub. See the next section for information on powered USB hubs.

>> Windows automatically enables USB power reduction when battery life becomes critical. This reduction means that any USB-powered peripherals are shut off when the battery gets low. Though this feature can be disabled, I don't recommend doing so.

Using a USB hub

Expandability is one key to the USB port's popularity. It may not seem practical, but your laptop can have as many as 127 USB devices attached to it at any given time. Yes, all at once. Imagine dragging that chain of goodies through airport security! You'd win a medal. Or be detained.

A USB *hub* is nothing more than a USB device with more USB ports on it. You plug the hub into your laptop's USB port. Then you can plug additional USB devices into the hub, depending upon how many ports it has.

>> If you get a USB hub for your laptop, look for a smaller, more portable, laptop-size model. It's quaint — and more portable than the desktop, or full-size, USB hub.

>> Two types of hubs are available: powered and unpowered. The powered hub must have its own power source. (It must be plugged into the wall.) Powered hubs are necessary in order to supply more power to certain USB devices.

>> Some devices cannot be run from hubs, such as high-speed hard drives. In this case, the peripheral must be connected directly into the laptop's USB port. Don't fret: A warning message appears and instructs you when such a thing happens.

>> Keep your eye out for *pass-through* USB devices. For example, a USB keyboard may sport more USB ports on its sides, so you can plug the USB device into your laptop and then plug more USB devices into the first device. This way, you don't run out of USB ports.

>> Every USB port on your laptop is considered part of the *root port*. The 127-device limitation is per root port, so if your laptop has two USB root ports, it can access as many as 254 USB devices. Golly.

Perusing potential USB goodies

I just checked with Google, the official source of all human knowledge, and it reports that over 14 gazillion different USB devices are available to attach to your laptop. Rather than list them all, I decided to present the most common and useful USB laptop peripherals in Table 12-2.

TABLE 12-2 **Typical, Plain, Boring Uses for the USB Port**

Device	Typical Boring Use
Phone, tablet, digital camera	Grab photos from the device's memory card and store them on your laptop. You can also do this directly, by removing the mobile device's digital storage media, which is covered in Chapter 9.
External storage	Use external hard drives, optical drives, thumb drives, and media card readers for storage. See Chapter 9 for more information on external storage.
Headphones	Though your laptop most likely has its own headphone jack, USB headphones are far more sophisticated (though wireless headphones are the bomb).
Network adapter	Add wired networking to your laptop, but also Bluetooth, as covered later in this chapter.
Printer	Print stuff on paper. See Chapter 11 for printer fun.
Legacy adapter	Connect *legacy* (antique) dialup modem, serial, parallel, joystick, or other devices to your laptop. Employ this adapter to continue to use antique computer hardware with your laptop.
Numeric keypad	Quickly enter values without having to toggle the main keyboard between numeric and alpha modes.
Scanner	Do your document scanning in a portable manner, especially if you're a lawyer.
Little light	Imagine! Plug it in, and it's powered by the USB port. Furthermore, imagine it with a stiff-yet-twistable neck so that you can see the keyboard when you use your laptop in the dark.
Game controller	Control your little man, pilot your spaceship, or wield that sword of truth.
Laptop cooler	Set your laptop on it, which acts like a fancy pad. It contains a tiny, quiet fan that helps keep your laptop cool, and it runs from the power supplied by the USB port.
Security device	Use the USB port to power an alarm on a cable lock, or plug in to the USB port and unlock (or unscramble) the laptop's data.

The Bluetooth Thing

Bluetooth refers to a wireless standard for connecting computer peripherals, as well as other, noncomputer devices. As long as your laptop is equipped with a Bluetooth radio, you can use various Bluetooth devices and gizmos with your laptop, including printers, keyboards, speakers, and automobiles.

>> The advantage of Bluetooth is that it lets you connect wirelessly to a variety of peripherals without having to use a separate wireless adapter for each peripheral.

>> Bluetooth began its existence as a wireless replacement for the old serial (RS-232) interface, popular with computers in the 1980s and 1990s.

TECHNICAL
STUFF

Checking for Bluetooth

Before you can get all excited about using Bluetooth, you need to ensure that your laptop has a wireless Bluetooth radio. Not every laptop does. You have two ways to check for this feature.

The first way is to look for the Bluetooth logo (shown in the margin) on your laptop. Bluetooth gizmos feature this logo, though your laptop may not.

The second way is to use Windows. Follow these steps:

1. Open the Settings app.

Press the Win+I keyboard shortcut.

2. Choose Devices.

3. On the left side of the window, ensure that Bluetooth & Other Devices is chosen.

The right side of the window indicates whether Bluetooth is on and lists any paired Bluetooth peripherals, as shown in Figure 12-2.

As long as you see something similar to what's shown in Figure 12-2, your laptop features a Bluetooth radio and it can connect with Bluetooth peripherals.

>> If your laptop lacks a Bluetooth radio, you can easily add one: The teensy Bluetooth radio dongle easily plugs into a USB port. As a bonus, USB Bluetooth dongles are relatively inexpensive. They also install all their own software, so you don't have to set up anything.

TIP

>> When Bluetooth is available and configured, a Bluetooth notification appears on the taskbar, in the notification area (on the right). If it's not readily visible, click the up-pointing chevron to see it. Click the Bluetooth notification to access commands on a pop-up menu.

Bluetooth radio is active   Available device

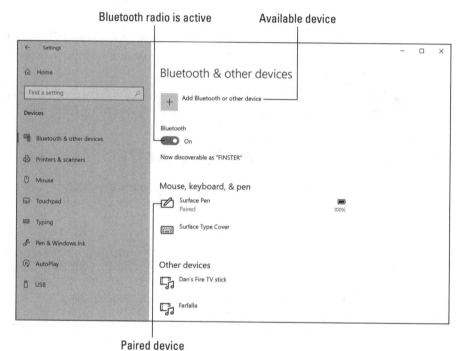

Paired device

FIGURE 12-2:
Bluetooth
options.

Pairing with a Bluetooth gizmo

Thanks to its wireless nature, connecting your laptop with a Bluetooth peripheral involves a specific dance with a willing partner. The dance is called *pairing*, and it works like this:

1. Turn on the Bluetooth peripheral and ensure that it's discoverable.

The Bluetooth device must broadcast its availability. For some devices, you turn it on. Other devices sport a Bluetooth button. When the Bluetooth peripheral is available, a lamp on the device blinks.

2. On your laptop, display the Bluetooth window in the Settings app.

Press Win+I to bring up the Settings app. Choose Devices. Choose Bluetooth & Other Devices from the left side of the screen. Refer to Figure 12-2.

3. **Ensure that the Bluetooth radio is active; set the toggle to the On position.**

4. **Tap the button Add Bluetooth or Other Device.**

5. **Choose Bluetooth from the Add a Device List.**

   The laptop actively scans for available Bluetooth peripherals, listing them in the window.

6. **Choose the desired Bluetooth device from the list.**

   Additional action may be required. For example, a Bluetooth keyboard requires you to type a PIN and press the Enter key on the peripheral.

7. **Tap the Done button.**

   The device is paired and ready to use. It appears in the list of devices in the Settings app.

The good news is that after pairing is complete, the peripheral and your laptop remain connected. To stop using the device, turn it off. When you turn it on again, it's instantly available.

>> Bluetooth devices are discoverable for only a brief length of time; usually, two minutes. If you fail to pair during this period, you must make the device discoverable again.

>> If you don't plan to use the Bluetooth peripheral again, unpair it: Select the device in the Manage Bluetooth Devices window (refer to Figure 12-2). Click the Remove Device button. Click the Yes button to confirm.

REMEMBER

>> Unpairing is required only when you no longer want to use the Bluetooth peripheral with your laptop. Bluetooth is a monogamous standard; devices are paired for life, until they're unpaired. No attorneys need be involved.

The Laptop Becomes a Desktop

If you plan to park your laptop in one place most or all of the time, you probably want to upgrade its teensy portable features with more-robust desktop counterparts. Specifically, I refer to the keyboard, monitor, and mouse. Any of these desktop-size items can be added to, and used with, a laptop. You can even take them with you, but don't expect your laptop bag to fit beneath the seat in front of you on an airplane.

Using a full-size keyboard and mouse

If you miss the full size and action of a real PC keyboard, get one! Ditto for a full-size computer mouse: Plug the keyboard into your laptop's USB port. Ditto for the mouse. You can start using the keyboard or mouse the second it's plugged in.

When you're done using the keyboard or mouse, unplug it. Once again, the laptop can roam free and untethered.

TIP

>> Often, adding an external keyboard doesn't disable the laptop's keyboard. Likewise, adding an external mouse might not disable the laptop's touch pad. You can use both! But you're probably not crazy enough to do that.

>> If all you're yearning for is to have a separate numeric keypad, consider getting only this peripheral. USB numeric keypads are available anywhere fine USB numeric keypads are sold.

Adding a monitor

Your laptop is readily able to handle two monitors: the laptop's own screen and an external monitor; almost all modern laptops feature an external monitor connector or port. The reason is so that you can use the external monitor or projector for making presentations. Even if you're not making a presentation, you can use the monitor connector to add a larger or second monitor to your laptop computer system.

To add the external monitor, locate the monitor connector on your laptop's edge. Plug in the monitor. (An adapter may be required.) Turn on the monitor.

After a successful connection, you may be prompted on how to use the second monitor, or the second monitor may duplicate the laptop's screen. Options for how to use the external monitor are summoned by pressing the Win+P keyboard shortcut and illustrated in Figure 12-3. Here are their descriptions:

PC Screen Only: Use only the laptop's display; ignore the external monitor.

Duplicate: In this mode, the laptop uses both displays at the same time, showing the same image on each. This option is chosen automatically when you attach an external monitor (or projector) to your laptop. It's ideal for running a slide show presentation.

Extend: This mode uses the second monitor to expand desktop real estate, combining both monitors into a single, larger desktop area.

Second Screen Only: Use only the external monitor; the laptop's screen is disabled (until the external monitor is disconnected).

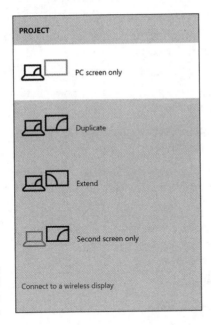

PROJECT

PC screen only

Duplicate

Extend

Second screen only

Connect to a wireless display

FIGURE 12-3:
The second
display projection
panel.

Further adjustment of the second monitor can be made in the Settings app: Right-click the desktop and choose Display Settings to get there quick. Use the icons presented to adjust each monitor's resolution, orientation, and position relative to each other.

TIP

If your laptop seems to lack an external monitor port, such as mini-DP connector, use the USB C connector instead. This connector can be fitted with an adapter, which translates the versatile USB signal for use with a DisplayPort or HDMI cable. These adapters are inexpensive and a must-have item for any road warrior's laptop bag.

Running the laptop with its lid closed

When you plan to keep your laptop in one spot and you've attached an external keyboard, mouse, and monitor, you can get away with closing the laptop's lid and using only the full-size desktop computer input devices. I've set up my laptop that way on many occasions, especially when it's been in only one spot for a long time.

To ensure that the laptop doesn't sleep or hibernate when you close the lid, you must configure the system so that the laptop does nothing when the lid is closed. Follow these steps:

1. **Tap the Windows key.**

    Up pops the Start menu.

2. **Type the text** change what closing the list does, **or enough so that you see a matching item in the search results.**

   The Control Panel opens, displaying options for the power button and lid. These options are arranged in a grid: rows for the power button and lid and columns for On Battery and Plugged In.

3. **From the Plugged In column, When I Close the Lid row, tap the menu button and choose Do Nothing.**

   You're directing the laptop to do nothing (don't shut down, sleep, or hibernate) when the laptop is plugged into a power source and you close the lid. This is the option you want.

WARNING

   I do not recommend that you choose this same option from the On Battery column. Ensure that the laptop either hibernates, sleeps, or shuts down when you close the lid on battery power.

4. **Click the Save Changes button.**

5. **Close the System Settings window.**

Of course, you may have to open the laptop to turn it on, but after it's on, you can close the lid and use the keyboard, monitor, and mouse just like you do on a desktop computer.

Chapter **13**

O the Places You'll Go

You can take your laptop here. You can take your laptop there. Go, go with your laptop anywhere.

Take your laptop to the park. Use the laptop after dark.

Bring your laptop on a plane. Walk your laptop down the lane.

Laptop with your cousin Ned. Sleep with laptop when in bed.

Laptop time while in Nantucket, on a hill, or in a bucket.

Take your laptop where you please. Wi-Fi access overseas.

Don't use laptop in the car. Drink with laptop in a bar.

Laptop with a cup of joe. Laptop, laptop, on the go.

Laptop here! Laptop there! Laptop, laptop, everywhere!

In the Bag

A laptop fashion accessory, bag or case, is a necessary thing to have. It allows you to comfortably store the laptop, to keep all the accessories in a single place — plus, you can carry other items in the bag. Without the bag, you'd have to tote around the laptop, its charger, and everything else stuffed into your pockets or balanced atop your head, which is an awkward thing to do. So, having a laptop bag also prevents you from looking like a dork.

Features to look for

Don't get all fancy. Sure, you can buy a brand-specific laptop case. You can go to some high-end, snooty store where the laptop bags offer shock absorption features. Me? I use a sturdy backpack and just toss in my laptop — plus other things I need, many of which are legal in all 50 states.

REMEMBER

The idea behind your laptop bag is to safely carry and protect the laptop while you're moving from point A to point B. Use the bag to carry all your laptop toys and other related goodies. Go nuts on the extra features, if you must. But, honestly, if you can find a solidly made case, bag, or backpack that does what you need, you're set.

Here are some thoughts regarding selecting a fashion accessory in which to place your laptop:

Size

The bag must close over the laptop without bursting at the seams. And you want more room inside the bag than you need. After all, you may not be toting around the same-size laptop in a few years.

REMEMBER

Keep in mind that when flying, your bag must fit beneath the seat in front of you on an airplane. Don't buy a bag so big that it must be stashed in the overhead bin.

Some laptop cases are tiny, but they're TSA-approved. This size means you can keep the laptop inside the case while advancing through the scanner at an airport. Is it worth it? No. Get a larger bag and accept that you may be asked to remove the laptop and have it scanned separately at airport security.

Style

If you desire the briefcase style, get a soft case-style laptop bag, not a hard model. If the case has a shoulder strap, use it.

TIP

My preference is for a backpack. The bonus here is that shouldering the backpack keeps both arms and hands free. This way, I can hold my phone with a boarding pass in one hand and coffee in the other and still carry my laptop.

If you know that you have to carry lots of stuff (extra material for your job or perhaps a heavy printer or video projector), consider getting a laptop case with wheels and a retractable handle.

Zippers are preferred over snaps, buckles, or latches. For me, it's easier to work a zipper when I'm in a cramped space like an airline seat or sitting in a crowded café.

WARNING

Avoid laptop cases and bags that have the word *Laptop* on them or feature a brand name. Such text advertises to thieves that valuable items lie within.

Pouches and places

Does the bag feature plenty of pouches? You need pouches for storing accessories, office supplies, thumb drives, manuals, Altoids, year-old receipts, and other items you plan to carry around with you. The pouches can also be used for smuggling.

Having an easy-access pouch on the outside of the bag or case helps with storing important documents and other information that you need to grab quickly.

Things to pack in your laptop bag

REMEMBER

A good laptop bag is useful for holding more than the laptop. Otherwise, it would be called a laptop *cozy* and not a case. When you're at a loss about what to put into your laptop bag, consider this list for inspiration:

>> Pack the power cord and AC adapter!

>> Bring headphones if you plan to listen to music or watch a movie. Noise canceling headphones are worth the extra price. Wearing any headphone style is more polite than sharing the noise with people sitting next to you.

>> Pack any necessary peripherals: mouse, keyboard, and removable storage, for example.

>> It seems anachronistic, but pack an Ethernet cable. I keep a 6-foot cable in my laptop bag, just in case.

>> Two words: office supplies. Pens. Paper. Sticky notes. Paper clips. Rubber bands. Highlighter. And so on.

>> If you're making a presentation, don't forget the presentation! If you need your own video projector, pack it too.

>> When you're traveling overseas, remember to bring along a power conversion kit or an overseas power adapter.

>> Ensure that you have some screen wipes.

>> Bring a deck of cards. That way, you'll have something to play with after the battery dies.

Also take a look at Chapter 25 for more goodies you may want to take with you.

Things to do before you leave

Here are some things you should consider doing before you toddle off with your laptop:

TIP

>> Charge the battery! In fact, this task is probably something you want to do long before you leave.

>> If you're lucky enough to have a spare battery, charge it as well.

>> If you haven't used the laptop in a while, check for Windows updates. You want to ensure that the update installation doesn't delay your work — or prevent it. See Chapter 19 for information about Windows updates.

>> Synchronize your files. Copy the ones you need to the cloud. See Chapter 18 for more information.

Flying with Mr. Laptop

Taking a laptop onboard a commercial airliner today is about as normal as bringing onboard a sack lunch or a crying infant. That's good news, unlike the old days, when having a laptop was cause for concern by airport security. Today, you most likely won't be the only person in your row with a laptop on the tray table during the flight.

Is your laptop case one carry-on bag or half a carry-on bag?

Despite what you may think, the laptop bag is considered a personal item. You're allowed a piece of luggage and a personal item. So the laptop case or bag is one of these two things. If the flight is full, however, don't be surprised if the airline actually enforces its own rules.

WARNING

>> Do not check your laptop as luggage! You don't want to subject the laptop to the kind of torture that most checked bags endure. You don't want your laptop to be stored in the subzero cargo hold, and you don't want to risk your laptop being stolen. Do not check your laptop!

>> When the plane is full and you've tried to sneak on too much carry-on luggage, remove the laptop and check the bag as luggage. Keep the laptop with you.

Laptop inspection

Security rules seem to change all the time. Always follow directions given at a security checkpoint. It doesn't matter whether the other airport did things one way or the security agents were more kind during your outbound trip.

Generally speaking, you must remove the laptop from its bag. The laptop must be placed into a bin, along with other electronics, change, keys, and so on.

If you've been pre-checked, you can keep the laptop in its bag. This rule may not hold at all airports.

If you have an approved laptop case, you can keep the laptop in that case. I don't recommend these cases (as mentioned earlier in this chapter), because keeping it in the case at a security checkpoint is really the case's only benefit.

After you've passed security, put the laptop back in its bag, reassemble yourself, and be on your way.

WARNING

>> Watch your laptop! The X-ray machine is a popular spot for thieves! Refer to Chapter 20.

>> X-rays don't harm the laptop.

>> If you're pulled aside for additional security, you may be asked to turn on the laptop. That's a good reason to have its battery fully charged. If not, be sure to pack the power cord. Most inspection stations have a wall socket you can use.

All aboard!

After taking your seat, store the laptop bag under the seat in front of you. That storage is easier to get to. Use the overhead bins only as a last resort; otherwise, you run the risk of having latecomers jamming their steamer trunks and body bags into the overhead bins and crushing your laptop.

Keep the laptop in its bag! Wait until you hear the announcement that you can turn on your electronic devices before you whip out your laptop.

>> Obviously, you should avoid bulkhead seats, which lack underseat storage.

>> When the airline offers an extended-legroom class, such as the exit row, take it! More room for legs means more room on the tray table for your laptop.

>> I prefer window seats for computing aloft. This way, I can control the window blind, to shield my laptop's screen from the sun. Plus, I can more easily angle the laptop toward me and away from prying eyes in other seats.

>> 3M makes a special laptop display cover, the 3M Laptop Privacy Filter. It prevents peering eyes from seeing the information on your laptop screen, which is a problem on airplanes. The filter can be found at office supply and computer stores all over the place.

TIP

Airplane mode

Like other wireless mobile devices, laptops feature an Airplane mode. (Laptops had this feature long before phones and tablets.) The key is to disable wireless radios, such as Wi-Fi, mobile data, and Bluetooth.

For some laptops, Airplane mode is a task handled by a physical on-off switch somewhere on the device or by pressing a special key combination, such as Fn+F5. Otherwise, you can use the Windows Action Center to control Airplane mode in Windows 10. Heed these steps:

1. **Press Win+A to summon the Action Center.**

2. **Click or tap the Airplane Mode tile.**

    When Airplane mode is active, an Airplane icon appears in the notification area on the taskbar, as shown in the margin.

If you need to use Wi-Fi while Airplane mode is active, press Win+A to view the Action Center again and choose the Network tile. Choose Wi-Fi to activate the laptop's wireless networking hardware. You can then connect to the plane's internal Wi-Fi service to watch movies or overpay for a slow and unreliable Internet connection.

Air power

The airlines have heard your cries for help, or at least those cries for in-flight power. Many commercial jets now offer AC power on many flights for use with your laptop. The most common form of power is provided by USB and standard power outlets on the back of the seat in front of you.

The USB power sockets provide power for phones and tablets.

The standard power outlets allow you to connect your laptop so that you may charge the battery in flight or just take advantage of the free power.

REMEMBER

>> In-flight power is great, but without it, your laptop runs just fine on its own battery.

>> You're required to disconnect your mobile devices from seat power during take-off and landing. Always obey instructions from the flight crew.

In-flight Wi-Fi

Many airlines offer in-flight Wi-Fi service. It might be free, primarily for airline-offered services such as flight information or video entertainment. Accessing the Internet, however, comes at a cost. Either way, your laptop accesses the in-flight wireless network just as it does at the local coffeehouse.

First, because you're flying in a plane, ensure that Airplane mode is active, as described earlier in this chapter.

Second, enable the laptop's Wi-Fi radio. In Windows 10, choose the Networking tile in the Action Center, and then click the Wi-Fi tile to turn on the Wi-Fi radio. Press the Win+A keyboard shortcut to view the Action Center.

Third, connect to the in-flight Wi-Fi base station. It's probably the only Wi-Fi signal you see on the screen.

Finally, use the laptop's web browser to navigate to any web page. You're redirected to the in-flight sign-up page. This location is where you either accept the terms or fork over a credit card number to access the service.

>> Specific directions for accessing in-flight Wi-Fi are usually found in the seat pocket in front of you.

>> The in-flight Wi-Fi providers don't like you using Skype or similar programs to make phone calls, but from my personal observations, this restriction doesn't seem to stop anyone.

>> In-flight Wi-Fi is inconsistent. In some spots the signal drops off, such as remote locations and over the ocean when you're flying overseas. So, if you're on a superlong flight over an ocean, don't get suckered into paying for several hours of in-flight Wi-Fi.

Café Computing

It used to be that you'd walk into a coffeehouse, order a cappuccino, sit around with artsy folks dressed in black, and discuss the plight of the common man. Today, you go to the coffeehouse, order your double-tall decaf machiatto, and discuss the plight of the common man while connected to the Internet.

This section mulls over a few of my observations while café computing:

>> It doesn't have to be a café. You'll find Wi-Fi access in just about any location frequented by the public, including parks, the dentist's office, and mortuaries.

>> You see one other difference between the cafés of yesterday and today: Whereas the café denizen of yesteryear could sit all day, the laptop user eventually gets up and leaves when the battery runs dry.

Find a good seat

The unofficial rules of café computer require that you stake out a seat *before* going to the counter to order a beverage or food. Finding a good seat is an art form, and you're competing with plenty of others who know the art well. Fortunately, you have this book.

The most important item is the wall socket. If you can use the café's power, great. Those seats next to the wall socket are best, and they usually go first.

You want a table, a flat surface upon which to set up the laptop. The alternative is balancing the laptop on your knees while you sit on a sofa or an old sack of Columbian coffee beans. If that's your thing, great!

Grab a table that's either away from the windows or facing the windows. You want to avoid having that bright light from the windows reflecting on your laptop screen and washing out the display.

When you really want to get work done, find a spot away from the door and away from the sales counter. Do the opposite if you prefer to be social.

> » Along with avoiding windows, keep an eye peeled for skylights or windows high up on the wall. As a sunny day grows long, the sun sweeps a slow swath of bright light across some tables, which can thwart your laptopping efforts.

> » After successfully finding a wall socket, plug in your laptop. Ensure that it's drawing power, as described in Chapter 10.

Other tips 'n' stuff

Don't be a moocher. If you've planted yourself in a café, order something to drink. Buy a snack. Tip the kind-but-underpaid employee who gave you the Wi-Fi password.

The management at some places enjoys having laptop and mobile users because they add to the location's trendy atmosphere. Keep in mind that the place is a business and that free Wi-Fi is a perk for supporting the business. Also, the courts have established that you can be thrown out for using the wireless networking if you don't buy something, so buy something!

Though you should avoid placing beverages near a computer, it's not an easy thing to do while using a laptop in a café. Therefore, ask for your beverage in a cup with a saucer. Grab several napkins, just in case.

WARNING

Never leave your laptop unattended! Though it might not be stolen, it's a distinct possibility. See Chapter 20 for more information on laptop security.

Sometimes, you may be asked to leave or relocate, especially when you're taking up an entire booth all by yourself. Be knowledgeable about this situation in advance. If you see the place filling up, move to a smaller table, or just pack up and leave.

In a Hotel Room

The hotel industry expects you to require Wi-Fi service in the room, just like you want fresh towels and an ice bucket. The desk in the room most likely has power sockets that are easily accessible and even a few USB connectors for phones and tablets. Welcome to the 21st century.

You obtain the Wi-Fi password from the front desk. It's probably on one of those bits of paper they gave you along with the room card key. If not, you'll find the password in the room on the desk. If not, you're probably in a cheap hotel or motel where you must pay separately for Wi-Fi services.

REMEMBER

TIP

>> When you first connect to the hotel's wireless network, you're prompted to set its security level. Choose the Public type of network. See Chapter 16.

>> If the room features an Ethernet port, try it out. The Ethernet connection is more reliable than the Wi-Fi connection, which can slow down from an abundance of mobile devices vying for the service. (This is the reason I recommend tossing an Ethernet cable into your laptop bag.)

>> Some hotels provide an Ethernet cable; look for it either in the desk drawer or (oddly) hanging in the closet.

>> When you have no choice but to pay for the hotel's Wi-Fi connection, buy as large a block of time as you can for your stay. If 24 hours is the largest block, start your 24-hour session at 6 P.M. This way, you can use the connection that evening and then the following morning and throughout the next day's afternoon.

Mind the Laptop's Temperature

One reason that your laptop lacks the latest, fastest microprocessor is heat. Even in a desktop PC, cutting edge technology generates lots of heat. Managing this heat in a desktop is a huge chore, so you can imagine the things your laptop has to do to keep cool, especially when you're on the road.

TIP

>> Your laptop comes with a wee li'l cooling fan. It may even have two speeds, one for normal operation and a faster speed to cool down the laptop quickly. Even so, don't let your laptop get too hot to touch. If so, turn it off at once.

>> Avoid putting your laptop where it sits in direct sunlight.

>> Do not store the laptop in your car's trunk.

>> Don't let the laptop run in a closet or in any closed environment where air cannot circulate.

>> Do not block the little vents on the laptop that help it inhale cool air and expel hot air.

>> When the laptop continually runs too hot, especially when the battery compartment becomes too hot to touch, phone your laptop dealer for service.

>> As a suggestion, consider buying your laptop a cooling pad. Chapter 25 covers this and other gizmos.

Chapter **14**

Presentation Information

For centuries, the point of having a laptop computer was to entertain, inform, and enlighten conference rooms packed full of people. Coupled with a video projector, the laptop would run dreaded Microsoft PowerPoint slide shows. The net effect was to blow away the masses with a smart, fresh presentation that informed and inspired without lulling anyone to sleep.

The Show Must Go On

To inform crowds of eager humans, you need a laptop. You need a digital projector. And you need a presentation, usually prepared by using the *PowerPoint* presentation application included with Microsoft Office. If it were that simple, this chapter would be done. It's not.

Giving the dog-and-pony show

PowerPoint creates documents generically referred to as slide shows. Each slide can contain text, graphics, or pictures, or any combination. You can add animations and sound effects, plus interesting fades and transitions between slides.

NOT THE ONLY ONE

The laptop is the traditional vehicle by which presentations are delivered, but it's not the only one: Thanks to advances in technology, digital projectors can now interface with a mobile phone or tablet or just a thumb drive. As long as the presentation software is on the device, say hello to the slide show.

Not only is the laptop only one of many vehicles ready for presenting a slide show, but PowerPoint isn't the only software tool. Another alternative is to use the Prezi program, which I confess presents information in a better and more visually interesting manner than PowerPoint.

Of course, the PowerPoint program isn't the point. The point here is the presentation, what's required, how to configure things, and how to be ready to impress the crowd.

>> PowerPoint must be installed on your laptop. Although . . .

>> . . . Microsoft offers PowerPoint Viewer, which lets you play, but not edit, PowerPoint presentations. The viewer comes in handy when you create a presentation using your desktop PC and then copy it to your laptop for a road show. This viewer program can be obtained for free from the Microsoft Store app in Windows 10.

>> PowerPoint takes advantage of sounds, fonts, and animation on your computer. When you create a presentation on your desktop, ensure that the same font or sound files exist on the laptop; otherwise, your presentation won't look the same.

TIP

>> My advice is to create the PowerPoint presentation on the same laptop you plan to use for making the presentation. If this arrangement isn't possible, don't employ fancy fonts or special sounds in your presentation.

>> The first slide of any presentation I make isn't the first slide shown. Instead, the first slide is used to help set up the laptop and video projector (covered in the next section). On this slide, I have a logo or my contact information to test the focus. It also helps to add to the slide some sort of sound effect so that you can test the audio system.

TIP

>> Yes, creating a backup copy of your presentation is an *excellent* idea. I keep a copy on cloud storage or a thumb drive. This way, if the laptop gets lost or malfunctions or if something is incompatible, you can rescue your show from the backup copy.

PowerPoint PRESENTATION KEYBOARD SHORTCUTS

Display next slide: spacebar; Enter; N; down arrow; right arrow

Redisplay previous slide: up arrow; left arrow; P; Backspace

Go back to the first slide: 1, Enter (press 1 and then the Enter key)

Go to slide number *n*: *n*, Enter

Display a black screen: B; . (period)

Display a white screen: W; , (comma)

Cancel the show: Esc

Display all slides: – (hyphen)

Hide the pointer or navigation box: A

Setting up your presentation

I suppose that the most nerve-wracking part about giving a presentation is ensuring that everything works. When the laptop, projector, and software sing in harmony, the speech itself should go smoothly, right? Even when well prepared, few folks enjoy speaking before large groups.

In most circumstances, you're allowed to set up your laptop and run a test to ensure that everything works before giving your presentation to an audience. A technician might be available and even do everything for you. That's great. But it still doesn't make the situation any less nerve-wracking.

For a presentation before a handful of people, viewing the PowerPoint slide show on your laptop screen and sitting at the end of a table is perfectly fine. Most of the time, however, you connect your laptop to a video projector or large-screen monitor. In this configuration, the video projector or monitor works like just like a second monitor on the laptop.

In Windows, the standard configuration is to mirror your laptop's display on the external monitor. That's exactly what you want: Start your slide show on the laptop, just as you rehearsed in the hotel room.

The only thing you must remember is how to start the slide show. Here's the secret: Press the F5 key. This key starts the slide show. Remember: F5.

>> Be aware that PowerPoint changes its presentation when you project the slide show. You see a control screen, from which you can manipulate the slide show. Don't let it freak you out.

>> Because most people forget (or don't know) the F5 keyboard shortcut, to present your slide show full-screen in PowerPoint, click the Slide Show icon on the status bar, as shown in the margin.

>> If you need to configure the external monitor/projector, press the Win+P keyboard shortcut. See Chapter 12 for details on using this shortcut.

>> It's Win+P, where P stands for *projector*. Or PowerPoint. Or "Please let it be over!"

>> Any audio in the slide show should be carried over the video cable to the projector. If not, use the laptop's audio-out or headphone jack.

>> Consider getting a presentation input device. It's a combination laser-pointer-and-mouse. The gizmo connects wirelessly to your laptop and allows you to stand at a distance and give the presentation, using buttons on the device to move the slides back and forth. Such devices can be found at any office supply or computer store.

VIDEO PROJECTOR SUGGESTIONS

Most locations where presentations are given already have video projectors. If not, you need to bring your own. As with buying a laptop, choosing a video projector can be frustrating and intimidating — not to mention expensive. Here are my suggestions:

- **You need a more powerful video projector when you frequent larger auditoriums.** Most low-end projectors handle small rooms well. The key word here is *lumens*. The more lumens, the better the projector can handle a larger venue.

- **Resolution is an issue.** If you plan to project to a larger screen, you need a higher resolution. Low-end projectors use a resolution of 1024 by 768 — or lower. Then again, don't go overboard with very high resolutions, such as 1080p or even 4K, when your presentations don't need it.

- **Buy an extra bulb — if you can afford it.** Nothing sucks more than having a bulb burn out before a presentation. But, dang — the bulbs are expensive! Half of what you pay for the projector is probably the price of the bulb. And, you cannot find replacement bulbs in the hotel's sundry store.

Printing out a slide show

A great way to spread the word is to provide hard copies of the slide show. You don't need to put one slide on each page. Instead, put six slides on a page to save paper. Follow these steps in PowerPoint:

1. **Save your presentation.**

   Always save!

2. **Click the File tab.**

3. **Choose Print.**

   The Print screen appears, as shown in Figure 14-1.

4. **Choose the number of slides per page.**

   I prefer six, which is illustrated in Figure 14-1.

Set slides per page   Preview

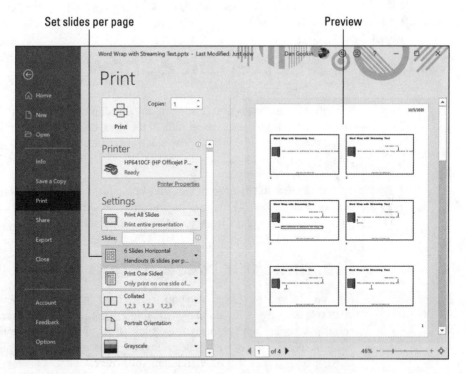

FIGURE 14-1:
The PowerPoint
Print screen.

5. **Set other options in the Print dialog box.**

   See Chapter 11 for details on printing when using a laptop.

   TIP

   Set the number of copies equal to the number of attendees or at least to a value you assume won't waste lots of paper.

6. **Click the big Print button to print.**

As an alternative to using your own printer, consider dropping off the hard copy at a print shop. Direct them to reproduce the show for you and to either staple or bind the pages.

TIP

If the boss is too stingy to pay for hard copies of the slide show, make them yourself. Go fancy and print the slide show on good paper stock and in color. Add a fancy cover and binding. And then charge adequately for each copy. Make them available before and after the show.

REMEMBER

Include contact information in the slide show handout.

To Create a Better Slide Show

Schoolkids use PowerPoint. They can quickly slap together a slide show, thanks to all the hints and fill-in-the-blank templates that the program provides. This accomplishment isn't difficult; the software is forgiving, and the parents are consistently overwhelmed.

The problem with PowerPoint software being forgiving is that it encourages plenty of lazy slide shows. To make your presentation shine, I offer a slew of slide show suggestions, from the spectacular to the subtly sneaky.

Starting your presentation

All your life, you've known who you are. All their lives, your audience hasn't a clue who you are. Even if you have considered yourself world-famous, published countless books, appeared on the *Today* show, and started your own YouTube channel, please do your audience a favor and introduce yourself. Give yourself a one- or two-sentence bio. Then begin your topic.

REMEMBER

>> Introduce yourself! This point is a pet peeve of mine. I don't know how many times I've sat in an audience and the presenter just starts talking without saying who they are.

>> Yes, even if the emcee says, "Here is Arthur Grockmeister," you must repeat: "Hello. I'm Art Grockmeister, president of Sterling, Worbletyme, and Grockmeister. I'm here today to talk about the earwig plague in Manitoba."

Driving home your point

To effectively communicate to an audience, tell them three times. It works like this:

1. Tell them what you're going to tell them.

2. Tell them.

3. Tell them what you've told them.

You can be subtle. You can be overt. Humor helps. Just don't be repetitive. For example, your talk's introduction takes care of the first time you tell them. That's it! As part of your introduction, you say, "Today I'm going to cover how most people spend their vacation dollar."

The second time, you tell them in more detail: Cover the topic. Give examples. Provide illustrations. People enjoy seeing examples, especially realistic ones.

For example (see how I did that?), don't say, "This is how a median-income white collar worker spends their vacation dollar." Instead, say, "Oscar is 34 and manages a pharmacy. Here is where he would like to go on holiday this year."

Finally, tell them what you told them. This is simply a summary, perhaps a quick bullet-point review of the topic. "So when you have money, you take a better vacation." Simple.

>> Two more things: When you're done, thank the audience and ask whether they have any questions — as long as that time is allocated for questions-and-answers.

>> You can opt to accept questions *during* the talk, but I recommend saving them until the end. That's because many questions are often answered during the presentation. If someone raises their hand, say, "If you could please hold that question until I'm done. Thank you."

TIP

Building a better presentation

My observation is that the best presentations involve about 60 percent speaker and 40 percent slide show. Those presentations where the speaker merely reads the slides would probably work better as a handout, not a slide show. Here are my words of advice:

>> **Don't read the slides!** The slides are the big picture. You provide the details when you speak.

>> **Keep text at a minimum.** Use bullet points, not paragraphs. The more text you add, the more difficult it is to read the slide. Seriously: Unless that quote from Marcus Aurelius is only a handful of words long, don't put it on a slide.

>> **Accept that the audience reads the slides before you do.** Use animation to reveal parts of the slide, or simply introduce the slide generally and then get to specifics. For example, "Here are three things you don't want to find in a jar of mayonnaise."

>> **Number the slides.** Especially if you plan on having a Q&A later, your audience can reference slides by their number as opposed to awkwardly describing a specific slide.

Keeping your audience awake

Your slides can be boring statistics, facts, and endless bullet points. That's fine because it's not the slide show that keeps the audience awake — it's you!

The best presentations are infused with personality. After the audience reads the slide — which should be brief — they focus on the presenter for attention. Give it to them!

If you find yourself coming up short on charisma, another trick is to be interactive. This technique avoids the milieu of a warm and quiet, dimly lit, after-lunch meeting room and the gentle pull of napping that it brings. My advice: Give your audience handouts.

Don't just print the slide show, either. Though handouts are a good thing to provide, as covered earlier in this chapter, I recommend instead creating a fill-in-the-blanks handout. For example, the handout reads:

Only ___ percent of American adults have been to a bookstore in the past month.

During your presentation, a slide gives the statistic — which is 16 percent and rather dismal. The audience stays awake because they're interacting with the show. As a bonus, they're taking notes, which is something most of them want to do anyhow.

The fill-in-the-blanks items need not be answered directly in the slide show. You can interactively ask questions of the audience, which also helps keep them awake: "How often did Americans buy books in the 1950s?" When you get the proper answer, reveal the slide.

Selling a presentation

The key to making a great presentation, and to truly sway an audience, is to use the finely honed sales-and-persuasion techniques categorized by one word: propaganda.

Yeah, yeah: *Propaganda* is a loaded term. It carries a lot of baggage, but it works, and everyone from the big evil corporation to your honest neighborhood preacher employs its methods in one way or another.

Beyond not using the word *propaganda* in your presentation, you can muster one or more of its common techniques when it comes to selling your presentation:

>> Testimonials

>> The bandwagon

>> Plain folks

>> Card stacking

>> Loaded language

>> Cute kids and animals

>> Sex

You may not recognize these terms, but you definitely know the techniques. Political campaigns thrive on these methods to coerce and convince voters. You can do so as well in your PowerPoint slide shows — and not feel bad about it.

Testimonials: The testimonial appears as expert or valued advice, as though it's from an independent authority. Examples include celebrities, sports figures, and actors in white lab coats who spew data. Even a quote from Shakespeare is considered a testimonial. It adds weight to your point by providing another perspective — even if the point is completely fabricated.

The bandwagon: As a tribal species, doing what everyone else is doing is important — whether people admit to it or not. Getting on the bandwagon is compelling; no one wants to be left behind. Central to this technique is the use of the words *everyone* and *everybody*. How often have you heard, "Everyone agrees . . ." in an advertisement? That's the bandwagon technique.

Plain folks: In a way, the plain-folks technique works best where testimonials work least. Everyday people, just like you or someone you know, offer their opinions and recommendations. Contrast a commercial with a doctor talking about a new drug (testimonial) with an elderly patient talking about how well it worked for her (plain folks).

Card stacking: The card stacking technique is a direct comparison, showing one item in a positive light while showing another in a highly negative light. This approach is overused for political campaigns, although the focus tends to be more on shedding negative light on the opponent and not on a balanced presentation.

Loaded language: This approach takes advantage of the rich variety of adjectives in the English language. Multiple words can describe the same thing but carry negative and positive connotations. For example, *enthusiast* versus *fanatic* or *public assistance* as opposed to *welfare*. The loaded language carries with it more information than it would otherwise.

Cute kids and animals: No one in vaudeville wanted to follow the dog act. There's a reason: People love cute animals and little kids. Politicians pose with their families or family pets. It softens their image.

Sex: Sex can sell, but it's not a guaranteed sale. The use of sex as a propaganda technique works well or terribly, depending on the audience. If you're unsure whether to use this technique, try something else instead.

Chapter **15**

A Laptop at Play

Forget about work. Your laptop is capable of intruding upon the leisure time domain of mobile devices, such as phones and tablets. These activities include listening to music, watching videos, and taking photos. The modern laptop (specifically, the tablet PC) is more than capable of handling these tasks — and of doing those business things.

The Laptop Media Player

To enjoy the pictures, music, and video on your laptop, you run a specific program or app. The traditional program is Windows Media Player, which still works great in Windows 10. For a more app-y experience, you can employ one of the newer apps, which may work better if your laptop is a tablet PC.

Exploring Windows Media Player

Media management programs are no longer the rage. Specific applications for certain types of media, such as music-playing and video-watching, are now more common. Still, the legacy Windows Media Player program handles many tasks in a single location.

To start Windows Media Player, follow these steps in Windows 10:

1. **Click the Start button.**

   Up pops the Start button menu.

2. **Type** windows media player **or as many letters as necessary to see the Windows Media Player item appear atop the search list.**

3. **Press the Enter key to start the Windows Media Player program.**

   Windows Media Player appears on the screen, although if it's the first time the program is run, you must do some configuration. Choose the recommended settings.

Figure 15-1 shows the Windows Media Player window. Media categories are shown on the left side of the screen, content in the middle, and special options on the right.

FIGURE 15-1:
Windows Media
Player.

TIP

Fret not when you find no media in the Windows Media Player window. You can easily add media as described in the later section "Expand the Laptop's Media Universe."

>> If you're an Android user, you can connect with your online media by using the laptop's web browser and visiting Google Play on the Internet.

>> iOS users can install the iTunes program for Windows, where you can access your iTunes library.

Running the Photos app

The Photos app has only one, obvious job: Display and manage photos found not only on your laptop but from online sources as well, such as Microsoft's OneDrive. The Photos app main screen is shown in Figure 15-2.

FIGURE 15-2:
The Photos app.

To start the Photos app, choose it from the Start button menu. You can press the Windows key on the keyboard to pop up the menu and then type **photos** to start the program.

Click or tap an image to examine it, as shown in Figure 15-3. Icons appearing atop the window let you manage or manipulate the image, as illustrated in the figure.

Click the Back icon to return to the Photo app's Album view (refer to Figure 15-3).

Using the Groove Music app

Windows 10 doesn't appear to have a native music-playing app. The only thing that comes close is Groove Music, which not only lets you buy and stream music online but also recognizes any music already stored on the laptop.

Figure 15-4 shows the Groove Music app's main screen. To listen to music, choose an album and then click the Play button that appears at the bottom of the app's window.

Choose a way to view your music

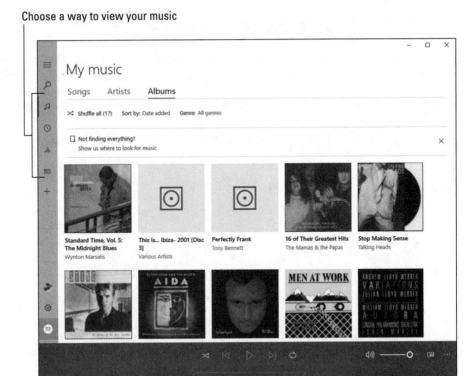

FIGURE 15-4:
The Groove
Music app.

Play controls

Expand the Laptop's Media Universe

Unless you have a really good memory, or you hang out only with musicians and artists all the time, it's important to pack your laptop with plenty of exciting media. The goal is to get that media — music, pictures, and video — into your laptop. You have two options:

>> If you have physical media, such as music on a CD, you can rip the music into the laptop. This media must be ripped, scanned, or otherwise sourced from the physical realm into the laptop's digital realm.

>> You can obtain digital media, either free or paid, from an online source. For example, the Microsoft Store features an Entertainment category from which you can retrieve movies or music or other media. If you lack an app to access the media, the store offers this software as well.

Ripping music from a CD

You can use Windows Media Player to copy music from your CD collection to your laptop. The process is called *ripping*, which seems violent and illegal, so it's probably a music industry term. With one of your treasured music CDs in hand, follow these steps to magically copy its contents from eternal plastic to sacred digital:

1. **Insert the music CD into the laptop's optical drive.**

If your laptop lacks an optical drive, connect an external optical drive.

2. **Ignore any AutoPlay notification.**

You could tap the notification to choose the Play Audio CD option to immediately listen to the CD. Don't.

3. **Open Windows Media Player.**

Directions are found in the earlier section "Exploring Windows Media Player."

4. **Choose the CD from the left side of the window.**

The CD's content — the music — appears in the center of the window.

5. **Select which songs you want to rip.**

All songs are selected, as shown in Figure 15-5. If you want only a few, remove the check marks by the songs you don't want to copy.

6. **Click the Rip CD button.**

The music is copied from the optical disc to the laptop's storage. While it's copying, the Rip CD button changes to the Stop Rip button. A progress bar appears by each track as it's copied.

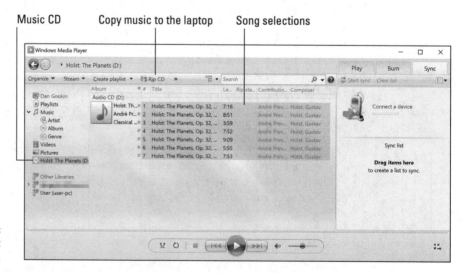

Music CD   Copy music to the laptop   Song selections

FIGURE 15-5:
Copying music
from a CD.

When the ripping is done, the songs appear in the Windows Media Player music library. Choose the Music category from the left side of the window to look for the album and locate its tunes.

>> To continue ripping your old CD collection, eject the disc and replace it with another one. Repeat the steps in this section to rip more music.

>> If you want to share the music with other devices, copy it to cloud storage. See the later section "Copying media to your OneDrive."

>> Any music you copy to your laptop is also available in the Groove Music app.

Uploading pictures and videos from a phone or camera

The best way to obtain a ton of pictures and videos is to connect a digital camera to your laptop and synchronize the images. To properly connect the device to your laptop, follow these steps:

1. **Ensure that the phone or tablet is turned on and unlocked.**

2. **Connect the phone, tablet, or digital camera to the laptop.**

Attach one end of a USB cable to the laptop and the other to the device.

3. **Ensure that the device is turned on and unlocked.**

4. **Ignore the notification.**

The notification generally doesn't help in Windows 10, at least not when you desire to import pictures and videos.

After the connection is made, you can use either the Photos app or the Windows Media Player program to import images. Using the Photos app is quicker, but the Windows Media Player program offers more options.

To import images when using the Photos app, follow these steps:

1. **Click the Import Photos button.**

Refer to Figure 15-2 for the button's location.

2. **Choose From a USB Device.**

Your phone, tablet, or camera is effectively a USB storage device, like a thumb drive.

3. **Continue to follow the onscreen directions to import photos and videos.**

A notification appears when the process is complete.

For more discrete control over which images are imported, and potentially a higher degree of success, use the Windows Media Player program instead of the Photos app. Follow these steps:

1. Choose the device's Pictures category from the left side of the window.

Look for your phone, tablet, or camera listed on the left side of the window, as illustrated in Figure 15-6. Expand this item to view the Pictures category, as illustrated in the figure.

Attached media device   Phone's pictures   Copy images to the laptop   Sync tab

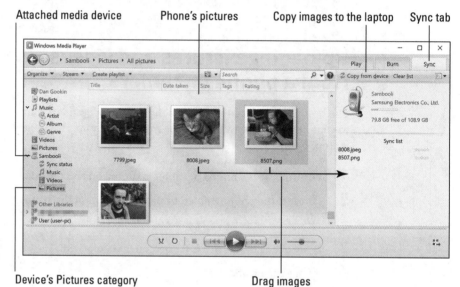

FIGURE 15-6:
Copying images from a smartphone to a laptop.

Device's Pictures category   Drag images

2. Click the Sync tab.

3. Select the images you want to copy from the center of the window.

Refer to Figure 15-6 for the specific location.

4. Drag the images you want to copy from the middle of the window to the Sync tab.

5. Click the Copy from Device button.

The images are copied from the other gizmo into your laptop.

The copied images are found in your laptop's main storage. Look in your User Profile folder, in the Pictures folder. Images are organized into subfolders given the month and year in which the images were taken.

TIP

» You can use the same process in the Windows Media Player program (the second set of steps) to copy over music and videos on a phone or tablet. Choose the proper category from Step 1 and then repeat the rest of the steps.

» Once you're done copying media from the device, disconnect it: Unplug the USB cable.

» If you want to share the music with other devices, copy it to cloud storage. See the later section "Copying media to your OneDrive."

Taking a picture

A common feature on today's laptops is the webcam, usually found squat above the screen. Tablet PCs might also feature a rear or main camera. Obviously, one solid way to get a photo into your laptop is to use this camera.

Follow these steps to use your laptop's webcam to snap a photo:

1. **Open the Camera app.**

   The app is found on the Start menu: Type **camera** and choose the Camera App item.

2. **Frame the picture.**

3. **Tap the Shutter icon to record the image for posterity.**

To record video, tap the Video icon. The app's window changes, replacing the Shutter icon with the Video Camera icon. Tap that Video Camera icon to begin recording. Tap the icon again to stop recording.

Figure 15-7 illustrates the Camera app's interface. Use the onscreen controls to snap an image or record a video. You can also make some photographic adjustments, though these are limited by your laptop's camera capabilities.

For example, to switch between front and rear cameras, tap the Switch Front/Rear Camera icon, as illustrated in Figure 15-7. If your laptop has only a front camera, this button doesn't appear.

» Pictures you snap and videos you record are saved in the Pictures\Camera Roll folder found in the User Profile area on the laptop's storage.

» Both the Photos app and Windows Media Player can be used to examine photos.

Camera options and settings

Switch to video

Switch front/rear camera

Previous image

Shutter icon

FIGURE 15-7:
The Camera app.

Media Sharing

Your laptop isn't the only device on which you store media. You most likely have a phone or tablet. You probably also use online storage for some of your media. Happiness occurs when all those devices can peacefully coexist and share their media in a pleasant and convenient manner.

Copying media to your OneDrive

Your Windows 10 computer works automatically with Microsoft's OneDrive cloud storage. Any files or media you copy to the OneDrive area on your laptop's storage are immediately shared with other devices you own that can access the storage — including any device connected to the Internet.

To make media from your laptop available to another OneDrive gizmo, copy that media to your OneDrive folder. Suppose that you have an album of music on your laptop and you want to share that music with other devices. Follow these steps:

1. **Open a File Explorer window.**

   Press the Win+E keyboard shortcut.

2. **From the left side of the window, choose your User Profile folder.**

   The folder is given the name of your account on the laptop. See Chapter 8 for more information on the User Profile folder.

3. **Double-click to open the Music folder.**

4. **Right-click the folder representing the music album you want to share from your laptop.**

5. **Choose Cut.**

   You're moving this folder to the Music folder on OneDrive.

6. **Choose OneDrive from the left side of the window.**

7. **Open the Music folder on OneDrive.**

8. **Click the Home tab and choose the Paste command.**

   The folder is moved to OneDrive cloud storage and synchronized with all other OneDrive devices.

Changing the album's location doesn't affect how it plays in either the Groove Music app or Windows Media Player program. The media is still available; only its storage location has changed.

These steps can be repeated for any media stored on your laptop. You can move photos from the Pictures folder in your User Profile area to the Pictures folder on OneDrive. Ditto for video. Just change the proper location in this section's set of steps.

See Chapter 18 for more information on OneDrive and cloud storage.

Adding media from your OneDrive

Though you have music, photos, and videos stored on your OneDrive cloud storage, that media may not show up in Windows Media Player. To ensure that it does, you must add the OneDrive storage location to those places where the program looks to find media. Follow these steps while using the Windows Media Player program:

1. **Choose Organize ⇨ Manage Libraries ⇨ Music.**

   The Music Library Locations dialog box appears. It lists the folders where Windows Media Player looks to find music or other audio files. The standard folder is the Music folder in your User Profile folder.

   If you see your OneDrive\Music folder in the list, you're good to go. Otherwise, continue with Step 2.

2. **Click the Add button.**

   The Include Folder in Music dialog box appears, which works like the standard Open dialog box.

3. **Choose OneDrive from the list of locations on the left side of the dialog box.**

4. **On the right side of the dialog box, choose the Music folder on your OneDrive storage.**

5. **Click the Include Folder button.**

   The OneDrive folder appears in the Music Library Locations window.

   You can add other folders — say, from Dropbox or Google Drive — by repeating Steps 2 through 4.

6. **Click the OK button.**

   Instantly, the online media is synchronized with Windows Media Player, and your online music populates the screen.

7. **Repeat these steps for the Videos and Pictures items.**

   Choose Videos in Steps 1 through 6 as well as Pictures to coordinate those items from your OneDrive cloud storage.

Music stored on OneDrive is automatically synchronized to the Groove Music app. The same holds true for pictures when using the Photos app.

Connecting to a network media player

The joy of sharing music, pictures, and videos is that it can work both ways. Your laptop can access other PCs on the network to view any media available for sharing. To do so, open Windows Media Player and choose a network media server from the list shown on the left side of the screen.

In Figure 15-8, two PCs are available for sharing media: User–PC and Tony. In the figure, Tony has been selected and its media appears categorized, just like media stored on your laptop. The Music category is chosen, and music from that PC appears in the center of the window.

Shared media libraries
on the local network

Music stored on Dan's PC "Tony"

Media from Dan's account on PC "Tony"

FIGURE 15-8:
Accessing media
on another
network PC.

Playing music or viewing photos or videos on the other computer works the same as accessing your laptop's media: Choose a song to play, view a picture, or watch a video.

>> You don't need to disconnect from the network PC's media server. Just close the Windows Media Player window.

>> To share your laptop's media with other computers and gizmos on the network, refer to the next section.

Sharing your laptop's media

Media sharing, or *streaming*, is normally disabled for Windows 10 laptops. To activate the feature and make your laptop's music, pictures, and video available to other computers on a private network, follow these steps:

1. **Pop up the Start menu.**

Press the Windows key on the keyboard.

2. **Type** media streaming options, **or enough of this text until you see the item Media Streaming Options Control Panel.**

3. **Click the Turn On Media Streaming button.**

   A list of network devices capable of accessing your laptop appears. On my screen, I see computers on the network as well as my Internet-ready HDTV and the Xbox One. You can remove items from this list by removing their check marks.

4. **Click OK.**

   Your laptop's media is now shared.

Pictures, videos, and music on your laptop are accessed by other network PCs, similar to the process outlined in the preceding section. Your Internet-ready TV and Xbox One use other techniques to access the media.

Laptop Phone Calls

If you recall laptop history (found in Chapter 1), you know that one pillar of laptop technology is communications. That means not only computer communications, networking, and modem use but also people communications. Yes, it's possible to use your laptop as a phone.

The go-to app on your Windows 10 laptop for chatting it up is Skype. You can connect with other Skype users to text-chat, voice-chat, and video-chat. If you already have a Skype account — great! Otherwise, you can use your Microsoft account to sign in.

To start Skype, choose it from the Start menu. It's appears in the list of apps, or you can type **skype** to quickly find it in the list. If you don't see the Skype app, look for the Get Skype app, which installs Skype.

After the Skype app starts, sign in or create an account.

You can use Skype to voice- or video-chat with other Skype users. To call a real phone with Skype, you need Skype credit, which is where you add money to your account. Only a small amount is necessary, because the calls are cheap, even for international calling. Use the dialpad to type the number and connect.

When you're done using Skype, you can set it aside or sign out.

To set Skype aside, close the app window. Skype stays active and catches incoming chats or video call requests. Click the App button on the taskbar to reactivate Skype, or choose the notification for an incoming message.

To sign out of Skype, click the Skype menu item and choose Sign Out. You hear the "Skype deflating" sound, and then the sign-in screen appears. You're officially signed out of Skype and can close the app window.

>> Click the Add Skype Credit link to add more credit to your account.

>> If you don't want to spend the money for Skype Credit, ensure that your pals have Skype on their computers, phones, or tablets. Then you can chat it up for free as long as an Internet connection is available.

WARNING

>> Though you can use inflight Wi-Fi to access the Internet, most airlines forbid you to use Skype while aloft.

>> When someone receives a Skype call on their phone, they see an unusual or unknown phone number appear on the caller ID. Therefore, I recommend first sending your friend an email so your Skype call isn't wantonly dismissed.

TIP

>> Get a good headset if you plan to use Skype for video chat or phone calls. Yes, the program works work with the laptop's built-in microphone, but a headset is so much better. Plus, a headset doesn't annoy everyone else in the room.

eBooks on Your Laptop

Another fun thing you can do on your laptop is read an eBook. I guess you're familiar with the whole reading thing. eBooks work similarly to real books, with the exceptions that the book appears electronically on your laptop screen and the publisher really screws the author on the royalty percentage.

eBook reading apps can be obtained from the Microsoft Store. Open the Store app and browse for eBook readers. Many of them are free, such as Amazon's Kindle app.

>> My advice is to obtain the eBook reader app for whatever electronic book library you already use. For example, if you have an Amazon account and have ordered eBooks there, get the Kindle app. Sign in to that app and behold your entire Amazon eBook library. Ditto for the Nook app.

>> If you use Google Play Books, you can access your eBook library by visiting the Play Books website: play.google.com/books.

REMEMBER

>> Download or synchronize your eBook library with your laptop before you leave on a trip. That way, you can read on the airplane without having to pay for the inflight Wi-Fi.

4

Laptop Networking

Understand wired and wireless networking.

Manage networks in Windows.

Access files from afar and on the cloud.

Chapter **16**

The Networking Thing

A
t the core of laptop communications is the computer network. A long time ago, the network was a mysterious technical thing that most people feared and few understood. Today, computer networking is the way people get on the Internet, though it also remains a mysterious technical thing that most people fear and few understand.

The Big Networking Picture

Computer networking is about communications and sharing. Different electronic gizmos communicate with each other, sending and receiving information. They share resources, which includes storage, printers, and modems.

Figure 16-1 illustrates a typical computer network, such as one you may desire for your home or that's already configured in the office. This type of network is known as a local area network, or LAN, though few people use this term.

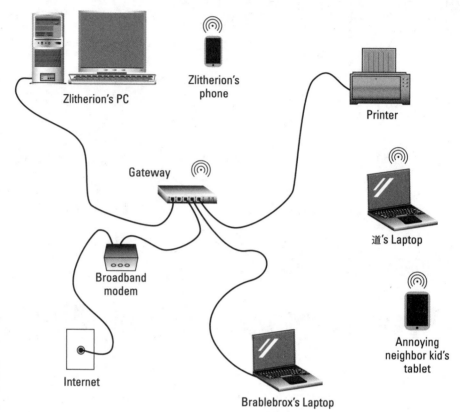

FIGURE 16-1:
A typical
computer
network.

Zlitherion's PC

Zlitherion's
phone

Printer

Gateway

道's Laptop

Broadband
modem

Internet

Annoying
neighbor kid's
tablet

Brablebrox's Laptop

Despite its octopus–like layout, the typical network connection works something like this:

Device ⇨ Gateway ⇨ Modem ⇨ Internet

Device: Your laptop, as well as other devices, contain networking hardware. This hardware connects the laptop to a central location, wired or wirelessly. Other devices can connect as well, including other computers, phones, tablets, printers, and so on.

Gateway: The gateway is a central location to which all network devices are connected. The gateway manages traffic between the devices. For example, your laptop can use a network printer, or you can steal files from Zlitherion's PC.

Modem: Internet traffic is forwarded by the gateway to a modem. It also receives Internet traffic from the modem and distributes it to those devices requesting the information.

Internet: The Internet is the great collection of computers in the world that all send, receive, store, and share information, most of which is not pornography.

When special software magic is applied, all these network hardware components work together. They help your laptop communicate with other computers, share information, and access the Internet.

>> The gateway is commonly called a router. It might also be known as a wireless base station or hub. See the later sidebar "Network terms to ignore" for more details.

>> In some network configurations, the gateway and modem are the same device.

>> Nearly all laptops are capable of connecting to both wired and wireless networks. Low-end laptops and tablet PCs offer only wireless networking.

>> Network software magic is supplied by Windows in conjunction with mythical pagan beasts and deities.

TECHNICAL
STUFF

>> Setting up your own network isn't that difficult, especially if you use an all-wireless configuration. I do strongly recommend that your first network action is to apply an administrator password to the gateway (router) and create a complex password for the Wi-Fi network.

TIP

>> Write down both the gateway and wireless network passwords! Be clear; don't write sloppy or so tiny that no one can read the passwords. Label each password, such as *Router password* and *Wi-Fi password.* Tuck the piece of paper beneath the router.

NETWORK TERMS TO IGNORE

Computer scientists have concluded that the basic networking concepts of communications and sharing are too easy to grasp. Therefore, they've invented some interesting terms and acronyms to describe computer networking, many of which were effectively designed for the purpose of confusing you:

802.11: This number refers to the current wireless networking standard. The number is followed by various letters of the alphabet. As long as you get the 802.11 part correct (say "eight oh two eleven"), the letters that follow are of concern only to the nerds.

(continued)

(continued)

Base Star: The bad guys' spaceship in *Battlestar Galactica*. This term has nothing to do with computer networking.

base station: A generic term that applies to a hub or gateway used as a central connection point in wireless networking.

Ethernet cable: This cable connects computers with networking equipment. The term *CAT* also refers to this type of cable, where *CAT* is followed by a famous number, such as 5 or 6.

gateway: The proper name for what's commonly called a router, it organizes and manages information on a local network. The gateway also serves as the interface between a local network and the Internet.

hub: A central location to which networked computers are connected, either wired or wirelessly. It allows the connected devices to communicate with each other. Unlike a gateway, a hub doesn't manage network traffic.

LAN: This acronym stands for local area network, which is how computer networking works in a home or office. Often just called "the network" or "my network" or "the neighbor's network because their gateway lacks a password."

modem: Originally a portmanteau of *mod*ulator/*dem*odulator, today's broadband modems provide high-speed Internet access to your home or office network.

NIC: This acronym stands for network interface card (or controller). It's the hardware in your laptop that provides the network connection — wired and wireless.

router: This is the common name for a gateway.

switch: Another term for a hub. You use a switch to add more wired network connections to a gateway.

Wi-Fi: This term refers to wireless networking. Supposedly, it stands for *wireless fidelity*, but various Internet nerds will argue that point with you.

Make the Network Connection

The only determination of whether your laptop uses wired or wireless networking is the hardware that's installed. Choosing one or the other doesn't affect the device's networking capabilities, but the technique for accessing each type of network is different.

Connecting the laptop to a wired network

To make the wired connection, locate the Ethernet port on the laptop's side. It looks like a telephone jack, though the shape is slightly larger. Plug the Ethernet cable into the jack.

The other end of the Ethernet cable plugs into a wall socket or directly into a hub or gateway. This plug-in arrangement is the extent of the physical, wired connection.

To complete the connection process, you must contend with Windows to configure the network. This process happens automatically (if the laptop is on). See Chapter 17 for information on network configuration.

>> Perhaps you're too young to remember what a phone jack looks like. Whatever. The Ethernet jack is rectangular in shape with a notch on one of the long sides.

>> Ethernet cables can be obtained at any office supply or computer store. Even Home Depot has them. Just ask a Home Depot employee. And if you can't find a Home Depot employee, you're in the right place.

>> If someone refers to the Ethernet port as an RJ-45 port, punch him in the nose.

>> It doesn't matter which end of the cable you use; you cannot plug in an Ethernet cable backward.

>> Network security experts tell me that the wired Internet connection is far more secure than a wireless connection. If possible, connect your laptop to a wire-based network.

Accessing a Wi-Fi network

Your laptop can make a wireless network connection anywhere the Wi-Fi signal is available. You need to know the network's name and its password. Upon success, your laptop can use the network and access the Internet without the burden of wires and other encumbrances.

WARNING

Avoid connecting to unknown networks in a public location. You're taking a security risk when you don't know exactly which network you're using.

In Windows 10, you access a wireless network thusly:

1. Click the Network notification icon.

The icon is shown in the margin. It appears whenever no network connection is active.

2. Choose a wireless network from the pop-up list.

Figure 16-2 shows what the pop-up list may look like.

Available Wi-Fi networks

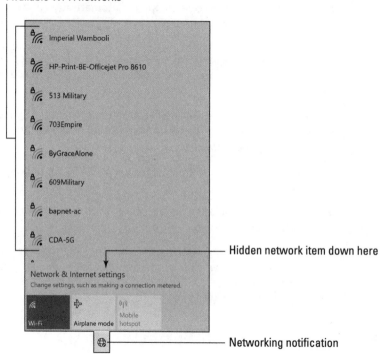

Hidden network item down here

Networking notification

FIGURE 16-2:
Selecting a Wi-Fi
network.

3. Place a check mark by the Connect Automatically option.

This option ensures that the laptop automatically reconnects to the network whenever it's in range.

4. Click the Connect button.

5. Type the network password and click the Next button.

6. **If you're on a home or work network, click the Yes button; otherwise, click No.**

    By clicking No, you add extra security to the connection. This is the choice to make for a public location, such as a café or the airport. Click Yes for your own, private network at home or at the office.

Your laptop is now connected to the wireless network. The networking notification changes to reflect the wireless connection, as shown in the margin.

By choosing the Connect Automatically option (refer to Step 3), you ensure that whenever your laptop is in range, it connects to, signs in to, and accesses the specific network. This way, you need to configure the network only once.

TIP

Connecting to a hidden Wi-Fi network

For security reasons, some wireless networks don't broadcast their network names. Obviously, you cannot connect to a network if you don't know its name, mostly because the unnamed network doesn't show up in the list of available networks.

To find the network name, you must ask someone, such as the network manager or perhaps the distracted young person who served you coffee and a biscotti. After you have the network name, plus other information, such as the password and security key, follow these steps:

1. **Choose the networking notification.**

2. **Scroll or swipe down the list of available networks to locate the last item in the list, Hidden Network.**

    No, Hidden Network isn't the name of an available network. It's the doorway into accessing networks that don't broadcast their names.

3. **Choose the Hidden Network item.**

4. **Click or tap the Connect button.**

5. **Type the network's name or SSID.**

6. **Click the Next button.**

    Windows goes out and finds the unnamed wireless network.

7. **Continue following the onscreen prompts to complete the connection.**

    You may need to type a password and choose other options, each of which is delightfully explained in the preceding section.

The network name is referred to as the SSID, where *SSID* stands for *service set identifier*.

Tethering to a smartphone

You might be able to use a smartphone as your laptop's modem. The process, called *tethering*, involves using the phone's mobile data signal to provide the laptop with Internet access.

Some might argue that tethering a connection is unnecessary because you can use the smartphone directly for Internet access. I would remind those folks that this type of tethering merely puts the smartphone in its place.

To make the connection, obey these steps:

1. **Use a USB cable to connect the smartphone to the laptop.**

2. **On the smartphone, activate the USB tethering feature.**

    On an Android phone, this feature is accessed from the phone's Settings app, in the Wi-Fi area or Wireless Networks area.

Once active, the laptop recognizes the smartphone as a modem. The process takes place automatically, and an Internet connection is immediately established.

To break the connection, either disable the USB tethering feature on the smartphone or disconnect the USB cable.

>> Not every smartphone is capable of USB tethering. If you attach your smartphone to the laptop and only the phone's digital photos or music are recognized, the phone probably cannot be used for tethering.

>> Some cellular providers enable USB tethering only when you subscribe to that service on your mobile data plan.

>> Another option, as opposed to tethering, is to create a mobile Wi-Fi hotspot. The smartphone acts as a wireless hub, which the laptop can connect to as it would any wireless network.

>> Be mindful of how much data the laptop uses! Data rates and surcharges from the phone's cellular provider still apply.

>> If you plan to tether the Internet connection quite often, consider instead obtaining a cellular modem for your laptop. These gizmos are obtained from the same locations where you can buy smartphones.

Break the Network Connection

The question may not seem necessary, but that doesn't stop people from asking: How do you and your laptop break a network connection in a friendly manner that won't incur the wrath of the network gods? Unlike human relationships, breaking the connection between a laptop and a network doesn't require counseling or a lawyer or making a cryptic social networking post.

Disconnecting from a wired network

To stop using the wired connection, unplug the Ethernet cable from your laptop. That's it.

WARNING

>> You can unplug the cable whether the laptop is on or off.

>> If an established Wi-Fi connection is available, the laptop instantly switches to using that connection as soon as the wired connection is terminated.

>> Don't break the connection while you're using the network to access files. If you're in doubt about whether files are accessed over the network, first close any applications and then unplug the cable.

Releasing the Wi-Fi connection

You don't need to take formal action to disconnect from a Wi-Fi network; simply moving out of range does the trick. The typical Wi-Fi network has a range of about 50 or so feet. So pick up your laptop and run 50 feet in any direction. Knowledgeable onlookers will recognize that you're trying to break the Wi-Fi connection, not that you've instead just seen an enormous spider.

Turning off the laptop, putting it to sleep, or going into hibernation also disconnects the wireless network. These actions seem less frantic to concerned onlookers.

It's possible to manually disconnect. Heed these steps in Windows 10:

1. **Click the Wi-Fi Connected icon in the notification area.**

   The Wi-Fi Connected icon is shown in the margin.

2. **Choose the currently connected wireless network.**

   The word *Connected* appears beneath the network name, and it's probably the item at the top of the pop-up list, similar to what's shown in Figure 16-3.

3. Click the Disconnect button.

With a heavy sigh, the network releases your laptop, letting go with an extended, open hand and a tiny lump in its throat.

Currently-connected network

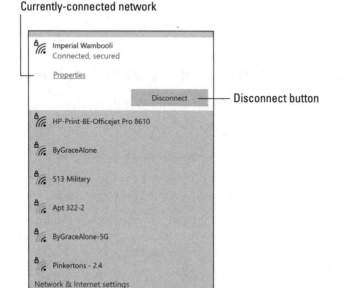

Imperial Wambooli
Connected, secured

Properties

Disconnect —————— Disconnect button

HP-Print-BE-Officejet Pro 8610

ByGraceAlone

513 Military

Apt 322-2

ByGraceAlone-5G

Pinkertons - 2.4

Network & Internet settings
Change settings, such as making a connection metered.

Wi-Fi   Airplane mode   Mobile hotspot

FIGURE 16-3:
Disconnecting
from a wireless
network.

————— Networking notification

REMEMBER

The network stays disconnected. If you move out of range and then move back into range, the wireless network is reconnected if you've configured it to automatically connect. Or you can reconnect by simply choosing the same network again, as described earlier in this chapter.

Chapter **17**

Network Life in Laptop Land

Out on the road, your laptop is a lone warrior, bringing you the power of the computer in a potent, portable package. After connecting to a network, the laptop becomes part of a team. You can access network resources, share files and printers, and do other networky things.

Network Configuration

If you just want to use the network to access the Internet, great! Otherwise, making a network connection opens your laptop to a world of networking opportunities. These include interacting with other devices on the network. Such frolic requires further configuration and oversight than required for using the Internet in your local café.

Locating network central

If you need to mess with network settings for your laptop, you must visit Network Central. Two locations are available, with the Settings app version shown in Figure 17-1.

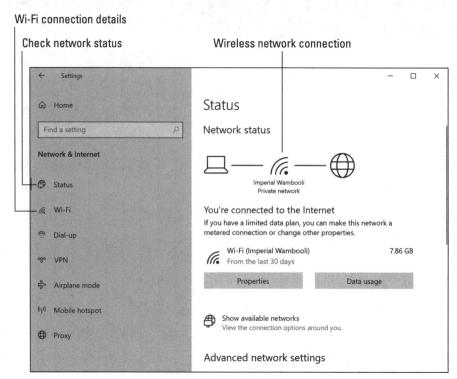

Wi-Fi connection details

Check network status   Wireless network connection

FIGURE 17-1:
The Network &
Internet Status
screen.

To display that window, heed these steps:

1. **Press the Win+I keyboard shortcut to summon the Settings app.**

2. **Choose Network & Internet.**

With the Status item chosen from the left side of the window, you see information similar to what's shown in Figure 17-1.

To see even nerdier information, scroll down the Status window a tad and choose the Network and Sharing Center item. You see the ancient Network and Sharing Center window in the Control Panel. It provides access to more networking features than the Settings app, which is why most of the nerds use both locations to fine-tune the network.

TIP

To quickly access the Networking & Internet status screen in the Settings app, click the networking icon in the taskbar's notification area. Choose the item Network & Internet Settings.

Setting the network security

Windows assumes that all wireless networks are public. For a wired network connection, you're asked whether the network is public or private. This setting determines the overall network security, as follows:

Private network: This setting implies that all computers on the network are accessed by you, your family, or others in your organization. Hopefully no one is going to do anything stupid. The Private network setting has the fewest network restrictions.

Public network: This setting offers the best security when accessing a network in a public location, such as a library, café, airport, dungeon, and so on.

The network-type question may be posed after the initial connection is made. Otherwise, for a Wi-Fi network, tap the wireless networking notification on the taskbar, shown in Figure 17-2. Choose the Properties item below the connected Wi-Fi network to review options, as illustrated in the figure.

Network security levels   Currently connected Wi-Fi network   Properties link

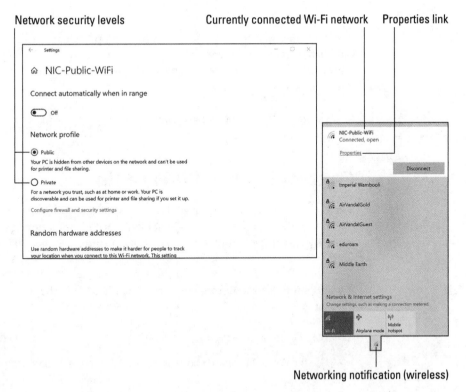

FIGURE 17-2:
The Public or
Private setting.

Networking notification (wireless)

To change the wireless-network security level, choose another option from the Settings window, as shown in Figure 17-2.

For a wired connection, review the security setting by following these steps:

1. **Press the Win+I keyboard shortcut.**

   The Settings app appears.

2. **Choose Network & Internet.**

3. **On the left side of the screen, choose Ethernet.**

   The right side of the screen changes to display the currently connected network. If not, choose the network connection, which you must do for systems that sport multiple network interfaces.

4. **Choose either the Public or Private option.**

   Just as Windows assumes Wi-Fi networks to be public, a wired network is assumed to be private. If not, you can change this setting in the Settings window.

Windows remembers which networks the laptop has used. The same settings are established when you reconnect to that network. Only by following the steps in this section can you change the network type for a remembered network after the initial connection.

REMEMBER

Always choose the Public Network option when you're using the laptop in a public location. This choice is the most secure.

Controlling the Wi-Fi radio

Some laptops have a handy On–Off button associated with their wireless radio. It could be a physical button or a special keyboard combination. Use this button to instantly disconnect from the network by turning off the wireless networking adapter.

If your laptop lacks a button, you can manually disable the wireless radio. Follow these steps:

1. **Display the Action Center.**

   Use the Win+A keyboard shortcut or swipe the screen inward from the right edge.

2. **Choose the Network tile.**

   A pop-up appears showing the connected network, any available networks, plus three tiles, as shown in Figure 17-3.

3. **Choose the Wi-Fi tile.**

   The wireless radio is disabled.

Currently connected Wi-Fi network

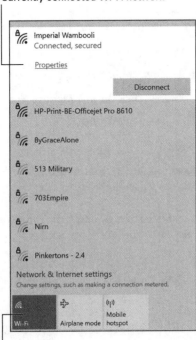

FIGURE 17-3:
Disabling the
Wi-Fi radio.
Disable Wi-Fi radio

Repeat these steps to enable the Wi-Fi radio. Once active, the laptop instantly re-connects to any previously connected, available wireless network.

Forgetting a Wi-Fi connection

The laptop remembers every wireless network you've connected to — if you've told Windows to remember the network. That's the advice I give in Chapter 16 when connecting to any Wi-Fi network.

Over time, the list of networks to which the laptop has visited grows. This process works well for you because it means as soon as the laptop is within range, a connection is made. Even so, you may find it necessary to remove a network from the list. A practical reason would be to reset the network type from Private to Public or vice versa, as described elsewhere in this chapter. Another reason is when the password has changed. In this instance, you must direct the laptop to forget the network so that you can reestablish the connection with the new password.

To forget a Wi-Fi connection, follow these steps:

1. **Press the Win+I keyboard shortcut to call forth the Settings app.**

2. **Choose Network & Internet.**

3. **From the left side of the window, choose Wi-Fi.**

4. **On the right side of the window, click the link Manage Known Networks.**

5. **Choose a remembered network from the list.**

6. **Click or tap the Forget button.**

    Windows forgets the network connection, discarding any saved information, which includes the saved network password.

Of course, you can always reconnect to any network. You'll need to supply the password again and set the network type. Refer to Chapter 16.

Getting the laptop's MAC address

Some wireless networks restrict access only to those computers that have been registered with the gateway. The ID used is the networking hardware's MAC address.

A *MAC address* is a unique number assigned to every networking adapter on Planet Earth, plus a few dozen networking adapters in orbit and on Mars. No two numbers are identical, and the MAC address is very difficult to fake. By using the MAC address, a wireless network can restrict access to only those computers that are known and registered.

To find your laptop's MAC address in Windows 10, follow these humble steps:

1. **Press the Win+I keyboard shortcut.**

    The Settings app appears.

2. **Choose Network & Internet.**

3. **Choose Wi-Fi from the left side of the window.**

4. **On the right side of the window, click the Hardware Properties link.**

   The MAC address is listed among all the trivial information displayed, labeled as Physical Address (MAC).

Provide the MAC address to the network administrator or to whoever is in charge of configuring the router so that your laptop gains access.

>> It should brighten your day to know that MAC stands for Media Access Control.

>> The MAC address is 12 digits long, broken up into pairs, like this:

   12–34–56–78–9A–BC

>> The MAC address is a base 16 value (also called *hexadecimal*), so the letters *A* through *F* are also considered numbers.

TECHNICAL STUFF

Your Laptop, Windows, and the Network

When your laptop becomes part of a network, it can share its resources and access network resources shared by other devices. These resources include storage, printers, file servers, and modems. The network hardware provides the physical connection. The software connection is provided by the Windows operating system.

Setting your laptop's network name

All devices attached to a computer network have their own names, or what the network nerds call *unique identification*. Your laptop is no exception.

To view your laptop's network name, visit the System window, shown in Figure 17-4. It lists the computer name, description, and workgroup, as illustrated in the figure. Display this window on your laptop by following these steps:

1. **Tap the Windows key to pop-up the Start menu.**

2. **Type** system **on the keyboard to search for items named "system."**

3. **Choose the item titled System.**

   This item will be down on the list, named just "System" with no other text.

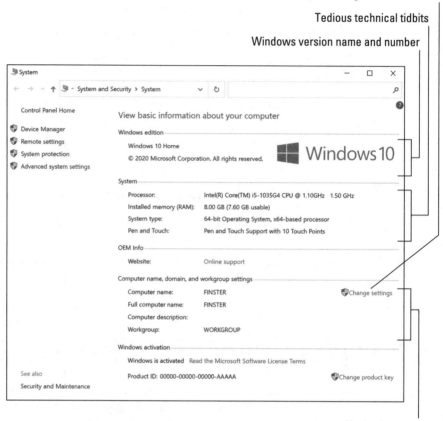

Change network names

Tedious technical tidbits

Windows version name and number

Network names

FIGURE 17-4:
The laptop's
network name.

The quick shortcut to display the System window is to press the Win+Break or Win+Pause keyboard shortcut, though most laptops lack a Break/Pause key.

The information in the System window is important, but not vital to know when operating the laptop. Four items describe your laptop on the network:

Computer Name: The name of the laptop as it appears on the network. Other computers see this name when they view devices on the network.

Full Computer Name: The name given to the laptop when you first set it up. It's probably your name or your company's name. It cannot be changed.

Computer Description: Optional text to describe your laptop or what it does or, if you're feeling saucy, text that's rude and pithy.

Workgroup: The name of the local peer-to-peer network to which your laptop belongs. Because few people bother to change this setting, the name WORKGROUP is used most often.

To set the network names, click the Change Settings link just to the right of where the names are found in the System window (refer to Figure 17-4). Clicking the link displays the System Properties dialog box. You can type a computer description into a text box or click the Change button to change the computer name or workgroup.

REMEMBER

If you elect to change the computer name or workgroup, keep in mind that the changes take place only after you restart the laptop.

Exploring the network

All computers on a private network can see each other. No, they don't look around the room. Instead, each computer can view the other computer's network presence. You can see these computers as well, if the network is private.

To view other computers and shared devices on the Internet, open the Network window. Follow these steps:

1. **Press the Win+E keyboard shortcut.**

   A File Explorer window appears. It opens to Quick Access view, which doesn't show network computers.

2. **Choose Network from the left side of the window.**

   You can also choose Network from the Address bar of any folder window.

The Network window appears, similar to what's shown in Figure 17-5. You see other computers, devices, file servers, printers, and so on. The variety depends on which devices are using the network and whether they've set themselves to be visible to other devices on the network.

To view shared folders on a network computer, double-click to open the computer's icon. You can access files in a shared folder just as though they were on your computer.

Media devices share music, photos, and videos. See Chapter 15 for information on sharing media.

Choose Network to view network devices

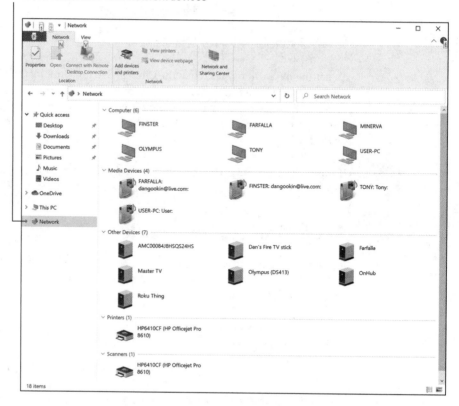

FIGURE 17-5:
Computers
sharing the same
local network.

Network printers are added automatically to your laptop's armada of printing devices. See Chapter 11 for details on printing.

>> Computers that are sleeping or hibernating or that have been turned off do not appear in the Network window.

>> Press the F5 key to refresh the Network window. A refresh is necessary to see any new computers that join the network.

>> Close a network folder when you're done using it. If you forget and don't close the folder, an error message appears when the other computer disconnects from the network or the network goes down.

REMEMBER

>> Seeing computers displayed in the Network window is a sure sign of success that the network is up, connected, and ready for action.

TIP

Checking the sharing status

To share resources between your laptop and the network, you must ensure that file and folder sharing is active. Obey these steps:

1. Press the Win+I keyboard shortcut to bring up the Settings app.

2. Choose Network & Internet.

The Network & Internet part of the Settings app appears, with the Status item chosen on the left side of the window.

3. From the right side of the window, choose Network and Sharing Center.

The ancient Control Panel appears. Marvel at its quaintness.

4. From the left side of the Control Panel window, choose the item Change Advanced Sharing Settings.

The Advanced Sharing Settings screen appears. The current network type is shown with two items visible: Network Discovery and File and Printer Sharing.

5. Ensure that both Network Discover and File and Printer Sharing are on.

Further, ensure that a check mark enables the item Turn On Automatic Setup of Network Connected Devices.

6. Click the Save Changes button to lock in any changes.

And close various open windows when you're done.

With network sharing active, your laptop can access other network resources and share its own resources over the local network.

WARNING

Do not activate sharing for public networks. Sure, it may be a kind gesture to everyone else at the café, but it's an unsafe computing practice.

Sharing a folder

It's possible to make the contents of an individual folder — and all its files and folders — available for others to access on the network. This type of sharing is designed primarily for use on private networks, such as in your home or office; you don't want to share a folder on a public network.

To share a folder with other computers on a private network, follow these steps:

1. **Right-click the folder you want to share.**

   It can be any folder, specifically one in your User Profile area.

2. **Choose the Properties command from the pop-up menu.**

   The folder's Properties dialog box appears.

3. **Click the Sharing tab.**

4. **Click the Advanced Sharing button.**

5. **Place a check mark by the Share This Folder item.**

   The rest of the dialog box lights up, appearing similar to what's shown in Figure 17-6.

   The name that appears in the Share Name text box is the same name that appears when someone clicks your laptop's Computer icon in the Network window.

The folder is shared on the network

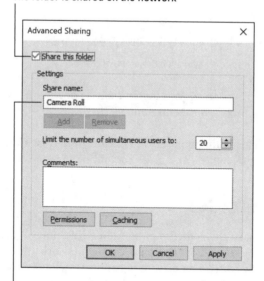

Folder's name as it appears to other network computers

6. **Click the OK button.**

   Ah! But the folder's Properties dialog box is still open.

7. **Click the Close button.**

The folder is now available for others to use on the network. It's set as read-only, meaning others can access files but not change them. (They can copy a file from your laptop's shared folder to their computer and then change it.)

>> To access a shared folder, refer to the section "Exploring the network," earlier in this chapter.

>> To grant full access to a folder, click the Permissions button in the Advanced Sharing dialog box (after Step 5 in this section). In the Permissions dialog box, place a check mark by the Full Control item in the Allow column.

>> To unshare a folder, repeat the steps in this section but remove the check mark in Step 5.

REMEMBER

>> Even on a local network, it's easier to share files by using cloud storage. See Chapter 18.

Chapter **18**

Your Files from Afar

B eing away or remote is what laptop computing is all about. As long as you pack your laptop bag with everything you need, you're all set. Yet though you may have all the hardware you need, you may not find all your files. The secret to a successful laptop adventure is to always have access to the files you need.

Files from Here to There

Oh, pity the poor protonerds from the dark ages of laptop computing. Like you, they desired to share files between computers — for example, to load up work for a trip or synchronize files between desktop and laptop after being on the road. The methods by which these hapless users accomplished the file transfer were crude and barbaric. Therefore, this section should not be read by the timid or by anyone easily upset by ancient technology.

Walking files between computers

The traditional way of moving information from one computer to another is to place the information on some type of removable media and swap the media between the computers. In the dark times before the PC, the media was magnetic or paper tape. Then came floppy disks, optical discs, and eventually media cards and thumb drives.

Because the information was carried from one computer to another, the name *sneakernet* was used to describe this file transfer. You can still use sneakernet today, though it's not the best way to move a file between two computers. It works like this:

1. You save or copy information from a computer to removable media.

2. You walk (in your sneakers) to the other computer.

3. You plug the media into the second computer.

4. You open the media (assuming that the second computer can read it in the first place).

In four steps, that's the process of *sneakernet*, or the physical, human-powered moving of data from one computer to another.

Using octopus net to connect computers

Before the Ethernet networking standard became widely adopted, computer users would use an ugly cable octopus to connect their desktop and laptop computers. Such a cable is shown in Figure 18-1. It would attach to either computer's serial or parallel (printer) ports.

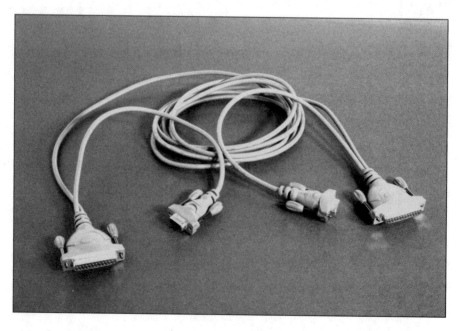

FIGURE 18-1: The ugly cable thing.

After the two computers were connected, special software was used to communicate between the systems and exchange information.

Although the octopus net method was more automatic than sneakernet, the complex hardware setup and software requirements meant that using such a thing was a major pain in the butt.

Quickly transferring files over Ethernet

The simplest way to send files between laptop and desktop is to place them both on the same computer network. After they're configured and connected properly, you can share and access folders on the storage system of both desktop and laptop to easily exchange files.

After the network connection is made, copying files between systems works just like copying files on a single computer — that is, if you've shared the necessary folders (covered in Chapter 17). Even then, you must still manually copy files — and ensure that you always have the most recent version.

Using the Windows Sync Center

For the longest time, Windows came with a utility called the Sync Center. It allowed you to coordinate files in two different locations, such as on a desktop and laptop computer. Updated files were immediately copied, which made the whole "which files to copy" question moot.

As with other methods mentioned in this section, the Sync Center required extra effort to get it to work. You had to deliberately set up and configure which files you wanted to use. If you accidentally modified another file outside of the Sync Center, it again had to be manually copied.

Windows 10 still comes with the Sync Center, but it's hidden deep within the Control Panel. The better solution is to use cloud storage to synchronize files, as covered in the next section.

Cloud Storage Synchronization

The best way to share files between various computers is to use *cloud storage*, which is a fancy term for file storage on the Internet. Any file kept on cloud storage is updated and made available to all computers, phones, tablets, and other devices that can access the Internet. It's a great way to share files between a desktop PC or any computer and your laptop.

Understanding cloud storage

Having nothing to do with atmospheric water vapor, cloud storage is an elegant solution for accessing files from multiple locations and devices. As far as your laptop is concerned, the cloud storage area on your computer looks like any other folder storage.

In Figure 18-2, you see the OneDrive cloud storage folders as they exist in my laptop's User Profile area. OneDrive automatically creates folders for Documents, Music, Pictures, Public, and Video.

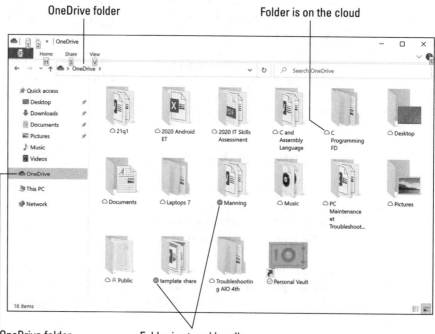

OneDrive folder   Folder is on the cloud

OneDrive folder   Folder is stored locally

FIGURE 18-2:
OneDrive folders
on a laptop.

The folders available in the OneDrive folder are also found on the Internet. To access them, visit onedrive.live.com. Use your Microsoft account to sign in — the same account you use to sign in to Windows.

On the Internet, the same files that appear on your laptop's OneDrive folder appear on a web page, as shown in Figure 18-3. You can view the pictures and videos, and even edit files. More importantly, you can download the files to whichever computer or device you're using.

OneDrive web page address

FIGURE 18-3:
OneDrive folders
on the Internet.

OneDrive folder contents

You can even see the same files on your mobile drives. For example, Android phones and tablets can obtain the OneDrive app to view, access, modify, or manipulate files and folders on cloud storage.

TIP

For expediency's sake, files on OneDrive are stored on the cloud and downloaded as you access them. In Figure 18-2, you see a Cloud icon by folders that are stored on the cloud only. Accessing them is natural — except when the Internet is unavailable. To ensure that the files are permanently stored on your laptop, right-click the file or folder icon and choose the command Always Keep on This Device. Such folders are flagged with a green check mark, as illustrated in Figure 18-2.

REMEMBER

>> Any time a file is added to your cloud storage, it's added everywhere. As long as that Internet access is available, other devices see the new file. With cloud storage, you don't have to synchronize anything; it's done automatically.

>> Another advantage of OneDrive is that it's tied in tightly with Microsoft Office. The backstage feature in Office lets you quickly access documents and projects stored on OneDrive.

Exploring cloud storage options

OneDrive isn't the only form of cloud storage. Its only advantage is that it's tied into your Microsoft account. This preference makes it a good choice, but if you desire more storage or different types of storage, you have plenty of options.

Dropbox: This cloud storage service is one of the originals. One Dropbox feature I enjoy is its capability to instantly share photos taken on a mobile device, which means that pictures from my phone and tablet are instantly uploaded to my laptop. You can obtain Dropbox from dropbox.com. Sign up for an account on that web page, and download the software for your laptop.

Google Drive: If you use Android mobile devices or have a Gmail account, you most likely already have Google Drive cloud storage. It synchronizes well with your phone or tablet and lets you share files from your laptop with those devices. Visit drive.google.com to sign in and download the program for your laptop.

iCloud: If your loyalties lie on the iOS side of the mobile planet, you can obtain a copy of iCloud Drive for your laptop: Visit icloud.com/#iclouddrive and follow the directions to download and install the cloud storage for your laptop.

Once installed, the cloud storage program creates a folder structure in the User Profile area on your laptop's primary storage device (the hard drive or SSD). The folders are created empty, or, if you already use the cloud storage service, they're instantly populated with all your personal files, folders, and whatnot.

>> All cloud storage services offer the same or similar features: a program to coordinate files and folders on your laptop with the Internet, plus apps for accessing files on a mobile device.

>> Cloud storage isn't unlimited. Most providers offer multiple gigabytes at no charge. If you want more, you must subscribe to the service.

Synchronizing cloud storage files

Here's the cinchy part: After you have cloud storage set up on your laptop, synchronizing files is a snap: Copy the files you need to a cloud storage folder.

For example, you create a spreadsheet using the office computer. Save the spreadsheet in your OneDrive storage. In Excel, follow these steps:

1. **Click the File tab.**

2. **Choose Save As on the left side of the window.**

3. **Choose OneDrive — Personal.**

4. **Use the folder structure on the right side of the window to browse to a location to save the spreadsheet.**

If you don't see the list of recent folders, shown in Figure 18-4, use the Save As dialog box to locate the folder.

5. **Type a filename into the Filename box.**

6. **Click the Save button to save your document.**

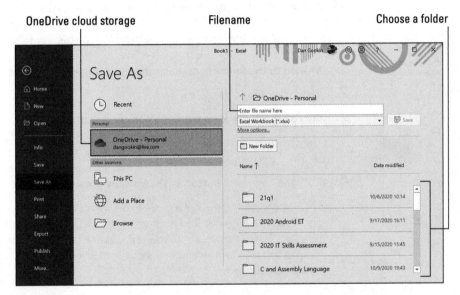

OneDrive cloud storage   Filename   Choose a folder

Because the file is saved on cloud storage, it's synchronized with the Internet. Eventually, all your devices that use cloud storage can access the file.

As an alternative, you can create the file anywhere on your laptop's storage system. To synchronize, copy the file to a cloud storage folder. That's all you need to do! The cloud storage software automatically synchronizes the file.

>> You can use any cloud storage folder on your laptop's storage system, including Google Drive, Dropbox, and others. As long as the file is copied to a cloud storage folder, it's synchronized.

>> The advantage of OneDrive is that it's well-integrated to Microsoft Office. Still, you can browse to your Google Drive or Dropbox folders to synchronize files on those services.

» Although creating a shortcut to a file works on your laptop, shortcuts copied to cloud storage don't work. Always copy the entire file to share it on cloud storage.

Sharing a file from cloud storage

Yet another advantage of cloud storage is that you can share links to your files. These links work like any web page link, allowing you to share a file with someone without having to manually copy the file for them or send it to them as an email attachment. You can even share full folders to more easily collaborate.

To share a file or folder from your OneDrive cloud storage, follow these steps:

1. **Browse to the folder containing the file or folder you want to share.**

2. **Right-click the folder.**

3. **Choose the Share item from the pop-up menu.**

The item features the OneDrive Cloud icon next to the word *share;* this icon is shown in the margin.

4. **Click the Copy Link button at the bottom of the Share window.**

The Share window looks like a mini-email composition window. It works, but only if you've configured the laptop with Windows Mail or some such similar program. Rather than frustrate yourself, click the Copy Link button so that you can paste the link into an email message composed on webmail or whatever email app you use.

When the recipient receives the link, they can click it to visit the document on the web, viewing its contents or even downloading the document to work on it.

You can also share files and folders on the OneDrive web page itself. After visiting onedrive.live.com, click to place a check in the box for the file or folder you want to share. Choose the Share command from the toolbar and click the Copy Link button. With the link copied, you can paste it into another application, email program, social networking post, or what-have-you.

The methods described in this section also apply to other cloud storage sites, with different specific steps, of course.

5

Security and Maintenance

Chapter **19**

Internet Safety

They say that the Internet was designed to withstand a nuclear attack. Yet computer scientists apparently never anticipated antisocial teenage pro-grammers who crave negative attention. If you are to participate in the goodness the Internet offers, you must defend your laptop from imminent peril.

Security Central

Without security, using your laptop on the Internet is like smearing your body with honey and walking through the bear cage at the zoo. Sure, you could get lucky, but why take the risk?

To help you thwart the bad guys, Windows offers a host of security tools. Fortu-nately, these tools aren't all stored in one location, which I suppose would make sense. Then again, often the Windows operating system isn't about making sense.

» A key part of laptop security is a healthy backup regimen. See Chapter 20.

>> Though my bear cage example may be humorous, it's actually quite true. People on the Internet do figuratively smear themselves with honey and walk into a bear cage. Oftentimes, it's their own silly or misadvised decisions that lead to trouble on the Internet. See the nearby sidebar, "The social engineering threat."

Viewing the Action Center

The first location for checking security issues is the Action Center. To view the Action Center in Windows 10, press the Win+A keyboard shortcut to swipe in from the far right edge of the screen.

The Action Center lists items requiring attention, such as updating software or checking the status of a failed backup. At the bottom of the Action Center lie the Quick Settings buttons, which provide shortcuts to common Windows features. Figure 19-1 illustrates the Action Center, though no important messages appear.

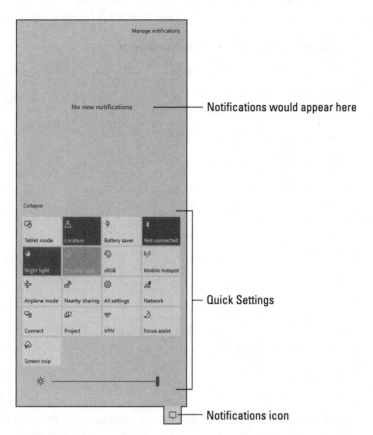

Notifications would appear here

Quick Settings

FIGURE 19-1:
The Action
Center.

Notifications icon

Checking the Windows Security Center

A recent update to Windows 10 moved all security related features to a single location. (Well, almost all the features.) This location is called the Windows Security Center, shown in Figure 19-2.

To access the security center, locate the Windows Security notification icon on the taskbar, as shown in the margin. Click this icon to display the Windows Security Center window. If the notification icon is hidden, click the chevron to the right of the notification area on the taskbar.

Green checkmark means things are good

The tile formerly known as Windows Defender

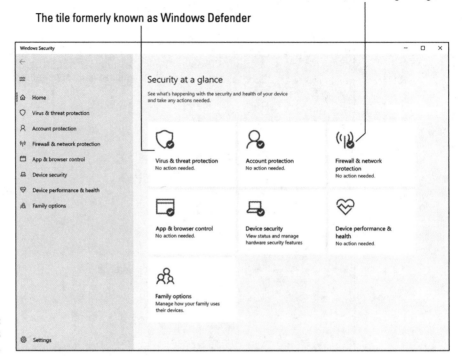

The Windows Security notification icon as well as the items in the Windows Security window feature tiny green check marks when no security issues are present. Otherwise, you see a yellow warning flag on the notification icon as well as on a specific tile in the Windows Security Center window. This yellow flag is your clue that an item needs attention: Click the flagged tile to receive more information and directions on what to do next.

>> Not every warning in the Windows Security Center window is serious. For example, the App & Browser Control item offers issues specific to the Microsoft Edge browser. If you don't use this browser, the issue is of no concern.

>> The other location where you can find security related features is the Settings app, covered elsewhere in this chapter.

TECHNICAL
STUFF

>> The old Windows Defender (antimalware) app is now part of the Windows Security Center, shown as the Virus & Threat Protection tile. In older versions of Windows, Windows Defender was a separate program.

Keep Windows Up-to-Date

One key to your laptop's software security is to ensure that you always have the most current version of Windows. This goal means installing the various updates and patches released by Microsoft to ensure that your laptop's operating system has all the latest security information and can meet any known, current, or looming threats.

Checking the update status

In Windows 10, updates are applied automatically. You can delay a pending update to a more convenient time, though I recommend that you install it after you're alerted — as long as you're not about to board a plane or go somewhere remote. The goal is to install the update when you have both time and an Internet connection.

To check for a pending update, follow these steps:

1. **Press the Win+I keyboard shortcut to summon the Settings app.**

2. **Choose Update & Security.**

   Windows Update should be chosen on the left side of the Settings app window. If not, tap that item.

3. **On the right side of the screen, click the Check for Updates button.**

   You are alerted to any pending updates that haven't already been queued for the day.

If updates are waiting, click the Install button to download and configure them. When critical updates are done installing, you see a Restart button. Click it to complete the process, which takes only a few minutes.

>> Some critical updates are installed automatically, even to the point of restarting the laptop for you. You see this type of automatic restart occur only if you leave your laptop on all the time. Otherwise, all restarts are prompted.

>> You can avoid clicking the Restart button — for a brief time. Eventually, Windows installs the update itself, usually automatically when you restart or shut down the laptop.

Postponing an update

Updates are important, so install them as they appear. Microsoft is understanding, however, especially for a laptop that may need to avoid an update while you're in an area with spotty Internet access or busy working or traveling and you don't want to wait for an update.

To postpone an update, visit the Windows Update screen in the Settings app; refer to Steps 1 and 2 in the preceding section. Choose the item titled Pause Updates for 7 Days. Upon success, you see an urgent-looking Resume button appear, which you click to resume the normal update schedule.

The Malware Scourge

Worry not your weary head over the prospect of nasty programs descending from the Internet and infecting your laptop. That's because Windows comes with an antivirus utility as part of the Windows Security Center. It protects against malware and spyware. It should be active and ready to work on your laptop.

>> The Windows antimalware program is commonly known as Windows Defender. This is its original name, though now it's officially called Virus & Threat Protection.

>> Rather than worry, be cautious. Computer security mustn't be taken lightly, even when using an antimalware program.

>> If Internet security is really, *really* important to you, you can obtain third-party antivirus programs, such as the popular PC security suites from Norton and McAfee. These can be used in addition to the protection offered from Windows.

WARNING

>> Some legitimate antivirus programs are available for free on the Internet. And quite a few illegitimate antivirus programs lurk out there as well, some of which are actual viruses themselves. Therefore, I advise that you either pay for the third-party antivirus software or obtain it from a reputable source.

Doing a virus scan

Windows constantly checks memory and files for signs of malware and other nasty items. You need not do a thing — unless the laptop has been turned off a while and an automatic virus scan hasn't been performed. If so, obey these steps:

1. Pop up the Start menu.

Press the Windows key on the keyboard.

2. Type Windows Security **to see a list of matching search results.**

3. **From the list of matching items, choose the Windows Security Center app.**

4. **Click the Virus & Threat Protection tile.**

   You see the Virus & Threat Protection screen, illustrated in Figure 19-3.

5. **Click the Quick Scan button.**

   Windows performs a quick scan of memory and files to ensure that no infections lurk undetected.

Scan for malware

Review quarantined files

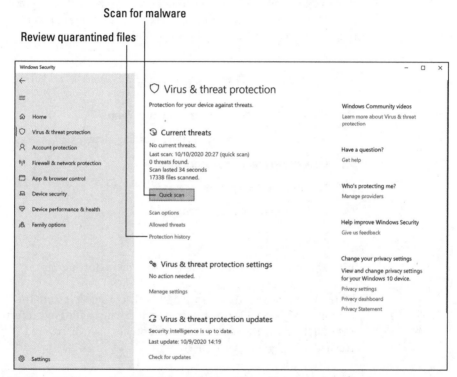

FIGURE 19-3:
Windows Security
Center antivirus.

If a suspicious file is located, it's placed into quarantine. See the later section "Dealing with a quarantined file" for what to do next.

Most other items on the Virus & Threat Protection screen are configured automatically. You can review them at your leisure to understand and appreciate the protection Windows offers. These items include Ransomware Protection, which helps guard against malware that locks your computer with a payment required to unlock it.

>> The malware most likely infected your system due to social engineering. See the sidebar "The social engineering threat," earlier in this chapter.

>> If you remain suspect about an infection yet the virus scan comes up empty, try running the scan again in Safe mode. See Chapter 21 for information about Safe mode.

Dealing with a quarantined file

When Windows antivirus protection locates a suspect file, it places it into quarantine. This placement doesn't delete the file, but it does prevent the malware from doing its nasty deed. It also allows you to rescue falsely accused files from imminent peril.

To review quarantined files, follow these steps:

1. **View the Virus & Threat Protection screen.**

Refer to Steps 1 through 4 in the preceding section.

2. **Click the Protection History link.**

3. **Ensure that Quarantined Items is selected.**

4. **Click the View Details button.**

You see a list of any suspect files.

It's okay to keep the files in the list; they do no further harm.

To rescue an incorrectly identified file, click to select it from the list and then click the Restore button. Please be extra certain that the file isn't infected! Do an Internet search on the filename to see what others have discovered. (That's how I once rescued a wrongly accused file.)

To remove actual infected files, select them in the list and then click the Remove All or Remove button. The infected files are obliterated and shall never harm your laptop.

Behind the Firewall

In the real world, a firewall is a specially constructed part of a building designed to impede the progress of a blazing inferno. The firewall acts as protection for whatever lies on the other side.

On your laptop, a *firewall* keeps nasty things on the Internet from either coming into or escaping out of your laptop. The firewall monitors the Internet's virtual doors, or ports. Each *port* is an individual Internet connection, and at any time your laptop may have dozens of ports in use or available.

When a network program knocks on a port's door, the firewall perks up and confirms that the program has permission to enter or leave. If not, a prompt appears, and you can decide for yourself whether to let the program in or out.

>> The official name of the Windows Firewall utility is Windows Defender Firewall.

>> Without a firewall in place, your computer is wide open to attack from any number of nasties on the Internet.

>> The best firewall is a *hardware* firewall. Most network gateways *(routers)* come with this feature installed and are more than capable of defending your Internet connection, as well as all computers on the local network, from incoming attacks.

>> A firewall cannot protect your computer from a virus. It may prevent the virus from replicating itself on other computers, but it doesn't stop the virus from coming in. You should use *both* antivirus software and a firewall.

Finding the firewall

The Windows Firewall is configured to be on and working all the time. To view the status of the Windows Firewall, obey these steps:

1. **Open the Windows Security Center app.**

Click the Start button on the taskbar and type **Windows Security**. Choose the Windows Security app item from the search results.

2. **Choose Firewall & Network Protection.**

The Windows Firewall window is rather plain. As long as each item shown in the window is On or active and no warnings appear, you're good; Windows Firewall protection is active.

If any options on the Firewall & Network Protection screen are disabled, enable them: Choose the option and set the master control gizmo to the On position.

REMEMBER

>> The key to setting the level of protection offered by Windows Firewall is to properly configure the network to public or private. That configuration takes place when you first connect to the network, which is covered in Chapter 16.

>> For a private network, the firewall is at its lowest setting. On public networks, the firewall is on full-bore.

Dealing with a firewall warning

Windows Firewall lets you know when suspicious Internet access takes place. Because Windows Firewall is paranoid, it flags a warning for Internet activity, both suspicious and suspect.

When Windows Firewall freaks out, a pop-up message appears, similar to the one shown in Figure 19-4. The message alerts you that either a program is attempting to access your computer from the Internet or a program on your computer is trying to access the Internet.

When the warning appears, *read it.* The name of the program is listed. In Figure 19-4, the *Red Dead Redemption 2* game is attempting to connect with the Internet. In this instance, I started the program myself, and it does request Internet access. Therefore, the warning is expected: Click the Allow Access button when you recognize why a program has triggered the firewall warning. Otherwise, click the Cancel button. You're safe.

REMEMBER

>> Take the firewall warning seriously! It's not a panic situation, because nothing bad has happened. Yet! Still, don't let yourself develop the habit of automatically clicking the Allow Access button.

>> It may seem like you see a lot of firewall warnings, especially for a new computer or new network configuration. This bombardment of warnings passes as you choose which programs to allow or deny. After you train Windows Firewall awhile, the firewall alerts appear less frequently.

FIGURE 19-4:
Is it okay for this program to access the Internet?

Safe and Private Browsing

Most web browsers feature tools that are useful for surfing the web without your having to worry whether anyone is snooping on you or trying to pull a fast one. These tools include private or incognito browsing, scanning for phony websites, and other tricks.

Browsing in secret

You can't avoid it. No matter where you go on the Internet, your web browsing history is being tracked. The web page ads record which ads you click. Online shopping sites remember which products you look at. Information from social networking sites targets advertising based on your age, sex, and likes, and even your friends' likes.

This type of snooping is nothing new. It's just a more sophisticated way to gather consumer information than has been previously available. You can avoid being tracked by using a private browsing window.

>> In the Windows 10 Edge browser, the feature is called Browsing InPrivate. To open a new InPrivate window, press Ctrl+Shift+N.

>> If you use the Chrome web browser, open a new Incognito window by pressing Ctrl+Shift+N.

>> Other web browsers feature similar, private windows. My guess is that Ctrl+Shift+N also brings up a secret browsing window in these programs as well.

The new, private browser window offers instructions on how it works. You browse in the window just as you would in a nonprivate window, though no cookies are tracked, cookies aren't remembered, forms aren't automatically filled in, and your website journeys aren't recorded in the browser history.

The good news is that none of your actions in the private window is tracked — supposedly. You can browse without a record being made of where you went or what you did. Even so, some websites and advertising links monitor your laptop's IP address, which is another way to track your activity.

End your private browsing session by closing the private window.

Purging your web browsing history

The web browser dutifully keeps track of every web page you've visited. The information is stored as your web browsing history. You can use the history to revisit web pages, create bookmarks, or see what your lying, cheating partner has been doing recently.

When you forget to use a private browsing window, you can review and purge the web page history. If you're using Windows 10 and the Edge web browser, follow these steps:

1. **Press the keyboard shortcut Ctrl+Shift+Del, where Del is the Delete key on the laptop's keyboard.**

   The Clear Browsing Data panel appears. It's chock-full of items that are recorded as you visit websites.

2. **Ensure that the Browsing History item is selected.**

   It's the only option you should zap; choose other items in the window at your own peril.

3. **Click the Clear Now button.**

   History is gone and doomed to be repeated!

In the Chrome web browser, follow these steps to purge historical information:

1. **Click the address box and type** chrome://history.

   Do not type a period after the word *history*.

2. **Press Enter to view the Chrome History screen.**

3. **Click the check box by those web page items you want to purge.**

4. **Click the Delete button.**

   They're gone.

REMEMBER

To prevent the web browser from tracking your web page visits, you can use a private browsing window. See the preceding section.

Location Information

One feature popular in cell phones and tablets is the GPS radio. The radio uses global positioning system (GPS) satellites to discover its current location on Planet Earth. Laptops lack GPS radios (though this feature may arrive soon), but its absence doesn't stop Windows from offering location services, similar to a mobile device.

Even though Windows recognizes that your laptop lacks a GPS radio, it can still guess your location and share that information with a variety of apps, place it on a photo, or share it with the Internet. If, like many mobile device users, you consider this type of sharing a security risk, I recommend that you disable Windows 10 location features. Follow these steps:

1. **Press Win+I to summon the Settings app.**

2. **Choose Privacy.**

3. **Choose Location from the left side of the window.**

4. **Click the Change button.**

   A teensy pop-up window appears with a single toggle switch.

5. **Set the master control to the Off position.**

6. **Click outside the teensy pop-up window to dismiss it.**

If you'd rather not disable all location information, you can select which apps or programs have access. At the bottom of the Location screen you find a list of apps that have requested to access the laptop's location information. Set the master control by each app, on or off, to enable or disable the app from accessing location information.

General Security Settings

The Privacy screen in the Settings app is festooned with settings that affect you, what you do on your laptop, and how that information is shared with other entities. For example, did you know that Microsoft tracks what you do, type, or even say to your laptop and makes that information available to advertisers?

Yeah, that sucks.

I recommend shutting off many of the preset privacy options in the Settings app. Open the Settings app and choose Privacy. Peruse the following items as listed on the left side of the window:

General: Disable every item: advertising, websites, app launchers and so on. Many security experts have termed the features displayed on the General screen as spyware, pure and simple. Microsoft has no business knowing what you do on your laptop.

Location: See the preceding section.

Camera: Leave the master toggle on, but peruse the list of individual apps that desire camera access. Turn off an app if you don't recognize why it would use the laptop's camera. For example, Skype obviously uses the camera, so leave this app on. When in doubt, disable an app's access to the camera.

Microphone: Follow the same rules on this screen as for the Camera screen. If an app such as Skype needs to use the laptop's microphone, set its toggle to Yes. Otherwise, set the toggle to No.

Speech: If you don't use Cortana, disable speech recognition. Even if you use Cortana, consider disabling this feature, which implies that the laptop's microphone is always on and listening to — and recording — what you say.

Activity History: No one needs to know what you do with your laptop. Disable this feature: Uncheck all the boxes.

Other items on the Settings app's Privacy screen also deal with items you may consider, well, private. My observation is that giving apps access to some information, such as contacts or calendar appointments, is okay. But if you find such information-sharing to be insecure, disable the item.

Chapter **20**

A More Secure Laptop

The convenience of portability leads to a common problem with laptop computers: theft. Portable things get stolen. It's easier to purloin a battery-operated drill gun than it is a standing drill press. Someone may steal a miniature Eiffel Tower from a souvenir shop, but the real thing is too big to swipe. And the French would notice.

Thieves are out for your laptop. You need to protect the device itself, protect your data, and try to get the thing back should it ever be liberated by one of society's lesser individuals.

The Hot Laptop

Sure, your laptop can get hot. Managing heat is one of the laptop hardware's primary duties. This section's title does not, however, deal with that kind of "hot." No, the topic here is hot as in stolen, pilfered, purloined. Bad Guys out there want your laptop more than you do. The lighter and more portable, the better.

Well, the Bad Guys don't want to use your laptop. They want to steal it and sell it for drug money. Some Bad Guys want the data inside your laptop, stored on the mass storage system. They want to access your data, look for passwords, and get into your online banking and investments.

The Bad Guys get what they want, mostly because the typical laptop owner doesn't think like a thief. In addition to being handsome, laptop users are a rather trusting lot. That trust is, sadly, what makes laptops easy to steal in the first place.

First, the good news: Most laptops are forgotten and not stolen. As silly as it sounds, people leave their expensive laptops sitting around unattended more often than someone sneaks off with them. Don't let that trivial tidbit lull you into a false sense of security; many laptops are stolen right out from under the eyes of their owners.

TIP

Think of the laptop as a sack of cash sitting around. To a crook, that's exactly what it is. Treat the laptop as a bag full o' money, and chances are good that you'll never forget it or have it stolen.

The best way to protect your laptop is to label it. Specific instructions are offered later in this chapter. Keep in mind this statistic: Ninety-seven percent of unmarked computers are never recovered. Mark your laptop.

Other interesting and potentially troublesome statistics:

>> The chance of your laptop being stolen is 1 in 10.

>> Most laptop theft occurs in the office. That includes both coworkers and Well-Dressed Intruders, or thieves in business suits.

>> Laptop theft on college campuses (from dorm rooms) is up 37 percent.

>> A thief who steals a $1,000 laptop typically gets about $50 for it on the street.

>> According to law enforcement, 90 percent of laptop thefts are easily avoidable by using common sense.

Before Your Laptop Is Stolen

Any law enforcement official will tell you that taking a few extra steps of caution can avoid a disastrous theft. Like any shopper, a thief enjoys convenience: If your laptop is more difficult to pinch than the next guy's, it's the next guy who loses.

Marking your laptop

You can help in the recovery of a stolen laptop if you mark your laptop. I recommend either engraving it or affixing to it a tamper-resistant asset tag. After all, the best proof that something is yours is your name on the item in question.

>> You can use an engraving tool to literally carve your name and contact information on your laptop.

>> I know some folks who are clever and merely write their names inside their laptops, either on the back of a removable door, inside the kick stand, in the battery compartment, or in other places a thief wouldn't check. Use a Sharpie or another indelible marker.

>> Asset tags are available from most print shops. The tags peel and stick like any stickers do, but cannot be easily removed or damaged. For an investment of about $100, you can buy a few hundred custom tags, for not only your computers but also other valuable items (cameras, mobile devices, bicycles, and TVs, for example).

TIP

>> The STOP program offers a bar code asset tag that leaves a special tattoo if it's removed. The program also offers a recovery system that automatically returns stolen (or lost) property directly to your door. STOP stands for Security Tracking of *Office* Property, although home users and (especially) college students can take advantage of the service. Visit www.stoptheft.com for more information.

Registering the laptop and its software

Be sure to register your laptop; send in the registration card or register online. Do the same for any software you're using. If the laptop is then stolen, alert the manufacturer and software vendors. If someone using your stolen laptop ever tries to get the system fixed or upgraded, the company cares enough (you hope) to help you locate the purloined laptop.

REMEMBER

Keep with you a copy of the laptop's serial number and other vital statistics — specifically, in a place other than in the laptop's carrying case. That way, you know which number to report to the police as well as to the manufacturer.

Paying attention to your environment

They say that a gambling casino is a purse snatcher's paradise. That's because most individuals with purses (okay, women) are too wrapped up in gambling to notice that their property is being pilfered. The purses can be on the floor, at their feet, or even in their laps. Thieves know the power of distraction.

When you're out and about with your laptop, you must always pay attention to where it is and who could have access to it. Watch your laptop!

For example, when you're dining out, put the laptop in its case beneath the table. If you need to leave the table, either take the laptop with you or ask your friends to keep an eye on it for you.

Take your laptop with you when you leave to talk on your cell phone. And, yes, you are leaving the restaurant dining area to talk on your phone, thank you.

WARNING

Be especially mindful of distractions! A commotion in front of you means that the thief about to take your laptop is behind you. A commotion behind you means that the thief is in front of you. Thieves work in pairs or groups this way, using the commotion to distract you while your stuff is being stolen.

Pay special attention at the airport screening station. Just one raised voice or "the woman in the red dress" can divert your attention long enough for your laptop to disappear. Also be aware of distractions on crowded escalators, where the movement of the crowd can knock you down and someone can easily grab your laptop bag and take off.

Attaching the old ball-and-chain

Chapter 6 takes you on a tour around your laptop's external places, pieces, and parts. One thing I point out over there is the place for the old ball-and-chain: a hole or slot into which you can connect a security cable. That hole has an official name: the *Universal Security Slot,* or *USS.*

The USS is designed to be part of the laptop's case. Any cable or security device that is threaded through the USS cannot be removed from the laptop; the cable itself must be cut (or unlocked) to free the laptop.

Obviously, the USS works best when the laptop is in a stationary place. Like using a bicycle lock, you have to park the laptop by something big and stable and then thread the cable through that big thing and the USS for the lock to work.

>> The best place to find a security cable for your laptop is in a computer store or office supply store.

>> Some cables come with alarms. You can find alarms that sound when the cable is cut, plus alarms that sound when the laptop is moved.

Protect Your Data with a Strong Password

Passwords protect only your laptop's data, not the laptop itself. Most thieves are looking to make a quick buck; generally, for drugs. They don't care about the contents of your laptop — they just want the cash it brings. But a data thief wants more.

Data thieves feast on information. They want your passwords. They want credit card numbers, which are valuable to sell. Furthermore, they can use your own computer to order stuff on the Internet or to make transfers from your online bank account to their own.

A *strong password* is long. It contains letters, numbers, and symbols. The letters must be in different cases. Yes, it's a pain in the rear to type, though it's possible to be clever. For example, consider a password as a collection of two or more regular words with a symbol separating the words.

Windows lacks a ready trick for revealing your account's current password. To change the password, follow these steps:

1. **Click the Start button.**

2. **Click your account picture at the top of the Start button menu.**

3. **Choose the Change Account Settings option.**

   The Settings app opens to the Accounts screen.

4. **On the left side of the window, choose Sign-In Options.**

5. **Choose Password and click the Change button.**

6. **Confirm your current password, and then click the Sign In or Next button.**

   If your laptop is protected with a PIN, you're prompted to type the PIN for security reasons.

7. **Type the same password twice, once in each box.**

   You type the password twice to ensure that *you* know the password.

8. **Type a password hint into the Password Hint box.**

   Hint: The password hint should not be the same as your password. Just a hint.

9. **Click the Next button and then the Finish button.**

   The new password is applied and used the next time you sign in to Windows.

I recommend that you immediately sign out of Windows and sign in again, just to get used to the password thing.

>> If you use a Microsoft (email) account to sign in to Windows, changing the password changes it for all your Microsoft services in addition to the laptop. These services include OneDrive, Microsoft 365, Skype, and so on.

>> Computer security nabobs say that you should change your password every few months or so, and more often in high-security areas. In fact, if you use your laptop with a corporate account, you'll probably be pestered to change your password on a regular schedule.

WARNING

>> If you forget your password, you're screwed. It's possible to recover Windows, but all your account information may be utterly lost and not retrievable. Keep this warning in mind when you're choosing a password.

TIP

>> When you have trouble remembering your password, write it down! Just don't keep the password list near your computer. I know folks who write their passwords on their kitchen calendars or in their recipe books. Random words and numbers there may not mean anything to a casual onlooker, but they're helpful when you forget the password.

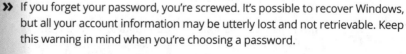

SILLY PASSWORDS

Data thieves steal passwords all the time and what they find isn't interesting. That's because people tend to use the same passwords over and over — and simple, predictable passwords as well.

After an online database was hacked, security experts examined the stolen data. What they discovered was that far too many people were using insecure passwords. In fact, most of the passwords were downright silly.

Here's a sampling of real passwords used by folks who should know better — no matter what, never use any of these passwords!

- 111111
- 1234567
- 2000
- 654321
- 696969

- abc123

- baseball

- dragon

- football

- iloveyou

- letmein

- master

- monkey

- mustang

- passw0rd

- password

- qwerty

- rockyou

- shadow

- sunshine

- superman

- trustno1

Back Up Your Data

If you ever lose your laptop, you lose not only the hardware but also all the stuff on your laptop. The best way to keep that stuff is to back it up; create a safety copy of all your data, files, videos, music, pictures, and so on. This safety copy is what backup is all about.

Multiple ways are available for you to keep a backup copy of your laptop's files. For example, any file you save on cloud storage is automatically backed up, as described in Chapter 18. For other files, called *local* files, you can use Windows to create a backup copy — providing that your laptop has external storage or access to external storage on the local network.

>> The Windows 10 backup program is called File History.

>> Internet backup services are available to help you with the backup chores. These may work better than the Windows 10 File History feature in that you use the Internet and cloud storage — not an external hard drive — to store the backup files.

Preparing for backup

To make a backup operation work, you need two things: one hardware and the other software.

The hardware thing is backup storage. You can use a portable hard drive, one that merely connects to the laptop by using a USB cable — no power cord. Or you can use storage on a network.

The software thing is supplied by Windows. The File History utility keeps track of your data, ensuring that historical copies are available for rescue, just in case.

>> Inexpensive, high-capacity, portable hard drives exist in abundance. If you find one, ensure that it runs from USB power; that the device doesn't require batteries or an external power source.

>> Network backup is fine, as long as your laptop is connected to a local network that offers such storage. For example, you may have a hard drive plugged directly into the network's router (gateway). Obviously, this storage isn't available while you're on the road. That's okay: The File History utility bothers you when it's away from the mothership, but it instantly connects upon your return and starts backing up right away.

>> See Chapter 12 for information on attaching and removing external storage.

Configuring File History

Unlike other, less useful Windows 10 features, the File History utility isn't activated automatically. You must deliberately set up and configure the tool, and I recommend doing so as soon as possible because disaster strikes like an empty room with only a lamp and a cat.

To get running with File History, follow these steps:

1. **Connect the portable, external hard drive to your laptop, if you haven't already. Or, ensure that network storage is available.**

The external hard drive is the easy option. To configure external network storage, you must ensure that the laptop has full access to the storage. This setup involves the proper permission to access the network storage and assigning the storage to a drive letter on your laptop. See the later sidebar "All that network backup stuff he wrote about in Step 1."

2. **Open the Settings app.**

3. **Choose Update & Security.**

4. **On the left side of the window, choose Backup.**

If you see a setting that says Automatically Back Up My Files, you're all set. Ensure that the toggle is set to the On position. You're done. Otherwise, continue:

5. **Click the Add a Drive button.**

Windows prowls for suitable locations, such as an external hard drive or network drive. The results are displayed in a list.

If no drives appear, you failed Step 1. Either the external drive is unavailable or the network lacks shared resources. Try again.

6. **Choose a drive.**

Click to select one of the choices.

After you choose a location, Windows activates the File History feature. At that point, your interaction stops. Continue reading in the next section.

>> You can confirm that File History is working: Follow Steps 1 through 4 in this section. Ensure that the toggle is set to the On position.

>> File History duplicates copies of your files to the storage location chosen in Step 6. This process takes place automatically, anytime your laptop is on. In fact:

>> Generally speaking, File History works on all your files and folders stored in the laptop's User Profile area. Program files and Windows are not backed up. That's why I recommend keeping copies of your program installation discs or downloaded installation files. See Chapter 8.

>> If you leave your laptop off for a while or you disconnect from the File History storage device, you're reminded by a notification to reconnect and keep File History up-to-date.

TIP

>> If you find your laptop unable to do hourly backups, set the schedule for a daily backup. This way, you won't be hounded on the road with incessant reminders to attach the backup drive.

ALL THAT NETWORK BACKUP STUFF HE WROTE ABOUT IN STEP 1

If you're one of the brave souls who uses network storage as online backup, well, may you be blessed. That is, blessed with a teenager or computer-knowledgeable friend who will help you configure things. The goal is to assign that storage to a drive letter on your laptop's storage system.

For your first attempt, open the This PC window: Press Win+E and choose This PC from the items listed on the left side of the screen. On that window, click the Computer tab and choose the Map Network Drive command button. Choose the Map Network Drive command from the menu. Use the Map Network Drive dialog box to choose a drive letter, and then browse for the server and folder for the network storage.

When you click the Browse button, you see available storage devices on the network. Click one to view shared folders. Choose the network folder for your laptop to use as backup storage.

Ensure that the folder is reconnected when you restart your laptop: Place a check mark in the box labeled Reconnect at Sign-In. Click the Finish button.

Upon success, you see the network drive appear in the This PC window, along with its assigned drive letter.

Checking the backup schedule

The File History feature works automatically, but if you're like me you probably don't trust computers any farther than you can throw them. To confirm that File History is up and running, follow these steps:

1. **Open the Settings app.**

   Press the Win+I keyboard shortcut.

2. **Choose Update & Security.**

3. **From the left side of the window, choose Backup.**

   The Back Up Using File History screen appears on the right side of the window.

4. **Click the More Options link.**

   The Backup Options screen appears, similar to the one shown in Figure 20-1.

Backup schedule

Backup info

FIGURE 20-1:
Checking File
History settings.

5. **Confirm the backup location.**

   You can check to ensure that the proper device is chosen. In Figure 20-1, the external drive Seagate Portable Drive is chosen. It has a capacity of 931GB, and the backup set is using only 5.30GB of storage. That's good.

6. **Confirm the backup schedule.**

   The standard setting is every hour, as shown in Figure 20-1.

If you need to back up right away, click the Back Up Now button. Windows culls through your files and copies the newer ones to backup storage. You can do this before you leave, for example, to ensure that the backup drive is up-to-date.

In Figure 20-1, you don't see the list of folders that Windows File History backs up. Scroll down the window to peruse those folders. You can add folders to the list by clicking the Add a Folder button. Or you can remove folders by choosing a folder's tile and then clicking the Remove button.

Restoring an older version

One of the great features of File History is that you can restore an older version of a file. Say you overwrite a file or you update it with a newer version, but you really need the older version. To recover an older version of a file, follow these steps:

1. **Locate the file you want to recover.**

   Open the file's folder.

   If the file has been deleted, you can try to restore it from the Recycle Bin. If it's not found there, you need to restore from a backup copy, as described in the next section.

2. **Right-click the File icon.**

3. **Choose the Restore Previous Versions option.**

   You see the file's Properties dialog box, with the Previous Versions tab forward. Shown in a list are previous versions of the file — its history. These versions have been saved and can be recovered — similar to what's shown in Figure 20-2.

   If you see no previous versions listed, the file is too new and hasn't yet been backed up. Also, files you moved from other locations may not show a history.

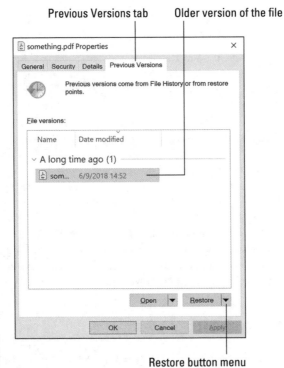

Previous Versions tab   Older version of the file

Restore button menu

FIGURE 20-2: Previous versions of a file.

4. **Click to select a previous version shown in the dialog box.**

Usually, the one you want is atop the list.

5. **Click the Restore button menu and choose Restore To.**

The menu is the triangle next to the button, shown in Figure 20-2.

6. **Use the Restore To dialog box to find a location for the restored file.**

Choose another folder than the one shown in the Restore To dialog box. If you don't, Windows can only overwrite the existing file. If that's what you want — great; otherwise:

7. **Click the Select Folder to set the new folder and save the restored file.**

If you merely desire that the restored version replace the existing version, click the Restore button in Step 6 and then choose the option to replace the existing file. The old file is restored.

Restoring more than a single file

Unlike more traditional file backup programs, the Windows 10 File History feature lacks a Restore mode. Its absence doesn't imply that you can't restore great swaths of missing files. You can! You just need to know where to look.

Follow these steps to restore more than a single file:

1. **Tap the Windows key on the keyboard.**

Up pops the start menu.

2. **Type** File History **to show a list of matching results.**

3. **From the search results, choose the item Restore Your Files with File History.**

The File History window appears, looking similar to Figure 20-3. This window is where you can select individual files or complete folders to restore from the File History backup.

4. **Choose a date.**

Tap the Rewind icon (refer to Figure 20-3) to page through older backups. The backup date and time appear atop the window, as illustrated in Figure 20-3.

5. **Choose a folder or file to restore.**

If you don't see the folder or file, open a folder on the screen. For example, double-click the Document's folder to view its contents. You can page back and forth to find the exact file you want.

File History backup date and time   Selected folder

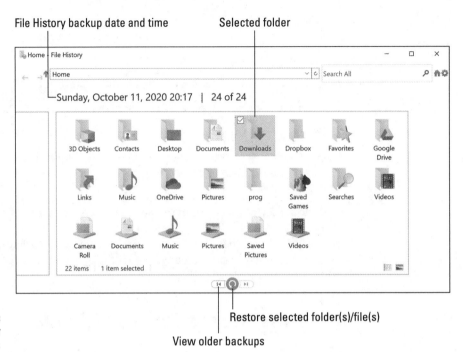

FIGURE 20-3:
The File History
window.

Restore selected folder(s)/file(s)

View older backups

6. **Click the Restore button.**

7. **Choose how to restore the file, if prompted.**

   You have three options:

   • *Replace the File in the Destination:* Choose this option if you want to overwrite any existing file or folder with the older copy.

   • *Skip This File:* Choose this option to ignore the operation and keep your existing file or folder as is.

   • *Compare Info for Both Files:* Choose this option to examine more details about the newer file that you're replacing with a backup.

   You're prompted for each file you restore if another file with the same name already exists.

8. **Close the various File History windows when you're done restoring files.**

REMEMBER

The File History restore procedure works only when you keep a backup drive attached to your laptop and you've enabled the File History feature, as described earlier in this chapter.

The Laptop Reset

The ultimate form of laptop security is to erase everything on your laptop, effectively returning it to the same (or similar) state when it first popped out of the box to greet you. I call this process the *factory data reset*, and it's a pretty drastic security step.

About the only time you'll want to perform a factory reset is when you sell or dispose of your laptop. The process erases all your files and restores the laptop to a bare minimum machine. Obviously, this isn't a task to be taken lightly, nor is it considered routine.

When it's time to reset your laptop, follow these steps:

1. **Open the Settings app.**

   Press the Win+I keyboard shortcut.

2. **Choose Update & Security.**

3. **On the left side of the window, choose Recovery.**

4. **On the right side of the window, below the Reset This PC heading, click the Get Started button.**

   An ominous window appears. Two options are available:

   Keep My Files: Apps are removed and programs uninstalled, but choosing this option doesn't erase your files. Windows settings are reset to the factory default.

   Remove Everything: Apps, programs, and all your data are removed from the laptop when you choose this option. Windows 10 remains, but in its raw, as-yet-to-be-configured state.

5. **Choose an option — and be careful.**

   You eventually see a Reset button and confirmation. Even so, do not choose any option casually!

WARNING

My advice is to choose an option only when you must do so. I don't know what happens after you click an option, because it appears to me that Windows plows ahead and does whatever deed you requested — with no confirmation!

TECHNICAL STUFF

>> If you're having laptop lamentations, read Chapter 21, on troubleshooting. That's where to look for fixing laptop issues and solving problems.

>> A third reset option may appear if you've upgraded from an older version of Windows. This option, Restore Factory Settings, restores the previously installed version of Windows.

Chapter **21**

Laptop Troubleshooting

There is one thing, and only one thing, that causes trouble in any computer: *change.* The change consists of new hardware, new software, or a setting or configuration you've just made. Of course, not all change causes a computer to go bonkers, but chances are good that when you have trouble, it was preceded by some kind of change.

Computer troubleshooting generally involves discovering what has changed in your computer. Oh, and there are random acts of God as well. Regardless, this chapter helps you to hunt down the change, fix the trouble, and get your laptop back up and running in working order.

REMEMBER

» Creating documents, moving files you've created, renaming files, or organizing files into folders doesn't generally cause trouble — as long as you're only messing with files you've created.

» Changing or modifying programs or parts of Windows is what can lead to trouble.

The Universal Quick-Fix

Before dropping into that deep pit of high-tech despair, you should try one thing first: Restart your laptop. Oftentimes, restarting the laptop unclogs the drain and allows your computer to work properly again. If there were a "take two aspirin and call me in the morning" laptop fix, restarting the laptop would be it.

Restarting the laptop

Follow these steps to restart your laptop:

1. **Ensure that you've saved your documents and closed your programs.**

   If you don't save you documents, you're prompted to do so after Step 4.

2. **Click the Start button.**

3. **Choose Power.**

4. **Choose Restart.**

   Windows closes open programs and shuts down its processes and services. After that's done, the laptop starts up again.

If Windows gets stuck on the restart, press and hold the power button. Eventually, the laptop turns itself off. Start the laptop again after it's been off a few seconds.

Signing out of Windows

Sometimes the problem doesn't require a full restart. A good thing to try before restarting is to sign out of Windows. This solution works well when you know it's a program you're running that's causing woe — for example, if it keeps reporting a file as "busy."

To sign out of Windows, follow these steps:

1. **Try to save your documents and close your programs.**

   Obviously, if one program is causing you distress, you won't be able to shut it down.

2. **Click the Start button.**

3. **Click your account button and name at the top of the Start button menu.**

NO, YOU DON'T NEED TO REINSTALL WINDOWS

Industry-wide, the average call for tech support is less than 12 minutes. When the call reaches 10 minutes, tech support people are often advised to end the call. One way they do that is simply to say that you need to reinstall the Windows operating system to fix your problem. Does this advice fix your problem? That's not the issue. It fixes *their* problem, which is to get you off the phone.

I've been troubleshooting and fixing computers for years. Only a handful of times has reinstalling Windows been necessary to fix a problem — and that's usually because the user deleted parts of the Windows operating system, either accidentally or because of a virus or another computer disaster. Beyond that, with patience and knowledge, any computer problem can be solved without replanting the operating system.

Reinstalling Windows is like rebuilding your home's foundation when all you need to do is fix a leaky faucet. When someone tells you to reinstall Windows, run. No, better: Scream and then run. Try to find another source of help. ***Remember:*** Only in drastic situations is reinstalling Windows necessary. If you can find someone knowledgeable and helpful enough, he can assist you without having to reinstall Windows.

4. **Choose Sign Out.**

Any programs you've opened are shut down and you're prompted to save any unsaved documents, in case you merrily skipped over Step 1.

5. **When you see the sign-in screen again, sign back in to Windows.**

Upon your return, things should be normal.

When you sign out, you're directing Windows to shut down only the programs you use. If one of them has run amok, signing out shuts down that program and solves the problem. Simply sign in again and things should be fine. If not, restart the laptop as described in the preceding section.

The Windows Troubleshooter

Windows comes with a troubleshooter tool. Thank you, Microsoft! You can use the tool to work through various laptop issues and resolve problems, assuming that the laptop is in good enough condition that the Troubleshooter is capable of doing its job.

To run the Troubleshooter, follow these steps:

1. Pop up the Start menu.

Press the Windows key on the keyboard.

2. Type troubleshoot settings **or just enough to see the Troubleshoot Settings System Settings item appear in the search results list.**

3. Choose the item Troubleshoot Settings System Settings.

The Settings app opens to the Troubleshoot screen, shown in Figure 21-1.

Recommended troubleshooting

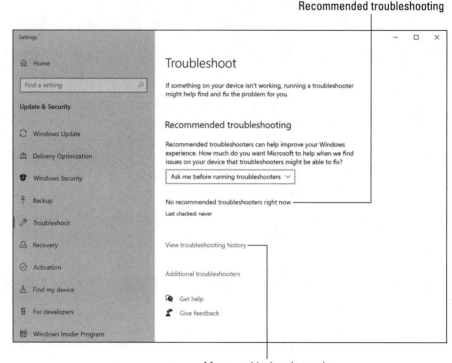

FIGURE 21-1: The Windows Troubleshooter.

More troubleshooting tools

Any recommended troubleshooting appears on the screen, though in Figure 21-1, things look good. Choose the Additional Troubleshooters link to peruse how Windows can help you resolve specific issues related to the Internet, audio, printer, and Windows Update service.

Restore the System

Windows offers two ways you can unwind the Windows update clock. The first is a rollback feature that lets you repeal a recent Windows update. The second is the traditional System Restore command, which is a bit broader in scope. Both of these tools work to restore the system, perhaps to an earlier time when things were working better.

Also see Chapter 20 for details on resetting your laptop. The reset procedure is normally done when you sell or give away the laptop. It can also be used when the system is so dreadfully dodgy that only starting over fixes a problem.

Doing a system restore

Windows employs a program named System Restore, which can be used to rescue Windows or even a specific program after a software upgrade or configuration change. It works by restoring Windows to an earlier point, back before the trouble started.

System Restore regularly sets *restore points*, especially before installing new software or updating Windows. It handles this job for you. Your job is to use System Restore when you need to recover from a weird or unusual event. To do so, follow these steps:

1. **Save your work and close all open programs.**

   The System Restore process eventually restarts your laptop, so be prepared and save now!

2. **Pop up the Start menu.**

   Tap the Windows key on the keyboard.

3. **Type** System Restore.

4. **Choose the item Create a Restore Point Control Panel.**

   The System Properties dialog box appears, with the System Protection tab forward.

5. **Click the System Restore button.**

   If this button isn't available, click the Configure button. In the dialog box that appears, choose the option Turn On System Protection.

   If the System Restore button is available, you see the System Restore Wizard. A recommended restore point is set based on the most recent activities in Windows.

6. **Click the Next button.**

The final screen describes what's about to happen: The laptop restarts, and the System Restore utility recovers Windows to an earlier point in time.

7. **Click the Finish button.**

The system restarts.

When the laptop starts up again, System Restore isn't quite complete. Go ahead and sign in, but wait until you see the confirmation message that the system has been restored. At this point, you can check to see whether the issue has been resolved.

>> If the issue hasn't been resolved, try running System Restore again, but choose an earlier restore point (after Step 5).

>> System Restore doesn't delete any new files you created. It affects only the operating system and installed software.

>> System Restore lets you reset the system to only a few days or so earlier. Attempts to use a restore point older than a week earlier generally don't meet well with success.

TIP

>> System Restore is a great way to return some of your personalized settings — desktop background, screen saver, window colors — when things get fouled up. I get email all the time from readers whose grandkids or other annoying relatives have screwed up their computer settings. System Restore is the solution.

>> You also have an emergency start-up System Restore option. You may see a text menu when the laptop restarts, identifying a potential problem. If so, choose the option Last Known Good Configuration or whichever option allows for a System Restore operation.

Restoring the previous version of Windows

If the latest version of Windows dislikes your laptop, you can reverse and reinstall an older version — before the recent Windows update. Be aware that these steps don't work if you've installed other user accounts on the laptop; remove those accounts before you follow these steps:

1. **Connect the laptop to a power source.**

You're asked to perform this step if you forget, so do it now.

2. **Press the Win+I keyboard shortcut to bring up the Settings app.**

3. **Choose Update & Security.**

4. **On the left side of the window, choose Recovery.**

5. **Below the heading Go Back to the Previous Version of Windows 10, click the Get Started button.**

6. **Continue following the onscreen directions.**

Eventually, the older version of Windows is restored. If this fix works, consider contacting your laptop's manufacturer or browsing their support website to see if others have a similar problem. Perhaps a solution is offered that may save you from having to take such a drastic step.

Common Problems and Solutions

It would be nearly impossible for me to mention every dang doodle problem your laptop can experience. So, rather than list every dang doodle one of them, or 1,000 or even 100, I've narrowed the list to 5.

"The keyboard is wacky!"

Keyboard problems happen more often than you would imagine, based on the email I receive. The solution is generally simple: You accidentally press the Num Lock key on the laptop's keyboard, and half the alphabet keys on your keyboard start acting like numbers.

The solution is to press the Num Lock key and restore your laptop's keyboard to full alphabetic operation.

Touchpad touchiness

Some laptop touchpads seem to operate merely by looking at them. I call them touchy touchpads. Rather than be frustrated, simply adjust the touchpad's sensitivity. Follow these steps:

1. **Pop up the Start menu.**

   Press the Windows key on the keyboard.

2. **Type** touchpad **and choose the item Touchpad Settings from the search results.**

   In the Settings app, review the settings available for the touchpad to see what you can adjust.

For example, you can change the cursor speed, adjust the touchpad sensitivity, and set optional features. To adjust sensitivity, use the Touchpad Sensitivity menu and choose an option that works best for you from low sensitivity to most sensitive.

"My laptop won't wake up"

A snoozing laptop can mean that the battery is dead. Consider plugging in the laptop and trying to turn it on. You may have to wait, because some laptops won't start unless the battery reaches a minimum charge.

When the laptop has trouble waking from Sleep mode — and you must turn it off and then turn it on again to regain control — you have a problem with the power management system in your laptop. See the next section.

Power management woes

When your laptop suddenly loses its capability to sleep or to enter Hibernate mode, it means that you might have a problem with its power management hardware or software.

First, check your laptop manufacturer's web page to see whether you can find additional information or software updates.

Second, ensure that power management is properly enabled, as described in Chapter 10.

Finally, confirm that other hardware or software isn't interfering with the power management software. If so, remove the interfering software or hardware or check for updates that don't mess with your laptop's power management system. A good trick to try is System Restore, just in case a recent update messed with the laptop's power management software. See the section "Doing a system restore," earlier in this chapter.

"The battery won't charge"

Batteries die. Even the modern smart batteries are good for only so long. When your battery goes, replace it with a new one — if you can. Most modern laptops, especially the 2-in-1 tablet PCs, do not sport removable batteries. In this case, you must replace the laptop.

Rules and laws govern the disposal of batteries. Be sure to follow the proper procedure for your community to safely dispose of or recycle batteries.

REMEMBER

Chapter **22**

Laptop Maintenance and Upgrading

The desktop PC owed its early success to the fact that it can be easily upgraded. New hardware can be added and old hardware replaced with ease. Sadly, the laptop computer isn't quite as versatile. Laptops are designed for portability, not for internal expansion. And if your laptop can't be expanded, you have the realm of maintenance to explore. Like upgrading, maintaining your laptop keeps it in tip-top shape and helps extend its lifespan.

New Laptop Hardware

You may have to surrender yourself to accept how internal expansion options are rare to non-existent on your laptops. I believe my 2-in-1 tablet PC is hermetically sealed. I can't even locate screws on the case.

Some laptops — specifically, the traditional notebook models that feature removable batteries — might have hardware upgrade options. Two items you can upgrade are the hard drive and memory (RAM). Other items, those often upgraded on a desktop PC — processor, motherboard, video card — have only rarely been available as upgrade options on a laptop.

Though the hard drive upgrade is uncommon (and complex), replacing or adding memory is common. In fact, you can use the online tools at `crucial.com` to determine whether your laptop's memory can be upgraded: The site features a configuration program that helps you select the exact amount of memory you need. The program is handy; plus, the memory chips you order come with detailed instructions on how to install them.

Beyond memory, your laptop is essentially a closed box, and no further upgrades are offered. Don't despair! Refer to Chapter 12 for various ways to expand your laptop without using a screwdriver.

REMEMBER

>> Tablet PCs, 2-in-1s, Ultrabooks, and netbooks rarely have the capacity for a hardware upgrade. The trade-off between weight and size usually means that prying open the case and adding or changing something just isn't possible.

>> Refer to the documentation that came with your hardware to find out exactly how to configure it. Note that the hardware you're adding might sometimes require its software to be installed first. Other times, it's vice versa.

How 'bout Some New Software?

I've changed my tune on software upgrades. Once I wasn't in favor of them, but today most upgrades address security issues. For this purpose alone, an upgrade is a must.

Upgrading your software

Not every program alerts you to a software update. A few do, which is good news: When you see the notification or when the program alerts you directly, follow the directions to install a new version. Often, all you need is an active Internet connection, although for some programs you may need your customer ID or an account number.

>> The newest software model is the subscription, such as Adobe Creative Cloud or Microsoft 365. In both cases, you are automatically notified of a new software version or upgrade and can install that version when you're ready.

>> I strongly recommend installing new software only when you can run the laptop from AC power.

TIP

>> Give yourself plenty of time for the upgrade. For example, if you're leaving for a trip, check for and install upgrades the day before you leave.

UPGRADES VERSUS UPDATES

Computer jargon can be confusing enough without having to deal with vague terms that also exist in English. Prime examples are the words *upgrade* and *update.* They might seem like the same thing, but in the computer world, they're not.

Upgrade means to install a newer version of a program you already own. For example, you upgrade from version 2.1 of a program to version 2.2. Specifically, that's referred to as a *minor* upgrade. Moving from version 4.0 to version 5.0 is a *major* upgrade. These days, all upgrades appear to be major.

Update means to improve an existing program but not change its version or release number. For example, Microsoft routinely releases security updates for Windows. These updates, or *patches,* are applied to your version of Windows to improve features, address security issues, or fix bugs.

In some universe somewhere, this stuff all makes sense.

>> You don't need to uninstall the previous version of a program when you're installing an update. The only exception is when you're specifically advised to uninstall any older versions.

>> Refer to Chapter 9 for information on installing and removing software from your computer.

Upgrading to a new version of Windows

The good news is that Microsoft has announced how Windows 10 is the *final* release of Windows. No new versions are coming, no upgrades are required, although they fully intend upon improving Windows 10 with frequent upgrades, patches, and fixes.

If Microsoft isn't holding a Windows 11 card up its sleeve (would that be a jack?), you're all set on Windows upgrades. Don't worry about them. Continue to install the updates as described in Chapter 19.

If you're holding on to an older version of Windows, that's okay for a laptop. Because a laptop's lifespan is usually three to five years, you'll get the latest version of Windows when you buy your next laptop anyway.

Laptop Maintenance

As with all things in the computer universe, there are two sides to laptop maintenance: hardware and software. The good news is that nothing will ever leak out of your laptop, nor will your laptop ever emit an odor strong enough to require the use of an air freshener.

Maintaining the storage system

Disk maintenance was once a routine activity, with nerds bantering back and forth about which utilities to use and how often to run them. All this talk is idle now. That's because Windows automatically handles all storage maintenance chores. These tasks include running disk tune-up and defragmentation programs. As long as you haven't disabled any of these utilities, consider your laptop's storage system to be adequately maintained.

>> One common storage maintenance task that's not automated is backup. See Chapter 20 for details on setting up the Windows File History program.

>> Unlike with an automobile, you have no reason to take your laptop into the dealer or a repair place for regular check-ups. Shun anyone who offers you such a program, which is often called a *maintenance contract* by some dealers. Your laptop doesn't need it, and you don't need to pay for it.

Keeping it clean

Laptops are robust beasts. They can go through a lot without cleaning. Well, any man will tell you that carpets can go for months with no vacuuming, but I digress.

After you've been out and about with your laptop a few times, you should do some minor clean-up. Look at those fingerprints! Yikes! If only your mother could see them.

The best way to clean a laptop is with a soft cloth. Use a nonabrasive cleaner like 409 or Fantastic. Spray the cleaner on the cloth, and then wipe down everything on the laptop except for the screen. A damp sponge also works best for cleaning a laptop. Be gentle as you wipe, and try not to get any moisture inside the laptop.

>> Consider washing your hands from time to time.

>> Turn off the laptop before you start cleaning it.

>> You might also want to use cotton swabs to clean some of the gunk from the cracks.

>> Do not clean inside any openings. Never spray any liquids into those openings, either.

>> If your laptop manufacturer has any specific cleaning instructions, directions, or warnings, please refer to them first before following the information offered here.

Grooming the keyboard

Every so often, I vacuum my laptop keyboard. I use the little portable vacuum with either the tiny (toothbrush-size) brush or the upholstery cleaning attachment. This technique effectively sucks up all the crud in the keyboard. It's amazing to watch.

Some people prefer to clean the keyboard by using a can of compressed air. I don't recommend this method because the air can blow the crud in your keyboard farther inside the laptop. Instead, use a vacuum.

Cleansing the screen

To keep the screen clean, use a microfiber cloth. Gently wipe away the dust and sneeze globs. If you need more power to clean the screen, use a liquid specifically designed for laptop screens — especially for a tablet PC (with a touchscreen). Using the wrong cleaner can damage the screen, rending its touch-powers useless or even making the screen difficult to see.

Let the monitor dry completely before closing the lid!

>> Oftentimes, the keyboard creates a shadow stain on the screen. It's difficult to avoid and impossible to clean off. To help prevent the stain, place a soft, lint-free cloth — like one you'd use to clean the monitor inside the laptop — between the keyboard and screen when the laptop is closed.

>> Office supply stores carry special LCD screen cleaners as well as the lint-free wipes you can use to clean your screen and the rest of your laptop.

>> One product I can recommend is Klear Screen, from Meridrew Enterprises (www.klearscreen.com). No, it's not cheap. You want *good,* not cheap.

>> Avoid using alcohol- or ammonia-based cleaners on your laptop's touchscreen! These harsh chemicals can damage the screen. Worse, they can render that expensive touchscreen monitor useless.

>> Never squirt any cleaner directly on a laptop's screen.

6

The Part of Tens

Discover useful battery-saving tricks.

Investigate some handy laptop accessories.

Consider some items to put into your laptop bag.

Chapter **23**

Ten Battery Tips and Tricks

Without a battery, your laptop would be merely a tiny, overpriced PC. You need the battery to give the laptop its power of portability. There also comes a battery of battery issues, most of which involve squeezing the largest amount of life out of a limited supply of battery juice.

TIP

Chapter 10 is chock full of battery information. Refer there for further battery-saving tips and suggestions.

Don't Drop the Battery, Get It Wet, Short It, Play Keep-Away with It, Open It, Burn It, or Throw It Away

Enough said.

SCARY LITHIUM-ION BATTERY TRIVIA

Lithium-ion batteries are what many of us humans aspire to be: smart and popular. But the lithium-ion battery has a scary side. Consider this frightening lithium-ion battery information designed to literally shock you away from any thought of messing with your laptop's battery:

- When a lithium-ion battery is overcharged, it gets hot. Then it explodes.

- The lithium metal in the battery burns when it comes in contact with water.

- The acid inside the battery is not only highly caustic, it's also flammable.

- I'm sure that the acid is poisonous as well, but — golly — that last sentence had me at *caustic.*

- You cannot recycle a used lithium-ion battery, so don't ever think of buying or using a "recycled" battery.

Reduce the Screen's Brightness

To save a bit on battery life on the road, lower the brightness level on your laptop's screen just a hair — or perhaps as low as you can stand. This reduction definitely saves the juice.

TIP

The quick way to set screen brightness is to summon the Action Center: Press Win+A to summon the Action Center. Use the Brightness slider to adjust screen brightness. This control might also be available on the laptop's keyboard. See Chapter 10 for more information on adjusting the screen's brightness.

>> Notebook laptops may sport brightness-setting buttons near the screen. Use these buttons to control the brightness.

>> Sometimes, the brightness is controlled by using special Fn-key combinations.

>> Your laptop's power manager might automatically dim the screen when the laptop is on battery power.

Power Down the Hard Drive

The motors in your laptop consume the most power. That's bad news. The good news is that many newer laptops have no motors. The only motor left is the hard drive, and this hardware is being replaced quickly by the SSD.

If your laptop does have a hard drive, know that disk intensive programs will keep the device active and that such activity helps drain the battery faster. Such intensive programs include databases or any program that frequently accesses storage. Larger programs also impinge upon the hard drive's motors; see the next section.

For laptops that sport optical drives — yikes! Those things draw a lot of power. I didn't use the optical drive while my laptop ran on battery power.

Add RAM to Prevent Virtual Memory Disk Swapping

One way that the laptop's mass storage conspires with the operating system to drain the battery quickly is when the virtual memory manager pulls a disk swap. The way to prevent it is to add memory (RAM) to your laptop.

Virtual memory has nothing to do with virtue. Instead, it's a chunk of storage space that Windows uses to help supplement real memory, or RAM. Mass chunks of information are swapped between RAM and your laptop's storage, which is why you never see any Out of Memory errors in Windows. But all that memory swapping drains the battery.

Windows does a great job of managing virtual memory. Though you can fine-tune the virtual memory manager, I don't recommend it. Instead, if your laptop features a hard drive lamp, you can use it to test the virtual memory manager this way:

1. **Run three or four of your most-often-used programs or apps.**

   Start up each program and get its window up and ready on the screen, just as though you're about to work on something. In fact, you can even load a document or whatever, to ensure that the program is occupied.

2. **Wait.**

   Wait until for hard drive access to stop and the computer is waiting. About five seconds should be long enough.

3. **Press Alt+Esc.**

   The Alt+Esc key combination switches from one program (or window) to another.

4. **Observe any delays as you switch between programs.**

   The delays may indicate that information is being swapped between hard drive storage and memory.

5. **Repeat Steps 3 and 4 until you cycle through all programs and windows at least once.**

What you're looking for is hard drive access. If you detect a noticeable pause or (if one is available) the hard drive light blinks as you switch between programs, it can be a sign that virtual memory is being used, by swapping from RAM to disk. Yes, your system is working harder than it should, and it affects battery life.

The solution to virtual memory disk swapping isn't to adjust virtual memory as much as it is to add RAM to your laptop and prevent virtual memory from ever taking over in the first place.

If your laptop lacks a hard drive access light, pay attention to how Windows behaves. Do you see a pause as you switch programs? Is the keyboard acting sluggish? If so, you're witnessing memory being written to and read from the laptop's storage. That action drains the battery.

See Chapter 22 for information on adding more memory to your laptop. Though not every laptop is capable of a RAM expansion, if yours is, consider adding more memory as a worthy undertaking.

Keep Memory Empty

Even when you cannot add more memory to your laptop, battery life can be extended by economically using the memory you have.

To optimize performance, I recommend running only a few programs at a time on your laptop when you're using the battery. For example, you might be reading email in your email program, browsing the web, editing a document in your word processor, and keeping a game of Spider Solitaire going in another window. All this activity is unnecessary, and shutting down the programs you're not using helps save battery life — not a lot, but some.

It may seem trivial, but when you don't set a background image or wallpaper, and especially avoid the slide show wallpaper, Windows spends less time updating the screen. And, time is battery life! Consider setting a solid-color background image on your laptop. See Chapter 9.

Guard the Battery's Terminals

Like a big-city airport or Frankenstein's neck, your laptop's battery has terminals. People don't traverse a battery's terminals; but, like Frankenstein's neck, electricity does. The terminals are usually flat pieces of metal, either out in the open or recessed into a slot.

If your laptop lacks a removable battery, you have nothing to worry about. If the battery can pop out, treat it with gentle, loving care.

>> Keep the battery in the laptop.

>> Outside the laptop, keep the battery away from metal.

>> Keep the terminals clean; use a Q-Tip and some rubbing alcohol. Do this whenever you succumb to the temptation to touch the terminals, even though you shouldn't be doing that.

>> Do not attach anything to the battery.

>> Do not attempt to short the battery or try to rapidly drain it.

WARNING

Avoid Extreme Temperatures

Batteries enjoy the same type of temperatures you do. They don't like to be very cold, and they don't like hot temperatures, either. Like Goldilocks, the battery enjoys temperatures that are *just right.*

Store the Battery if You Don't Plan to Use It

Don't let a battery sit. If you keep the laptop deskbound (and nothing could be sadder), occasionally unplug the thing and let the battery cycle, just to keep it healthy. That's the best thing to do.

When you would rather run your laptop without the battery inside, or when preparing a spare battery for storage, run down the battery's charge to about

40 percent or so and then put the battery in a nonmetallic container. Stick the container in a nice, cool, clean, dry place.

>> Like people, batteries need exercise! Try to use your laptop battery every two months or so whether you're using the laptop remotely or not.

>> The recommended storage temperature for lithium-ion batteries is 59 degrees Fahrenheit or 15 degrees Celsius.

WARNING

>> A lithium-ion battery has an expiration date! After several years, the battery dies. This is true whether you use the battery or store it.

Understand That Batteries Drain Over Time!

No battery keeps its charge forever. Eventually, the battery's charge fades. For some reason, this surprises people. "That battery was fully charged when I put it into storage six years ago!" Batteries drain over time.

Yet just because a battery has drained doesn't mean that it's useless. If you stored the battery properly, all it needs is a full charge to get it back up and running again. So, if you store a battery (see the previous section), anticipate that you'll need to recharge it when you want to use it again. This process works just like getting the battery on the first day you set up your laptop; follow those same instructions for getting the stored battery up and running again.

Deal with the Low-Battery Warning

Thanks to smart-battery technology, your laptop can be programmed to tell you when the juice is about to go dry. In fact, you can set up two warnings on most laptops (refer to Chapter 10). The idea is to act fast on those warnings when they appear — and to take them seriously! Linger at your own risk. It's your data that you could lose!

The real trick, of course, is to ration the battery power you have. Here's a summary of tips, some of which are found elsewhere in this book:

>> **Be mindful of power-saving time-outs.** Setting a 15-minute Stand By time-out may work well in the office, but on the road you may want to adjust those times downward. Refer to Chapter 10.

>> **Mute the speakers!** This strategy not only saves a modicum of power but also prevents the ears of those next to you from hearing the silly noises your laptop makes.

>> **Save some stuff to do when you get back home or reconnect to a power source.** Face it: Some things can wait. If that 2GB project file upload isn't needed immediately, save it for when you're connected to the fast Internet line back at your home or office.

REMEMBER

>> **Hibernate!** When time is short and your laptop has the Hibernation smarts, just hibernate. Refer to Chapter 10.

Chapter **24**

Ten Handy Laptop Accessories

The spending doesn't stop after you buy the laptop. Nope — many, many laptop toys are available for purchase. Beyond software are gizmos and gadgets galore. Some are standard computer peripherals, like media cards, but most are wonderful and useful items you can get to enhance your laptopping experience.

Laptop Bag or Travel Case

A handsome laptop traveling tote is a must. Chapter 13 offers some useful suggestions and recommendations.

Spare Battery

Nothing cries "Freedom!" to the laptop road warrior more than an extra battery. Having a bonus battery doubles the time you can compute without that AC wall-socket umbilical cord. Some laptops even let you hot-swap from one battery to another while the laptop is still running, which means that the total length of time you can use your battery greatly exceeds your capacity to do work.

WARNING

>> Sadly, the current trend is for laptops not to feature a removable battery. Curse those manufacturers!

>> Ensure that the spare battery is approved for your laptop, coming either directly from the manufacturer or from a source that is reliable and guarantees compatibility. Using the wrong battery in your laptop can be disastrous.

External Storage

Obtain a USB-powered hard drive or SSD for your laptop. This portable storage device's purpose is to serve as a backup drive, as covered in Chapter 20. Even if you use cloud storage, even if you have local network storage, an external hard drive or SSD comes in handy.

Cooling Pad

The ideal accessory for any well-loved laptop, especially the larger models, is a cooling pad. It's a device, similar to the one shown in Figure 24-1, on which your laptop sits. The *cooling pad* contains one or more fans and is powered by either the laptop's USB port or standard AA batteries. Your laptop sits on the pad, and the fans help draw away the heat that the battery and microprocessor generate. The result is a cooler-running laptop, which keeps the laptop happy.

>> Heed whether the cooling pad runs from the power supplied by the USB port or from its own batteries.

>> If you're getting a USB-powered cooling pad, buy a model that has a pass-through USB port so that you don't lose a USB port when you add a cooling pad.

>> Some cooling pads also double as USB hubs.

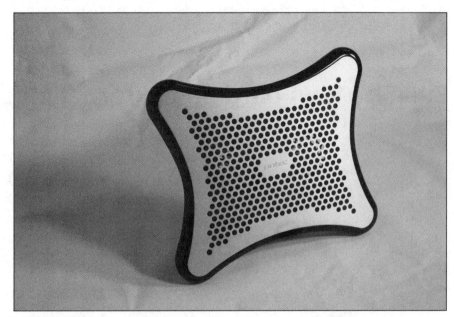

FIGURE 24-1:
A cool cooling pad.

Minivac

Useful for cleaning your laptop, especially the keyboard, is the minivac. This item is found in most office supply stores, and many are portable (battery powered). You'll be surprised (and disgusted) by the gunk that the minivac can suck from your laptop.

USB Lamp

Your laptop's screen is illuminated and even shows up in the dark. Sadly, most laptop keyboards don't light up. To help you see the keyboard as well as other important areas around your laptop, you can light things up with a USB-powered lamp.

The lamp plugs into a standard USB port on your laptop. It has either a stiff, bendable neck or a clamp so that you can position it. Flip the switch and let there be light!

>> Some laptops might already have built-in keyboard lights. Check for an LED lamp on the screen, or perhaps the keys themselves are illuminated. A special Fn key combination may be used to activate the keyboard lights. If this feature isn't available, get a USB lamp for your laptop.

>> Even when the keyboard is illuminated, a USB lamp helps you see things near your laptop, such as a notepad or reference.

Full-Size Keyboard and External Mouse

I'm certain that you don't want to tote one around with you, but there's a measurable pleasure to be had when you're using a laptop with a comfy, full-size keyboard and a mouse. The mouse need not even be full-size; plenty of laptop-size mice are available.

>> Did I say *wireless?* If you really want to be free of those pesky wires, get a wireless or Bluetooth keyboard and mouse. Wires belong back in the office, not on the road.

>> Maybe you don't want a full-size PC keyboard. Perhaps you just need a numeric keypad? If so, buy a USB keypad for your laptop.

>> When you use your tablet PC as a tablet, consider getting a digital stylus or pen. It works a lot like a mouse; plus, it's a better input device for creating text on a touchscreen — much better than your stubby fingers. See Chapter 7 for pen input info.

Privacy Screen Filter

Being in public with your laptop means, well, that you're in public — out amongst the rabble. Though you won't get the same curious stares I received when I took my old NEC UltraLite to a coffee shop back in 1989, you will get various looks from nosey people wanting to see what's so important that you have a laptop in a plane or in a hotel lobby.

To keep the snooping eyes at bay, get a privacy screen filter for your laptop. These devices are composed of a thin mesh that hugs the laptop's screen. From straight-on, you see the information on the screen. Move away from the screen at even the shallowest angle and you don't see anything. That's why it's called a *privacy* screen filter.

The good news: Privacy screen filters are available all over. Find one that fits your laptop's screen.

The bad news: These devices don't work well with tablet PCs. The screen interferes with your touch-input. This hindrance might be okay for a while, and most tablets let you attach a keyboard, so it's a frustrating trade-off.

ID Card or Return Service Sticker

Way back when, your mom would probably write your name on your laptop, just like she wrote your name on your underwear. And, seriously, Mom: Who was going to steal my underwear? Did they do that in the old country?

My point is that your laptop is yours only because you keep it with you. What it needs is your name on it somewhere. For example, businesspeople commonly tape their business cards somewhere on the inside of their laptops, such as slightly to one side of the touch pad.

The idea here is not only to claim ownership of the laptop but also to pray that if the laptop is ever lost or stolen, it will be recognizable as your own. A good citizen will contact you and offer to return the laptop that he or she found with your name emblazoned on an ID card.

>> While you're at it, attach a business card to other portable devices you might leave behind, like external storage, power supplies, and video projectors.

>> A better solution is to use a return service and take advantage of its tamper-resistant asset tags. Refer to Chapter 20 for more information.

Theft-Prevention System

The perfect gift for your dear laptop: some type of cable to keep it from walking off, one of those annoyingly loud my-laptop-has-been-moved alarms, or that special software that tries to "phone home" when the laptop is purloined. Ease your fears! Refer to Chapter 20 for more information on laptop security — specifically, these types of devices.

» A spare battery

» A wireless mouse

» Laptop cleaning supplies

» Security devices

» Removable media

» A set of headphones (or two)

» General supplies

» Cables, cables, and more cables

Chapter **25**

Ten Things to Throw in Your Laptop Bag

'm hoping that you follow my advice in Chapter 13 and purchase your laptop a handsome bag. And after you have the bag, and all that room, what are you going to put in it? Well, yes, of course: The laptop goes into the case. Duh. What else? Anything you truly need? Anything you might forget? Here's a list of ten items you should consider throwing (or gently tossing) into your laptop's case.

Power Cord and Brick

This item is one that even I forget. Sometimes I think, "Oh, I'm only going to be gone for an hour, and the battery lasts for three hours, so I don't need the power cord." Then an appointment is canceled and I have more time but regret not taking the power cord with me.

Always take your power cord and its adapter, or "brick," in your laptop bag. You just never know when a wall socket will appear. Take advantage of it!

Spare Battery

If the laptop is blessed with the capability to use a spare battery, put it in the bag!

REMEMBER

» Don't forget to charge the spare battery before you leave.

» Don't forget other batteries, such as a AAA battery for the wireless mouse, batteries for the digital pen and portable printer, and so on.

» Also refer to Chapter 10 for more information on your laptop's battery.

Mouse or Digital Pen

I figured I'd never forget my wee li'l wireless laptop mouse — until I actually did. I even toyed with the notion of buying another laptop mouse as opposed to using the touchpad for my entire trip. Since then, I've not neglected to keep the mouse in the laptop bag.

The laptop's pen or digital stylus is also an input device — one that probably costs more than the mouse. Don't forget it, and especially don't lose it. If your laptop has a pen dock or clip, use it to keep the pen handy.

Screen Wipes and Cleaner

Go to the office supply store and buy some screen wipes. Ensure that they're safe for a laptop screen, and for tablet PCs, ensure that they work properly on a touchscreen. Toss 'em in your laptop bag and keep them there.

Laptop Lock

Don't forget your laptop's antitheft device. Whether it's a cable you can connect to something solid or one of those loud, loud audio alarms, you probably want to pack it in your laptop bag. Refer to Chapter 20 for more information on laptop security.

Removable Media

Saving your stuff to the laptop's primary storage system often isn't enough. It helps to have an assortment of alternatives to get that information out of the computer, especially when your laptop isn't connected to a network for easy file transfer.

>> Label the media cards and thumb drives. That way, you can keep them straight.

>> I keep MicroSD cards in their tiny, plastic cases. They're more difficult to lose that way.

>> It may not be necessary to carry with you an external storage device for backup, such as a USB hard drive or SSD. Even so, the laptop's bag is an ideal place to put it.

Headphones

Consider two types of headphones for your laptop bag. First are the common earbud-style headphones, which you probably use on your cell phone. These are fine for a laptop and, if they have a microphone, you can use them to Skype or for other voice input.

A second type of headphone is the more complex, full-size model. Also known as a *headset*, this headphone includes full-size ear cans and a separate microphone. This headphone also goes well into a laptop bag, especially if you plan to Skype somewhere noisy or just need a better way to listen to things.

TIP

My favorite headphone features noise canceling capabilities. Though it's difficult to hear anything in an airplane, listening to music or watching a movie on my laptop is far more enjoyable when I activate the headphone's noise canceling feature.

Office Supplies

Yeah, this is supposed to be the "paperless" age. Whatever. You still need a pad of paper and a writing implement, despite the redundancy and its overall anti-21st-century nature. I keep two pens, one highlighter, sticky notes, a small pad of paper, and a legal pad in my laptop bag. Although it's not intentional, my laptop bag has also collected various paperclips and rubber bands.

TIP

>> Another must-have item: business cards.

>> Also consider copies of your presentation (if you're making one) and perhaps some magazines or reading material.

>> Surprisingly, also available at an office supply store are a deck of cards, Band-Aids, aspirin, and other sundries. These too make excellent items to keep in your laptop bag.

Cables, Cables, Cables

Cables are good. When you can, bring any spare Ethernet, phone, USB, or other type of cables you can muster. You might never use them, but then again, you never know.

>> You never know where the Internet lurks! Taking along a goodly length of Ethernet cable with your laptop is always a good idea. Then you can instantly connect to any available Ethernet network without having to wait for or (worse) rent a cable.

>> A goodly length is about 6 feet.

>> A phone charging cable is also a handy thing to keep in the laptop bag.

Not the End of the List

You can pack your laptop bag full of so much stuff that the bag eventually weighs more than you do. Weight is the practical limit on what you can put into a laptop bag. The list is long and gravity is persistent.

The items mentioned in this chapter are good to *always* have in your laptop bag. Add the other stuff as you need it. Or, when you're traveling, consider putting in your checked luggage the extra things you don't immediately need so that you're not toting their extra weight.

Index

About the Author

Dan Gookin has been writing about technology for nearly three decades. He combines his love of writing with his gizmo fascination to create books that are informative, entertaining, and not boring. Having written over 170 titles, and with 12 million copies in print translated into over 30 languages, Dan can attest that his method of crafting computer tomes seems to work.

Perhaps his most famous title is the original *DOS For Dummies*, published in 1991. It became the world's fastest-selling computer book, at one time moving more copies per week than the *New York Times* number-one bestseller (though, as a reference, it could not be listed on the Times' Best Sellers list). That book spawned the entire line of *For Dummies* books, which remains a publishing phenomenon to this day.

Dan's most popular titles include *PCs For Dummies*, *Laptops For Dummies*, and *Microsoft Word For Dummies*. He also maintains the vast and helpful website www.wambooli.com.

Dan holds a degree in Communications/Visual Arts from the University of California, San Diego. He lives in the Pacific Northwest, where he enjoys spending time annoying people who deserve it.

Publisher's Acknowledgments

Acquisitions Editor: Kelsey Baird

Managing Editor: Kristie Pyles

Senior Project Editor: Paul Levesque

Copy Editor: Becky Whitney

Production Editor: Mohammed Zafar Ali

Cover Images: Modern Laptop isolated on white background © rasslava/Getty Images, Color soft background with circle and halftone © Goja1/Getty Images, Abstract speed motion of a highway tunnel © FotoMak/Getty Images

Take dummies with you everywhere you go!

Whether you are excited about e-books, want more from the web, must have your mobile apps, or are swept up in social media, dummies makes everything easier.

Find us online!

Leverage the power

Dummies is the global leader in the reference category and one of the most trusted and highly regarded brands in the world. No longer just focused on books, customers now have access to the dummies content they need in the format they want. Together we'll craft a solution that engages your customers, stands out from the competition, and helps you meet your goals.

Advertising & Sponsorships

Connect with an engaged audience on a powerful multimedia site, and position your message alongside expert how-to content. Dummies.com is a one-stop shop for free, online information and know-how curated by a team of experts.

- Targeted ads
- Video
- Email Marketing

- Microsites
- Sweepstakes sponsorship

20 **MILLION**
PAGE VIEWS
EVERY SINGLE MONTH

15
MILLION
UNIQUE
VISITORS PER MONTH

43%
OF ALL VISITORS
ACCESS THE SITE
VIA THEIR MOBILE DEVICES

700,000 NEWSLETTER
SUBSCRIPTIONS
TO THE INBOXES OF
300,000 UNIQUE INDIVIDUALS
EVERY WEEK

# of dummies

Custom Publishing

Reach a global audience in any language by creating a solution that will differentiate you from competitors, amplify your message, and encourage customers to make a buying decision.

- Apps
- Books
- eBooks
- Video
- Audio
- Webinars

Brand Licensing & Content

Leverage the strength of the world's most popular reference brand to reach new audiences and channels of distribution.

For more information, visit dummies.com/biz

PERSONAL ENRICHMENT

Staying Sharp
9781119187790
USA $26.00
CAN $31.99
UK £19.99

Facebook
Carolyn Abram
9781119179030
USA $21.99
CAN $25.99
UK £16.99

Guitar
Mark Phillips
Jon Chappell
9781119293354
USA $24.99
CAN $29.99
UK £17.99

Investing
Eric Tyson, MBA
9781119293347
USA $22.99
CAN $27.99
UK £16.99

Beekeeping
Howland Blackiston
9781119310068
USA $22.99
CAN $27.99
UK £16.99

Digital Photography
Julie Adair King
9781119235606
USA $24.99
CAN $29.99
UK £17.99

Meditation
Stephan Bodian
9781119251163
USA $24.99
CAN $29.99
UK £17.99

Pregnancy
ALL-IN-ONE
9781119235491
USA $26.99
CAN $31.99
UK £19.99

Samsung Galaxy S7
Bill Hughes
9781119279952
USA $24.99
CAN $29.99
UK £17.99

iPhone
Edward C. Baig
Bob "Dr. Mac" LeVitus
9781119283133
USA $24.99
CAN $29.99
UK £17.99

Crocheting
Karen Manthey
Susan Brittain
9781119287117
USA $24.99
CAN $29.99
UK £16.99

Nutrition
Carol Ann Rinzler
9781119130246
USA $22.99
CAN $27.99
UK £16.99

PROFESSIONAL DEVELOPMENT

Windows 10
Andy Rathbone
9781119311041
USA $24.99
CAN $29.99
UK £17.99

AutoCAD
Bill Fane
9781119255796
USA $39.99
CAN $47.99
UK £27.99

Excel 2016
Greg Harvey, PhD
9781119293439
USA $26.99
CAN $31.99
UK £19.99

QuickBooks 2017
9781119281467
USA $26.99
CAN $31.99
UK £19.99

macOS Sierra
Bob "Dr. Mac" LeVitus
9781119280651
USA $29.99
CAN $35.99
UK £21.99

LinkedIn
Joel Elad, MBAs
9781119251132
USA $24.99
CAN $29.99
UK £17.99

Windows 10
ALL-IN-ONE
Woody Leonhard
9781119310563
USA $34.00
CAN $41.99
UK £24.99

SharePoint 2016
Rosemarie Withee
Ken Withee
9781119181705
USA $29.99
CAN $35.99
UK £21.99

Fundamental Analysis
Matt Krantz
9781119263593
USA $26.99
CAN $31.99
UK £19.99

Networking
Doug Lowe
9781119257769
USA $29.99
CAN $35.99
UK £21.99

Office 2016
Wallace Wang
9781119293477
USA $26.99
CAN $31.99
UK £19.99

Office 365
Rosemarie Withee
Ken Withee
Jennifer Reed
9781119265313
USA $24.99
CAN $29.99
UK £17.99

Salesforce.com
Liz Kao
Jon Paz
9781119239314
USA $29.99
CAN $35.99
UK £21.99

Coding
Nikhil Abraham
9781119293323
USA $29.99
CAN $35.99
UK £21.99

dummies.com

dummies
A Wiley Brand

Learning Made Easy

ACADEMIC

9781119293576
USA $19.99
CAN $23.99
UK £15.99

9781119293637
USA $19.99
CAN $23.99
UK £15.99

9781119293491
USA $19.99
CAN $23.99
UK £15.99

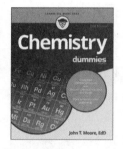

9781119293460
USA $19.99
CAN $23.99
UK £15.99

9781119293590
USA $19.99
CAN $23.99
UK £15.99

9781119215844
USA $26.99
CAN $31.99
UK £19.99

9781119293378
USA $22.99
CAN $27.99
UK £16.99

9781119293521
USA $19.99
CAN $23.99
UK £15.99

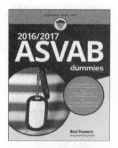

9781119239178
USA $18.99
CAN $22.99
UK £14.99

9781119263883
USA $26.99
CAN $31.99
UK £19.99

Available Everywhere Books Are Sold

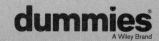

Small books for big imaginations

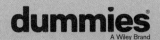